Understanding Israel

The Church, the Jewish People, and the Struggle for Identity

I0142434

Andrew M. Sibley

Fastnet Publications

ISBN: 978-0-9562146-2-1

Published by:
Fastnet Publications
Mill Close
Colyton
Devon
EX24 6EU
England

Printed by Lightning Source

By the same author:

> *Restoring the Ethics of Creation*, Annomundi Books, 2006.
> *Cracking the Darwin Code*, Fastnet Publications, 2013.

The cover picture is by Alexander Louis Leloir 1865 *Jacob Wrestling with the Angel* (public domain). It was after this incident that God gave Jacob the name Israel. Jacob had come to realise that God was the source of his blessing, and in wrestling with God actually come into submission to God.

Contents

Contents...iii

Preface.. 7

Acknowledgements 8

Chapter 1 Introduction... 9

PART I – THE CURRENT DEBATE............................... 17

Chapter 2 Replacement Theology........................ 17

The Church Fathers... 20

Calvin's Covenantal Theology 26

Modern developments 28

Chapter 3 The Roots of Christian Zionism 31

Promoting Christianity Among the Jews 32

Edward Irving.. 32

John Nelson Darby 36

Darby's Theology.. 38

Benjamin Wills Newton and the Open Brethren............. 42

Cyrus Scofield 44

Development of Political Zionism...................... 45

Hal Lindsey and Friends.................................. 46

The Teachings of John Hagee......................... 48

Other Denominations and Theologians 55

Summary 56

PART II – UNDERSTANDING ISRAEL............................ 59

Chapter 4 Israel and Biblical interpretations..................... 59

Chapter 5 The People of Israel in the Old Testament 65

Israel and the Birthright 67

Amos 71

Hosea 72

Isaiah 75

Micah 78

Jeremiah 79

Ezekiel 81

Zechariah 84

Chapter 6 Restoring Israel to the Land 87

Chapter 7 Israel in Matthew's Gospel 93

Matthew 1. Jesus' birth 93

Matthew 10. Shepherding the Lost Sheep of Israel 94

Matthew 13. Kingdom Parables 94

Matthew 21. Jerusalem and the Fig Tree 95

Matthew 23. A Desolate House 96

Matthew 24. End Time Prophecies 98

Chapter 8 Israel in Romans 101

Letter to the Romans 101

The Elect of God and Israel 103

All Israel? 106

Chapter 9 Israel in Galatians and Ephesians 111

Letter to the Galatians 111

Letter to the Ephesians 115

Chapter 10 Israel in Hebrews 117

Chapter 11 Israel in 1 Peter 123

Chapter 12 Who Owns the land? 125

The Jewish Claim 127

Jewish - Christian Presence in Palestine...................... 129

Chapter 13 What Promises Remain for Jews?............... 135

Chapter 14 Conclusions... 141

A Vision for the State of Israel 146

Appendix 1. Jerusalem Declaration on Christian Zionism 147

Appendix 2. Israel in the Prophets (table) 149

Appendix 3. The Lost Tribes of Israel............................. 151

Appendix 4. Questionable Documents 153

Selected Bibliography 157

Scripture References 161

Index 171

Preface

This book started out as a revision of *Zion's New Name*, a previous book on Israel. However, it became apparent that a new title was necessary instead. Again, it is written in a spirit of respectful dialogue in order to build understanding and unity in the Church over a controversial area of study, but also with the desire to interpret Scripture in the right theological context. The continued desire is to write in response to developments in Christian Zionism that seem to me to be moving away from God's grace and the gospel of Christ, for instance following John Hagee's book *In Defense of Israel*, and the growing promotion of a dual-covenant theology. Furthermore, the injustice against Palestinians, including Palestinian Christians, is often overlooked. On the other side of the debate, there is sometimes a failure to see the genuine pain and hurt amongst Jewish people. We need to acknowledge that Jews have suffered greatly through history. Messianic Jewish believers can also find themselves isolated from both fellow Jews and Gentile Christians - they are often torn between love for national Israel and their spiritual commitment to the Messiah. Incidentally, the first century Jewish Christians found a similar dilemma when they had to choose to flee Jerusalem prior to its destruction in AD70.

There are varied opinions on the question of the legitimacy of the modern State of Israel in the Church today, and I hope in this discussion to offer a bit more clarity. I also hope to have avoided careless use of language. When Jews were suffering greatly during the rise of fascism, many Christians in Europe rightly went out of their way to help them. Some German Christians formed the Confessing Church, signed the Barmen Declaration, and opposed the brutality of Nazi Germany, some even paying with their own lives for their stand. In the same spirit of concern for the victims of violence and oppression, many Christians now feel duty bound to speak up for the Palestinians, others feel the need to speak up for Jews. We should be critical of the violence by Palestinian authorities and militant groups, such as Hamas, against Jews. Instead we ought to work for peace, justice and reconciliation between both communities.

I would also urge those who might disagree with some of these things to check them out for themselves as use of labels has become very confused in this area. I want also to say as well that I am not going to argue for Replacement Theology, although I would note that the term is used polemically against anyone who is sceptical of Christian Zionism. My argument in this book is that the Christian Church is in continuity with God's purposes as revealed through the blessings given to Abraham, Isaac, Jacob-Israel, Joseph, Ephraim and Judah. All Christians therefore form the *One-New-Man* of Ephesians 2; that is Jewish and Gentile believers enjoying fellowship together in the Messiah, and looking forward to the return of Christ and the New Jerusalem in a single covenant of grace.

I would agree that we need to question Greek influences in the Church that take away from the Hebraic New Testament thinking, particularly Platonic dualism and Gnosticism. But we also need to avoid being led back to some of the traditions of the Scribes and Pharisees that were somewhat removed from the purity of the Mosaic Law. I want then to embrace the Hebraic foundations of Christianity, but in a true Mosaic sense that understands the spirit of the Law and the inclusive purposes of God for Israel and all nations. I believe therefore that the Messianic-Christian Church is the natural home for all people, Jews, Israelites and Gentiles.

Acknowledgements

The following acknowledgements carry forward from *Zion's New Name*. I would like to thank Dr Farid Abou-Rahme for encouraging me to write *Zion's New Name* and for writing a Foreword for that edition. It was already a concern upon my heart, but a shared desire gave the impetus to write. Thanks also to Farid and Ilham for their kind hospitality, and thanks to Dr Nabil Abou-Rahme who kindly reviewed an earlier draft and provided some useful feedback. Nabil also understands the relationship between Christianity and biblical Israel in terms of continuity. Also thanks to Dr Stephen E. Jones of God's Kingdom Ministries for his books and teaching material. Although there may be points of disagreement, his writing has encouraged me to research the Old Testament in much greater depth than I previously have done, especially as it relates to Joseph's birthright and the question of the northern Israelite exiles. Other works that have provided important material include study notes from Paul Wilkinson on Replacement Theology, together with further works cited in the footnotes and bibliography. Mike Gascoigne has also provided advice on setting up a publishing title, and advice on formatting the book, as have Lightning Source.

Chapter 1

Introduction

The overall purpose of this book is to seek to build unity and understanding within the Church on the question of Israel through a careful study. The questions that need to be asked first relate to the relationship between Christianity and the modern State of Israel. Does the State of Israel still have a purpose within God's plan today, or is the Christian Church the spiritual representation of Israel in the world? Questions such as these arise in terms of eschatology, (the end-times), how the old covenant Mosaic requirements are to be interpreted within the Christian Church, and how they relate to the person and work of Jesus the Messiah. It also arises when we question the nature of modern Israel in terms of political status, ethnic identity and in terms of legal claims and spiritual reality. There is divided opinion within the evangelical community over this relationship, and different opinions over how events will play out in the end-times. But as the sub-title of this book suggests, the struggle between both sides is really one of identity, and identities are deeply felt and held. So, the question arises; is the Christian Church and the Messianic community truly Israel today, or do the Jewish people still have a legitimate claim apart from Jesus?

I want to stress from the start that this study is written on the understanding that God loves both Jews and Palestinians equally. Furthermore, we need to approach this debate within the context of the great commission of Jesus; that is to preach the gospel to all nations (Matt. 28:19), and thus make disciples of all people groups within God's kingdom. If the modern State of Israel is a legitimate nation on earth, as Christian Zionists claim, then it is included in the sight of this commission. Sadly, some pro-Israel Christian teachers overlook or play-down the significance of this commission in their writing, as I will discuss in this book.

Through a study of Christian history two basic views can be identified and broadly categorised in regard to the place of Judaism and Israel in relation to the Christian Church. The first position is usually referred to as *Replacement Theology*, the second more recent view is *Christian Zionism*. These characterised positions however mark out polarised viewpoints, and this is causing division in the Church. In light of these different and opposing views that have arisen in Christian history, and brought to the fore in recent years, it is necessary to seek to find where the truth lies through a careful study of Scripture. Scripture though needs to be interpreted within the correct context; that is with consideration of its historical, social, spiritual and political setting. In doing this we may get to the heart of the intended meaning of the authors. The purpose here then is to ask, what or who is Israel?

The Bible does in fact have a lot to say about the promises that God made to Israel through biblical history. In examining these promises of God it is not the intention here to deliberately engage in contentious disagreements for the sake of it, but to simply examine the Scriptures and to ask what they say about this subject so that a better understanding might be developed. However, this is a difficult subject because views are often strongly held, and each side believes they are committed to Christian orthodoxy. But there are legitimate questions concerning the danger for Christians of wrongful theology. One further concern that appears to me to be real, is that many Christian Zionists have placed such great faith in Israel that if something were to happen to the state, something that doesn't fit their preferred eschatological scheme, then their Christian faith might be severely shaken.

As noted, the debate also seems quite polarised with many supporters of Christian Zionism continuing to support the dispensationalism of John Nelson Darby.[1] This theology was quite divisive when first proposed in the nineteenth century, being partly responsible for the split in the emerging Brethren movement. Other Christian supporters of Zionism further suggest that those opposed to Zionism in any form are anti-Semitic, this on the basis that the Jews have a right to their homeland and this should not be opposed at all. Not even apparently on the basis of a reasoned theological argument that notes the conditional nature of God's promises regarding occupation of the land in the Law of Moses. This approach also confuses and conflates Israel as a political secular state with Judaism as a religious movement or identity. It is indeed possible and important to love Jews as a people, without necessarily supporting political, nationalistic Zionism. Being opposed to the latter doesn't have to collapse into anti-Semitism.

On the other side, even someone of the stature of Jimmy Carter has suggested that the Zionist' policies of the State of Israel are in effect a form of apartheid because they seek to exclude Palestinians from the land.[2] The inference is that those Christian supporters of Israel, who then accept that Jews have pre-eminent rights over the land, are guilty of supporting apartheid policies by association. Each side then is

---

[1] Wilkinson, P.R. *For Zion's Sake, Christian Zionism and the Role of John Nelson Darby*, London: Paternoster, 2007.
[2] Carter, J, *Palestine: Peace not Apartheid,* New York, Simon and Schuster, 2006, reported in Sizer, S., *Zion's Christian Soldiers?* IVP, 2007, p. 15

Introduction

effectively accusing the other side of racism by calling into question the beliefs of the other. It is to be hoped here though that a reasoned discussion can be had without using emotive language that doesn't really facilitate respectful dialogue. In this book I don't want to accuse Christians of racism because I don't think that is the intention of believers on either side. However, I will question whether it is right for Christians to support militant nationalism of any kind, whether Israeli or Palestinian, and this is from a theological position. Christians are being caught up into a heavenly spiritual kingdom and thus called to make disciples of all nations as we bring God's love into the world. Love and support for Palestinians and Jews as people and communities is part of the gospel, and it is necessary to recognise that the issues are very important in terms of righteousness and justice for all.

This study stems from a personal quest to understand the issues, partly as a result of dissatisfaction with existing ideas on both sides of the debate, but also out of an understanding that a few passages in the Bible do seem to speak of the reappearance of a state of Israel in the last days. Although equally many passages now attributed to the modern State of Israel have historically been interpreted in terms of the Church as being the spiritual manifestation of Israel. Furthermore, there are other questions about the interpretation of Old Testament prophecies that speak of the restoration of Israel.

Many Christians have also rightly hoped and prayed for the Jews, both through Christian history and in the present time, that they will come to see Jesus as their own promised Messiah and King. I would encourage this aspect of concern for Jews. Many Christians have also rightly rejected anti-Semitism and expressed concern for the suffering of Jews in history as well.

For many years I personally accepted some of the moderate Christian Zionist arguments, perhaps similar to those espoused by David Pawson in his recent book *Defending Christian Zionism*,[3] and believed that God had a divine purpose for the nation of Israel in this present time. Jews were seen to be experiencing the biblically promised resettlement in their own land before our eyes, and afterwards I believed they would one day experience a national revival. Such mass conversion would mean life from the dead for all (Rom. 11: 15). However, this is the moderate view concerned with love for Jews as human beings. Other teachings of Christian Zionists have been developed that are of concern. Mainly because they turn love for Jews into nationalistic support for the

---

[3] Pawson, D., *Defending Christian Zionism*, Terra Nova Publ., 2008; See also Torrance, D.W., & Taylor, G., *Israel God's Servant*, London: Paternoster Press, 2007.

State of Israel, a state that is believed to be fulfilling God's purposes today even though it is secular. But in recent years an increasing number of Christians have become dissatisfied with this and believe that these views need to be questioned for various reasons, as characterised below.

Firstly, the violence brought to bear against Palestinians in recent years (many of whom are Christian, but now largely Muslim due to different rates of exile and birth rates) by the Israeli authorities cannot be overlooked by those committed to the teachings of Jesus Christ. Of course Palestinian terrorists have caused much suffering to the Israelis as well, through rockets and suicide bombings for instance, but it is only necessary to look at the death toll on each side to see which side has the greater firepower and is causing the greater suffering. Of course some may argue that the Palestinian side often instigates the violence, which is true in part, although this may be debatable in totality. It was initially Zionist' terrorism that sought to drive the British Mandate forces out of the land, and forced Palestinians from their historical lands. Today Palestinians continue to lose their land with forced expulsions, and many are living in a virtual concentration camp under siege conditions in Gaza with their human rights and liberty to travel denied. Any reading of the Gospels, or the Old Testament prophets such as Micah (Mic. 6: 8), shows that God has always required justice and mercy from his people the Israelites, even to the non-Jews who lived amongst them. In other words, it may be asked whether the current policies of the State of Israel are in fact in accord with the Mosaic Law, let alone the New Testament interpretation of the Law and teachings of Jesus Christ.

Some have suggested that inciting child suicide bombers against Jews is a form of child sacrifice, and inferred that because of this Palestinians are rightly being exiled from the lands. In the Old Testament the Israelites were sometimes told to wipe out those people and nations who were engaged in idolatry with their practices of self-mutilation and child sacrifices. But that is hardly applicable to the Palestinians today, many of whom are Christians, or to the Muslims who claim allegiance to some of the Old Testament prophets through Islam. As far as I know Palestinian Muslims do not worship pagan gods such as Baal, Molech or Ishtar, but claim to worship the God of Abraham, who they identify as Allah.[4] And many are opposed to militancy and suicide bombings even though they have not yet come to understand and accept the full knowledge of God as Father through the work of Jesus and the indwelling Holy Spirit. I would suggest that some individual Muslims ought to be categorised in the same way as

---

[4] A further claim is that 'Allah' is really the pagan moon god. I have not studied this claim in depth and offer no further thoughts.

Introduction

Cornelius who was said to be devout and God-fearing and diligent in doing good deeds and prayer (Acts 10: 2). However, even Cornelius was in need of salvation through Christ, as are Muslims. Other Muslims though preach violence and hatred and some Islamic institutions seem to be bordering on the demonic by encouraging children to hate Jews and non-Muslims and become suicide bombers. Inciting children to blow themselves up is indeed abhorrent and cowardly, but using this argument against all Palestinians is weak for a number of reasons. The Palestinians were being expelled before the suicide bombings started, and I would hope that most Palestinians do not support it.

Secondly, the history of Christianity in Palestine can be traced back to the time of Christ and the early Church, and it has been a large Christian community that has been reduced severely since the creation of the State of Israel. The rights of the Christian community in Palestine need to be acknowledged and respected by Christians in the wider world. While many Christians in Palestine are of Arab descent there is a strong contingent of Levantines, the pre-Arab Christians, and some Maronites, whose presence as a community pre-dates the coming of the Arabs with the Islamic conquests. There is concern that unless a permanent peace settlement is reached between Israel and the Palestinians the Christian community might disappear altogether. A brief history of the Christian community in Palestine, and the scale of the decline, is discussed more fully in chapter twelve.

Thirdly, the State of Israel, as a nation, shows no outward sign of repentance and conversion to Christ despite existing as an independent state in the land for over sixty years. It may also be noted that repentance was a pre-requisite for resettlement in the land according to the Law of Moses, as an example consider the way in which God brought Judah back from Babylon. There are also social and political pressures against the evangelism of Jews in Israel, and Messianic Jews are not really considered true Jews by the Jewish religious leaders and authorities. In other words, modern Israel is extremely resistant to the gospel of Jesus Christ and is often hostile to Palestinian Christians, and also to Jewish Messianic believers. However, there are reports that some Jews are converting to Christ despite the restrictions, which is encouraging indeed.

Fourthly, the teachings of some leading Christian Zionists, such as John Hagee for instance, are questionable as they are arguably moving away from traditional Christian theology and the core positions of the Church. It is claimed for instance that Jews do not need to come to Christ because of a national 'election' following the covenant given to Abraham. This needs to be questioned in detail in light of the gospel of Christ. The American branch of the Lausanne Consultation on Jewish

13

Evangelism has also recently pronounced in favour of spreading the gospel to Jewish people in its *Resolution on Christian Zionism and Jewish Evangelism*.[5] This calls on those who love and work amongst Jews to seek to bring the gospel to them.

Fifthly, some Zionist positions require the formation and continuation of the State of Israel so that it may experience destruction through another holocaust in the final battle of Armageddon, after the Christians are taken away in the rapture. While most of us have little influence over political and military activity, some of those who support Israel do have significant influence in American politics and use that influence to support their militant Christian theology. But whatever is to happen in the future, the Christian mandate is to make disciples of all nations, thus bringing peace and justice to all, and not to seek the ultimate destruction of a Jewish state and their Muslim neighbours through war. In response to this a detailed examination of Scripture is important to determine exactly what the Bible says about Israel.

Sixthly, the origin and nature of the Talmud, and Jesus' condemnation of the 'Tradition of the Elders' that was nullifying the authority of the writing of Moses and the Old Testament prophets is also relevant and ought to be questioned openly. The Talmud is considered to be more authoritative than the Torah, the five books of Moses, by many Jews today, although importantly there are some Jews who reject the Talmud in favour of the Torah. Without going into detail, it may be noted that many Jews do not base religious authority upon the Law of Moses, but upon an interpretation of Moses that Jesus rejected. Many Christian Zionists are not aware of this distinction. This is also borne out in the symbolic six-pointed Star of David that does not seem to be an Old Testament symbol, but one of questionable origins. The seven-candled Menorah would be a more appropriate symbol for the Israeli flag.

The seventh question is more theological, and relates to the claims of Jesus and the ability of Israel to bear spiritual fruit. Jesus said; 'I am the vine; you are the branches. If you remain in me and I in you, you will bear much fruit; apart from me you can do nothing' (John 15:5). How then may a state that denies Jesus bear spiritual fruits of righteousness? The concern is that it cannot. Furthermore, we need to look in depth at the Old Testament prophets and the New Testament authors, and consider how they saw the restoration of Israel.

It is such observations as these that I believe call us to question the true nature of the State of Israel in its standing before God. It ought

---

[5] 26th Annual meeting of the American branch of the LCJE, held at Phoenix, Arizona 2-4 March 2009. [http://www.lcje.net/statements/resolution.html]

to be questioned how a largely secular, nationalistic Zionist movement can be fulfilling God's purposes today. If it is a religious movement it is not in accord with Jesus' teachings, and arguably not in accord with the Mosaic teachings either. Perhaps the Israelis will experience a great revival in our time, and that is to be hoped for and prayed for, but from a human perspective such a national revival doesn't look very likely at present. The purpose of the reappearance of a state called Israel in the present time then is not entirely clear and as noted above there are a number of unresolved theological issues that ought to be addressed openly in light of Scripture.

Some Christians have accepted Israel as a legitimate Jewish state before God, and lost sight of the Jewish origin and nature of Christianity. They have perhaps not studied and understood the prophets and apostles in sufficient depth. Importantly, Old and New Testament biblical writers have commented widely on this subject, and it is necessary to weigh the evidence carefully and therefore avoid an incomplete understanding of Scripture. As a result of the misunderstanding of God's purposes in the world today Christians run the risk of being misled by poor doctrines and theology.

So common questions that are being considered concern the promises that God has given to Israel, and how these promises are to be fulfilled in history and in the present time. General comments from leading Christian Zionists suggest that there are age-old promises that are only now being fulfilled in our present time as a result of the restoration of the State of Israel in the last sixty years. Comments by some other Christian Zionists are perhaps more extreme and require a thoughtful response. Perhaps unwittingly, and with zeal for a Zionist state, they are downplaying the position of Christ and introducing questionable teachings into the Church. Some of this represents a new development in studies relating to the State of Israel and end-times prophecy, although it was also present in the nineteenth century discussion. At the very least this teaching should be examined in a proper theological manner.

The purpose in the following two chapters is to examine the teachings on both sides. Then through a careful study of the Old and New Testament text in later chapters we will examine how closely each line up with what the biblical writers actually believed and taught. Although the interpretation of biblical prophecy is not always easy, it is possible to begin to build towards a more consistent picture through careful study. The desire here is to reach a more complete, or better understanding of Scripture that is more coherent than current divided opinion allows. And it is also to be hoped that re-examining the theological issues will lead to an improved understanding between supporters of Christian Zionism and those falsely accused of adopting Replacement Theology.

It must also be remembered that Christians are called to love all people and nations, and that includes the Jews as well as Palestinians. However, that love can only be expressed within a context of honest dialogue, especially in light of the State of Israel's treatment of Palestinian people, many of whom are Christian. We must not forget to also challenge the terrorism and violence against the Jews by Palestinian or Islamic extremists as well. Christians need to show Christ's love to both communities by working for peace, understanding and justice so that both sides can enjoy peace and security.

While it is true that many Christians hold to moderate theological views in this area, as noted each side also has its more extreme elements. Sadly, through history, Christian authorities have often failed to live up to Christ's commands to love the Jewish people in exile, and have persecuted them down through the ages. Luther for instance initially embraced the Jews when it suited his rise to power, but once his position was secure he turned against them, perhaps through malicious negative reports by their opponents.[6] Jews have suffered much through the last two thousand years, being exiles and wanderers throughout the world. In the last century Hitler too turned against the Jews and suggested that Luther would be with him, although Hitler, being an atheist or pantheist, was really no friend of Christianity either. He claimed that he would abolish the established churches in Germany having nationalised large sections of it under the banner of the German Church. Hitler's real beliefs are notoriously difficult to interpret, but his stated position was that of 'Positive Christianity.' This was really a materialistic belief system devoid of any real spiritual significance or reality.[7] Hitler tried to maintain some aspects of Christianity, but within a severely nationalistic and brutal context where Christianity was denied any real spiritual significance and meaning. Other German Christians of the Confessing Church, such as Karl Barth and Dietrich Bonhoeffer, signed the *Barmen Declaration* and in fact rejected Hitler's fascist state.

---

[6] To be fair to Luther and the Reformation it may be noted that there was also persecution against Calvinists and the Anabaptists; and Protestants and Catholics were being executed across Europe for their faith during this time.

[7] Positivism, (sometimes known as scientism) is the assertion that only objectively verifiable statements can be accepted as true, although as this statement itself is not objectively verifiable, then the position is self-refuting.

PART I – THE CURRENT DEBATE

Chapter 2

Replacement Theology

The claim is often made by Christian Zionists that through much of Christian history the Church has taught that it has superseded or replaced Judaism, and that this represents a persistent problem in the Church that needs to be addressed. This claim sometimes seems more important than offering support to Israel, and is often made very dogmatically with the inference that it leads to anti-Semitism. Those who seek to hold to Reformed evangelical theology then are slandered by travelling ministries and videos on Christian TV. The reason for this is perhaps a struggle for the identity of Israel between Jews and Christians, but it leads to division in the Church. Although I think such teaching does exist, and needs to be challenged, the charge of being an advocate of replacement theology is often given to anyone who is sceptical of the Zionist' claims, irrespective of their actual teachings. The claim can then become a dismissive straw-man argument against one's opponents, thus avoiding the need to engage in careful analysis that might call one's own beliefs into question. Replacement theology is sometimes known as supersessionism in America, supercessionism in Britain, and substitution theology in parts of Europe.

On the other hand there are some theologians who discuss replacement theology in a more careful manner. R. Kendall Soulen, who is apparently not a Christian Zionist, discusses this question at length, and I will refer to his work through much of this chapter. However, it is notable that Soulen does not address the theology of John Calvin.[8] Soulen's work does however have some interesting points that need to be considered.

The New Testament has much to say about the relationship between Jews and Gentiles in the Church, although Soulen doesn't really address Pauline theology in much depth. But after the New Testament period, the early Church continued to try and fit the emerging Christian faith within an historical and global context as it was losing its initial Jewish identity. The Church Fathers were also facing a number of challenges, especially from the continuation of Judaism that was

---

[8] Soulen, R.K., *The God of Israel and Christian Theology*, Minneapolis: Fortress Press, 1996

resisting the gospel message, and from Greek paganism and various forms of Gnosticism. There was then an increasing tendency to respond to the pagan and Greek challenges to Christianity, and in order to convert Gentiles it was thought necessary to present the faith in a more Greek minded manner, as opposed to one based upon the Hebraic foundation. As part of this endeavour Christianity's Jewish roots were increasingly overlooked. The other concern of the early Christian community involved responding to the Jews who stubbornly rejected the gospel.

Soulen believes that there are basically three views of supersessionism amongst Christian theologians.[9] Starting with the Church Fathers, Soulen comments that historically some argued for a punitive supersessionism where God was believed to have first condemned the Jews for rejecting Jesus as the promised Messiah. Subsequently there was believed to be an ongoing divine punishment against them. In this teaching it is held that God rejected the Jews because they stubbornly turned away from his work of salvation. Soulen comments that although this teaching is more obviously hostile to the Jews it is not so deeply engrained that it cannot quite easily be given up. On the other hand he believes that there is a more general belief amongst non-Zionist theologians that focuses on the practical purposes of God; that is economic supersessionism. In this light God's economy of salvation is seen to run through the Church, as it is now believed to represent the true spiritual Israel in Christ that has replaced carnal Israel. The third view is identified by Soulen as structural supersessionism where he argues that many Christians have rejected the Old Testament altogether considering it to be of little historical importance to Christian faith.

Soulen notes that none of these views are mutually exclusive. From later discussions I hope to show that the Old Testament has much to say about God's continuing purposes for Israel, but that these purposes are being worked out through Christ and the Church. While recognising the Greek influence in the Church, I do not believe that structural supersessionism need be accepted as endemic. This is because the older Hebrew Scriptures and the life of Israel before Christ have much to say to us today; and the Scriptures are recognised in this light by many evangelical Christians. Although perhaps some sections of the Church have failed to address the Old Testament teaching adequately I don't think this is universally the case.

What is of further interest is that some supporters of Christian Zionism seem to adopt aspects of these positions, especially in terms of

---

[9] Soulen, *The God of Israel and Christian Theology*, pp.30-31, 181 n.6.

Replacement Theology

Soulen's punitive form. Pawson for instance, while arguing that the Jews are still a people before God, also comments that presently it is in a negative sense because they have been hardened.[10] It is possible to believe that the Jews are still in covenant relationship with God, but as a people they are presently being punished for their unfaithfulness. There is then the possibility of developing a theology of what might be termed punitive non-supersessionism. It could be argued that God is punishing the Jews because they are still in covenant with him through the Law of Moses. There are dangers in arguing for such a punitive theology I believe, because it can easily descend into a call to persecute Jews as has happened in history (although Pawson is clearly not advocating this).[11] But is God actively punishing rebellious Jews today because they are still in covenant with him and because of their rejection of Jesus? I will leave this question aside for now because of the difficulties it presents, but will comment that I would suggest that according to Scripture the glory of the Lord, and his presence, have departed from old Mosaic covenant ways of Judaism and its system of worship. Jesus for instance commented to the Pharisees that their 'house will be been left to them desolate' (Matt. 23), and instituted a new covenant. I would suggest that Jews have to some extent removed themselves from the protection of divine grace by rejecting Jesus.

Novak has developed a different approach to the question of replacement theology.[12] He considers what is meant by the 'new covenant' mentioned in Jeremiah (Jer. 31:31). He notes three interpretive options. Firstly, that the new covenant is an extension of the old; secondly that it is an addition to the old covenant; or thirdly that it is a replacement of the old covenant. Novak notes further that in the New Testament the new covenant was considered either an addition to or a replacement of the old covenant. Novak further argues from this that there are essentially two forms of replacement theology, a soft form and a hard form. The soft form sees the new covenant as an addition to the old covenant; the hard form considers it as a replacement to the old covenant. Novak comments that the soft form asserts that Jesus came to fulfil the old covenant promises, first for the God fearing Jews who

---

[10] Pawson, *Defending Christian Zionism*, pp. 73-93

[11] Pawson, *Defending Christian Zionism* p. 15, also categorises those who reject present day Zionism into supporters of liberal theology, replacement theology, fulfilment theology and finally liberation theology.

[12] Novak, D., (2004) 'The Covenant in Rabbinic Thought,' in Korn, E.B. (ed.), *Two Faiths, One Covenant?: Jewish and Christian Identity in the Presence of the Other*, Rowman & Littlefield.

accepted him, then also for the Gentiles who accepted the covenant through him. For those Jews who rejected Jesus, Novak comments that they should be seen as being under the old covenant because God's promises are irrevocable. Hard supersessionism on the other hand is the argument that the old covenant has been abolished once and for all, and Jews who continue to follow it are living in rebellion for rejecting Jesus. Many Christian Zionists in fact follow Novak in arguing that the claim that the new covenant is somehow an extension, addition or fulfilment of the old is still a form of replacement theology, even if only in a soft form. But if words mean anything is this fair or appropriate? I believe we can find a way forward that is faithful to Scripture, expresses a proper love and respect to the Jewish people even though rejecting Christian Zionism, and at the same time avoid the charge of replacement theology. So that is a fairly brief overview of ideas relating to replacement-type theology. I will now consider the historical development in more detail from the time of the Church Fathers onwards and begin to respond to these challenges.

The Church Fathers

Soulen deals at length with perceived supercessionism in the teaching of early Christianity. Justin Martyr lived in the first-half and middle period of the second century at a time when the Christian community was coming to terms with its faith, without the direct oversight of the apostles. Justin wrote a number of works including *First and Second Apologies* that were aimed at paganism, and *Dialogue with Trypho a Jew*, in which he responded to the continuing place of Judaism in relation to the Church. Soulen points out that the meta-narrative Justin adopted in his thinking involved an initial consummation of creation with Adam and Eve, followed by the Fall, then the redemptive work of Christ and the final consummation of all things in Jesus. In Justin's framework there was a tendency to subordinate the Old Testament life of Israel to the needs of the Church where the older prophetic writings were believed to have pointed towards Christ. In his *Dialogue* he argued that the Church had become the true spiritual Israel through the work of Christ as one crucified and resurrected.[13] The writings of the Old Testament then were believed to be pointing to the coming of Jesus and to his work, where Justin believed the Church was the new spiritual representation of Israel.[14] He further argued that in

---

[13] Justin Martyr, *Dialogue With Trypho* Chapter, 11 and 16, in *Ante-Nicene Fathers: The Writings of the Fathers Down to A.D. 325* 1:200.

[14] Soulen, *The God of Israel and Christian Theology*, pp. 34-40

God's justice and fairness there was now punishment for the Jews, with exile from their historical lands. This was for killing the prophets and the Messiah, but that God in his mercy and grace had spared them as a people. The Jews were then seen in terms of a continuing carnal people, while the Church was considered to be spiritual Israel.

Irenaeus of Lyon followed a generation after Justin and adopted a broadly similar framework in his major work *Against Heresies*. In this work against Gnostic heresies he wanted to show that the old covenant pointed towards the work of Christ. He tried to show more strongly that God's activity for the consummation of creation was through the Old Testament patriarchs of Abraham, Isaac, and Jacob, thus linking the old and new covenants.[15] Israel's place in this though remained subordinate to the overall purposes of God. There was a sense then that the status of Israel in the Old Testament was that of immaturity and childhood with an-ongoing process of training towards maturity. This process he believed reached its fullness in Christ, but that the Jews failed to respond to their natural calling. By dividing the old and new covenant he believed that God's economy of consummation involved a preparatory dispensation, or measure of grace as a training exercise for the Jewish people in the period before Christ.[16] Soulen writes that Irenaeus in effect sought to unify God's economy of salvation through Abraham and Israel towards Christ, but that the Jews rejected the gospel even though it had been prepared for them first. What was loss for the Jews was gain for the Gentiles. Thus, in Irenaeus' thinking, there was believed to be a unity in God's spiritual purposes through both covenants, but a carnal division had developed between Jews and Gentiles.[17]

Origen, in *Contra Celsus*, argued that the Jews couldn't be restored to God apart from Christ, because of the crime they had committed against him.[18] Origen believed also that God has now divorced the Jewish nation and married the Gentile Church under the new covenant. Perhaps with some influence coming from the Greek neo-Platonism of his time Origen further spiritualised or allegorised the promises relating to Israel and applied them to the Church. There was a tendency in Origen's thinking then to allegorise Israel's blessings with application instead given to the Church, but to interpret punishments

---

[15] Irenaeus *Against Heresies* 1.22.1 in Soulen Op. cit. p. 41

[16] Irenaeus *Against Heresies* 4.14.2 in Soulen Op. cit. p. 46

[17] Soulen, *The God of Israel and Christian Theology*, pp.40-48

[18] Origen, *Against Celsus* 4.22, in *Ante-Nicene Fathers: The Writings of the Fathers Down to A.D. 325* 4:506. Some references in this section are sourced via Paul Wilkinson's notes on replacement theology.

spoken against Israel as being literal. Cyprian of Carthage, a pupil of Tertullian who lived in the third century, also taught that the Jews had departed from God and thus lost God's favour, but subsequently Christians had 'succeeded in their place.'[19]

Augustine of Hippo argued that the Christian congregation was the true manifestation of Israel in the world commenting that; '…if [Christians] hold with a firm heart the grace of God which hath been given us, we are Israel.' And that 'The Christian people then is rather Israel.'[20] Augustine thought the Jews had become blind to their own Scriptures, but that in God's grace he had turned their offence into the 'salvation of the Gentiles.'[21] In *On Christian Doctrine*, Augustine argued that the Church had now possessed the Promised Land in a spiritual sense as spiritual Israel.[22]

As for the Jews who rejected Jesus, Augustine thought that the persistence of the unbelieving Jews, and the Old Testament Scriptures, were both a testimony to the Church that was spreading throughout the nations. This, Augustine believed, provided evidence to the world that Christians had not merely made up their faith concerning Christ, but that it was attested by Jewish history and prophecy.[23] A long and noble heritage was important for a faith system in those times and the continuation of Jews as a people was considered advantageous, especially as the Christian Church was becoming more influential across the known world.

Augustine thought that although God had dispersed the Jews, he had not destroyed them as an entire nation, but allowed them to exist as a separate group. Therefore their presence was a useful testimony for Christians in the world. Christians should therefore not harm or kill Jews. Pope Alexander II in the eleventh century even thought it a blasphemy to do such a thing because it would go against God's mercy. A number of scholars have noted that Augustine's comments had important social ramifications for the Jews as Christians permitted Jews to continue to live amongst them because of their apologetic value as a

---

[19] Cyprian of Carthage in the Preface to *Three Books of Testimonies Against the Jews*.
[20] Augustine, *On the Psalms* 114.3 in *Nicene and Post Nicene Fathers* 8:550
[21] Augustine, *City of God*, Book XVIII Ch. 46.
[22] Augustine, *On Christian Doctrine*, Book 3: Ch. 34
[23] Augustine, *The City of God*, XVIII Ch.46. in *Nicene and Post Nicene Fathers* 2:389

testimony to the truth of Christianity.[24] However, it is clear that at other times Christian leaders ignored Augustine's advice.[25]

So it would appear that the early Church Fathers were arguing that the increasingly Gentile Church now represented the true manifestation of Israel on the earth because of the historical work of Christ, but largely in a spiritual sense. It would however I think be wrong to categorise their beliefs too strongly as representing a single, unified position. Soulen though is quite critical of the Church Fathers and suggests that the standard theological framework that they developed was really a weak form of Gnosticism because it effectively divided spiritual Israel from carnal Israel. In this sense Soulen believes it represents structural supersessionism because it is a flight from history with the Church saved apart from its historical Jewish roots. This claimed semi-Gnostic belief was due to a failure to fully recognise the historical role of Israel in the Old Testament, and instead it relegated the place of Israel in the meta-narrative of the standard framework to an understanding of God's work in creation.[26] Although clearly the Greek thinking was coming to the fore it would be wrong to overstate the case. In Augustine's later work, *The City of God* (*de Civitas Dei*), he shows the growth of the divine city through the Old Testament, and in his own time overcoming the corruption of Rome that was collapsing.

It was at first recognised in the apostolic period by Paul that Gentile believers had been grafted into the Israelite olive tree alongside the Jewish believers in Christ (Rom. 11:11-24). However, as time progressed and the culture of Christianity became more and more Gentile in character and outlook, recognition of the Jewish origin and identity of Christianity was gradually downgraded. Instead of viewing the Church as an outgrowth from a Jewish root, the Gentile Church perhaps came to see that it had replaced Israel in God's plan. The suspicion is that replacement theology developed along non-scriptural lines and in later centuries was used to justify the maltreatment of Jews

---

[24] See for instance: Cohen, J., 'Introduction', in Jeremy Cohen (ed.), *Essential Papers on Judaism and Christianity in Conflict: From Late Antiquity to the Reformation*, New York: New York University Press, 1991, pp. 13–14 ; or Hood, J.Y. B., *Aquinas and the Jews*, (Philadelphia: University of Pennsylvania Press, (1995), p. 12f ; or Carroll, J., *Constantine's Sword: The Church and the Jews*, Boston: Houghton Mifflin, 2001

[25] Schama, S, *The Story of the Jews, by Simon Schama – extract*, from The Story of the Jews: Finding the Words (1000BCE–1492CE) by Simon Schama, published by Bodley Head. Published in the Daily Telegraph, August 2013

[26] Soulen, *The God of Israel and Christian Theology*, pp. 48-56

by Christian authorities.[27] I think that believers ought to take seriously Soulen's claim that some areas of Christian thought have developed a semi-Gnostic theology by forgetting the historical Hebraic roots. Perhaps there is at least some merit in this claim, although it is relevant to note that Soulen doesn't engage with Pauline theology in any real depth, and ignores Calvin altogether.

There was evidentially a developing separation between Judaism and Christianity that was at least in part the work of the Church, but also I believe in part due to the actions of the Jewish authorities who had persecuted the early Jewish Christian community. For instance by throwing James the half-brother of Jesus off the roof of the temple, and then stoning him to death. Christians perhaps also recalled that Stephen had been stoned to death as well, and the ongoing struggles helped to deepen the sense of separateness and division between Jews and Christians. As a result of this division there was, I believe, a developing neglect and misunderstanding of the full knowledge of Old Testament Scriptures by an increasingly Gentile Church.

Once the Roman Empire had legitimised the presence of Christianity, the Roman Catholic Church further worked to consolidate its power by enforcing acceptance of its central dogmas. With the conversion of the Roman Emperor Constantine to Christianity there was a desire to bring harmony to various theological disputes. One response was the Council of Nicea that was called to standardise theology and reject heresy, with the Arian controversy being a major problem at the time. Thus the power of the Roman Church became increasingly centralised, especially in Rome, and the Jews were gradually marginalized and separated from the Christian community. The initial Jewish identity of Christianity was slowly eroded. Eventually the Bishop of Rome came to take the place of the Roman Emperor and ascended over the other bishops, claiming jurisdiction across the whole of the known Christian world. With the Catholic Church exercising so much power, there were many opportunities for abuse, especially against the Jewish communities across Europe. The central dogmas of the Church were then imposed by force, which really ran against the teachings of Christ. This abuse of power also raised its head with the forced conversion of many Jews, for instance in Spain and the later

---

[27] It may be noted also that Judaism was developing away from its historical roots, with the Pharisaic Talmud becoming more and more authoritative in the lives of many Jewish people, over and above the Law of Moses, and the writings of the prophets. This may be seen as another form of replacement theology where the tradition of the elders was replacing the Law of Moses.

Inquisition. Some perhaps remained only nominal Christians and therefore did not come to love Jesus as their own Messiah. When Luther and the Protestant reformers later challenged the authority of Rome, there was much bloodshed across Europe. Luther at first embraced the Jews, but when his own power was secure he turned against them.[28] Jews have therefore suffered under Protestant and Catholic rulers.

This is of course only a brief outline of Church history in relation to Jews, but a couple of points may be noted from this short historical sketch. Soulen, as well as many supporters of Christian Zionism, makes the claim that much of this antagonism against Jews is because of replacement-type theology that is believed to have arisen from the time of the Church Fathers. While I think that there is some partial truth in this claim the real causes run deeper. These causes also seem to involve a struggle over Church authority and power, together with a lack of understanding and trust in both directions. But questions remain around the nature and adequacy of replacement theology.

Soulen also refers to the thinking of two Germanic theologian-philosophers of the Enlightenment, Immanuel Kant and Friedrich Schleiermacher. He believes that they went further in removing the historical aspect of Judaism from Christianity, what he terms the 'de-Judaization' of Christianity.[29] The reason for this was due to their desire to develop a purely rational basis for Christian faith, and thus they believed that regarding Christianity in its historical Jewish root was an anachronism. Soulen argues that whereas the Church Fathers merely subordinated Judaism to Christianity, Kant and Schleiermacher went further and expelled Judaism from having any place in Christian thought at all. And that which was believed to have been expelled from God's plan in this way may be seen to have no future place in society and may therefore be allowed to wither away.[30]

Soulen does have important things to say about the development of Christian theology in terms of a gradual loss of understanding of its Jewish roots. However, I think his assessment of the problem is incomplete. Kant and Schleiermacher were of course products of the Enlightenment, which has itself worked to undermine Christianity. He

---

[28] Luther also turned against the non-conformist Anabaptists, and there was tension and hostility between the Lutherans and Calvinists.
[29] Soulen, *The God of Israel and Christian Theology*, pp. 57-80
[30] It has also been argued, for instance by Wiener, that the rise of anti-Semitism in Germany was due to the strong opposition to Jews by Luther. Wiener, P.F. *Martin Luther: Hitler's Spiritual Ancestor*, Gustav Broukal Press, 1985. Originally written during World War II as a Win the Peace Pamphlet, No 3, Hutchinson and Co., London, (nd).

doesn't engage with the teachings of Paul in any great depth and ignores the type of covenantal theology developed by Calvin, which I think is a major weakness of his wider claims. Soulen's claim about the theology of the Church Fathers concerning structural supersessionism and a latent semi-Gnosticism in the standard framework, one that divides spiritual Israel from carnal Israel, does need to be taken seriously though. The question I want to ask now is how this divide between spiritual Israel and carnal Israel is being closed. In order to begin to answer this question it is first necessary to look at the covenantal theology of Calvin in order to understand his thinking with greater depth.

Calvin's Covenantal Theology

As noted in the previous section Soulen does not address the theology of John Calvin at all, or of Paul's teachings with any great depth. However, according to some other Christian Zionists, Calvin's covenantal theology is really no more than a form of replacement theology, and thus a rejection of the covenant made by God to Jews. Wilkinson for instance comments that the 'adversus Judaeus' (against the Jews) tradition is enshrined in Origen and Augustine's allegorical theology, and that this is central to the Reformed covenant theology later taken up as part of the *Westminster Confession of Faith* of 1646. Wilkinson expresses regret that Calvin remained influenced by the theology of Augustine even though he rejected the authority of the Roman Catholic Church. Augustine therefore continued to shape Calvin's view of the Church and Israel. Wilkinson further calls Covenant theology a 'philosophical system' and notes that it teaches that God has only ever had one people under an overarching covenant of grace that embrace all the biblical covenants.[31] There are though, I believe, some important differences between the types of replacement theology characterised by Soulen, and Calvin's covenantal theology. Identifying the Church as a continuation of God's plan regarding Israel is not an argument that is against the Jews, but one that is in continuity and unity with at least one part of the Jewish community; perhaps only a remnant part, but a part nonetheless. It is the continuity of a remnant of Jews from the Old Testament to the New that is of importance to a proper understanding of this discussion. Neither is it fair to label replacement theology a 'philosophical system' as it is clearly a well-developed theological system. And perhaps ironically it may have

---

[31] Wilkinson, *For Zion's Sake*, pp. 42-43.

formed in part the basis for Darby's dispensationalism. It is worth now looking a little deeper into Calvin's teaching.

Hans-Joachim Kraus has conducted an interesting study of Calvin's belief.[32] Calvin appears to have engaged with the Hebrew Scriptures seriously and showed a determination in reading the original writings of Jewish scholars such as Ibn Ezra and Rashi in order to gain a better understanding of the Old Testament. Calvin believed that salvation was from the Jews (John 4:22), and that God had called them as a people to reveal his glory to the world. Kraus believes that Calvin's high view of the Old Testament scriptures in fact led to greater respect for Jews in those countries that were under the influence of the French-Swiss reformer, as opposed to those nations that were influenced by Luther.

For Calvin, Jesus was considered to be central to a correct understanding of theology and the one who united the Church and Israel. Jesus was seen as the fulfillment of the Old Testament promises and one who took up the perfect role of prophet, priest and king of Israel. Thus for Calvin, Christ became the lens through which to view the whole of the Old and New Testaments.[33] Calvin for instance quoted from Matthew (Matt. 8:11) and noted that Jesus Christ promised his followers that the only kingdom of heaven is one in which Christians may sit down with Abraham, Isaac and Jacob,[34] and Calvin, like Luther, believed that Paul's use of 'Israel' in Romans (Rom. 11:25-26) referred to the union between Gentile and Jewish believers.[35] He believed further that the covenant that God had made with the Patriarchs was one that could not be broken because it was dependent solely upon God's mercy, the *sola gmita*.[36] There was then considered to be a family unity between Jews and Gentiles within God's covenant of grace that is fulfilled in and through Christ, but stretches back to Abraham. So Calvin believed that God retained a place for Israel in Christ, a commitment that could never be overthrown, because it was dependent upon God's faithfulness alone.

---

[32] Kraus, Hans-Joachim, 'Israel in the Theology of Calvin - Towards a New Approach to the Old Testament and Judaism', *Christian Jewish Relations,* Vol. 22, nos. 3 & 4, 1989

[33] From Augustine *Christus universae scripturae scopus est.*

[34] Calvin, J., *Institute of the Christian Religion.* (IV.XVI.14) (Garland, TX Galexie Software, 1999. Quoted in Sizer, S., *Christian Zionism: Road Map to Armageddon,* IVP, 2004, p. 27

[35] Sizer, S., Op. cit., p. 27.

[36] Kraus, '*Israel in the Theology of Calvin...*'.

However, Calvin also believed that the unity between the Church and Israel was because God had established an eternal Church, the *ecclesia aeterna* from the beginning of creation. Calvin therefore believed that the true Church or congregation (Gk. Ekklesia)[37] existed amongst the Jews and Israelites in the Old Testament, as well as in the New Testament. But the Church under the old covenant was in the form of childhood compared to the coming-of-age of adulthood that was enabled by the new covenant.[38] This was also the view of Irenaeus and the purpose of this structure was to train and educate the people towards maturity in Christ. The Law was thus appropriate for the old covenant, with the fulfilled gospel of grace necessary for maturity, although Calvin did not see a strong separation between law and grace even under the old covenant.[39] Calvin pointed out that the prophets looked forward to the restoration of the Church of Israel according to the everlasting covenant that God had promised to David and the earlier Patriarchs.[40] The overarching covenant was with Abraham, but that the outworking was in different modes of 'dispensations.'[41] Calvin then had a respectful approach to the Jews believing that God's promises to Israel could not be broken even though he believed that God's purposes in this plan were being worked out through the universal and eternal Church. This Church of Israel consisted of the Old Testament Israelites, and Jews and Gentiles united in the new covenant.[42]

Modern developments

In more recent years a strong movement in opposition to Christian Zionism has developed that seeks to counter the perceived politicisation of Christian belief that strongly supports the Israeli state.

---

[37] The Septuagint (LXX) uses the Greek word Ekklesia to refer to Israel as the congregation of the people of God in the Old Testament, and is used for the Church subsequently. See for instance Ladd, G.E., *The Gospel of the Kingdom*, Grand Rapids, Eerdmans Pulb., 1959, pp. 112-114

[38] Calvin, J., *Institutes of the Christian Religion*, (IV.II.7)

[39] See Kraus, Op. cit. Calvin, *Institutes,* (II.XI.2)

[40] Calvin, *Institutes,* (II.VI.4)

[41] Calvin, *Institutes,* (II.X.2). Calvin also influenced the *Westminster Confession of Faith* of 1643. Chapter VII *Of God's Covenant with Man* for instance states that the same covenant of grace has operated through history under various 'dispensations.' Chapter XIX *Of the Law of God* comments that God gave to the '…people of Israel, as a church under age, ceremonial laws…now abrogated, under the New Testament.'

[42] Kraus also notes that Calvin wrote a dialogue with an unnamed Jew entitled *A quaestiones et objects Judaei cuiusdam*

Replacement Theology

This is described and critiqued most clearly in two books by Stephen Sizer, *Zion's Christian Soldiers* and *Christian Zionism: Road Map to Armageddon*. Sizer is critical of the development of Christian Zionism because of this apparent right-wing political support. Sizer argues instead for Calvin's type of covenantal theology where the Christian Church should be seen as being in unity and continuity with biblical Israel, not a replacement of Israel. Although Sizer doesn't deny the right of Jews to a homeland in the Middle East he is a supporter of political campaigning for Palestinian rights. There have been some robust responses to these developments against Christian Zionism; for instance *The Jews, Modern Israel and the New Supercessionism* edited by Calvin L. Smith and Paul Wilkinson's *For Zion's Sake*. The claim is that those who strongly resist the policies of the State of Israel are in fact advocating replacement theology. It is clear I think that both sides in this modern dispute are engaged in political activity because of their theological beliefs. However, I believe that we should be careful to separate the theology from the politics here in order to ask whether those opposed to Christian Zionism are really arguing for replacement theology. I believe the evidence suggests that Sizer's theology is really in line with Calvin's beliefs, and the opposition is to a political theology that is perceived to be denying human rights to Palestinians. While I believe there is a place for a prophetic ministry that brings God's word to governments and politicians, and on both sides to Jews and Palestinians, I believe Christians do need to be careful that it doesn't become one-sided and descend into worldly political manipulation.

But leaving the politics aside, there have also been a number of other recent theological studies that broadly follow Calvin's theology. David Holwerda argues that there is only one covenant and not two in his book *Jesus and Israel: One Covenant or Two?* From this he provides a clear defence of the classical Reformed theology of Calvin that includes a place for Israel within the meta-narrative of salvation. Tom Wright also has a strong place for Israel within his new perspective on Paul, although like Calvin's belief it is one where Israel's position today is fulfilled within Christ and through the Church. Wright believes that Paul's teaching involved recognition that God has only ever had one single plan of salvation for the whole world, and that this plan was through Israel as the descendents of Abraham.[43] Wright rejects what he sees as the error of neo-Marcionism, where recognition of the Church's Jewish foundations is lost and the covenant of Abraham is forgotten. Instead, he reaffirms that the new covenant is the fulfilment of God's

---

[43] Wright, N.T, *Justification: God's Plan and Paul's Vision*, London: SPCK, 2009, pp. 18-19, 49, 74, 171

promises in the old; that Paul's teaching on justification was not an attack on Judaism; and that Christianity was not meant as a replacement of the Jews. Instead, the message that Paul taught was one that sought to embrace the Jewish people as the gospel was going out into the wider world.

Today we should view the whole world as the Holy Land, and the restoration of Israel that the disciples were looking for was fulfilled in Jesus. Wright is however critical of Christian Zionism because he believes it is repeating the error that Paul challenged in Galatians. It therefore renders the redemptive work of Christ incomplete and often has a rather callous disregard for Palestinians, including those within the historical Christian community. He argues that we should not overlook the suffering of Palestinians, but our response to the pain and suffering in the Middle East should be one of prayer.[44]

So whereas national Israel had failed in it's calling, Jesus as the promised Messiah of Israel completed the work as the legitimate seed of Abraham. Furthermore, the argument of Holwerda is that Jesus in effect became Israel through his life, death and resurrection, and that within the new covenant the place of Israel is located solely in and through the Messiah. Whereas Israel of old had failed, Jesus succeeded, and all those who came to accept Jesus as the Messiah, whether Jew or Gentile, were effectively grafted into Israel. This comes from Isaiah where the Messiah is seen as the root of Jesse, a tender shoot growing out of the remnant stump of Israel. This is not replacement theology because that ethnic part of Israel that has faith in Christ is included in him, as are all the Gentiles who too have become the seed of Abraham (Gal. 3:29). In this sense then there is unity in the Church between Jews and Gentiles.

So my contention in this chapter is that it is possible to develop a theology that avoids the errors of replacement theology. This can be done by embracing the Hebraic root and foundation of the Christian Church, and by recognising the continuity of God's purposes through Abraham and Israel in the Church, even if only through a remnant that is centred in Christ.

---

[44] Wright, N.T., *Way of the Lord: Christian Pilgrimage in the Holy Land and Beyond*. 1999, London: SPCK; Grand Rapids: Eerdmans, pp.119-130. Marcion, who lived during the 2nd century, believed that the loving God of the New Testament was different from the apparently cruel God of the Old.

Chapter 3

The Roots of Christian Zionism

The other view that is common today is the belief that God still has a purpose for the Jews and a Jewish state today. This purpose is considered by some to be apart from the Christian Church because ethnic Israel is still believed to be in covenant relationship with God. This is demonstrated, it is claimed, by the formation of the modern State of Israel on the 14th May 1948. Moves to restore the Jewish State of Israel began in the early nineteenth century, as evidenced for instance by the establishment of a British Consulate in Jerusalem in 1838. A group from the Church of Scotland also wrote a report, published in 1840, entitled a *'Memorandum to Protestant Monarchs of Europe for the Restoration of the Jews to Palestine'* arguing for the re-establishment of a State of Israel. In this chapter I am going to examine the rise of Christian Zionism amongst Christian non-conformists, and also related theological positions that have developed within some of the more mainstream Protestant denominations.

One of the main theological influences for a renewed interest in a state of Israel came through Edward Irving and Henry Drummond who were instrumental in forming the Catholic Apostolic Church. Also influential was the Plymouth Brethren leader, and former Church of Ireland Minister, John Nelson Darby. Darby later adopted and developed the pro-Israel theological framework of dispensationalism from Irving and Drummond's Zionist foundations. Darby it would seem was developing his dispensationalist theology through the 1830s and early 1840s with influence coming from both Irving and Drummond, although the origin of the theology of Christian Zionism and dispensationalism is often wrongly attributed primarily to Darby and therefore misunderstood. The root of this emerging theology appears to stretch further back in time; Wilkinson for instance argues that various puritans believed that Jews would be restored to the land in the last days.[45] It is therefore important to look at the influences that led to the development of dispensationalism and Christian Zionism as theological concepts afresh to see if it is possible to understand their origin a little better.

---

[45] Wilkinson, *For Zion's Sake*, pp. 135-161

Promoting Christianity Among the Jews

Some of those who promoted the idea of the restoration of a Jewish state were involved with the London Society for Promoting Christianity Among the Jews (LSPCJ). The LSPCJ was formed in on the 4th August 1808 under the leadership of Joseph Frey, the son of a German Rabbi, with the original grand title of 'London Society for the Purpose of Visiting and Relieving the Sick and Distressed and Instructing the Ignorant especially such as are of the Jewish Nation.' On the 1st of March 1809 it was changed to the slightly easier LSPCJ, and within a few years had attracted some very notable supporters and patrons, including from the evangelical community. In 1815 it was taken over by the Anglican Church as a result of debts and mounting costs of administration. Officially it did not take a view on the correct interpretation of eschatology, writing a disclaimer to that effect on the 27th October 1823, although many supporters believed in the physical restoration of the Jews to the land of Israel. As a result of the disclaimer the Vice President Lewis Way resigned because of his commitment to the return of Jews to the land before conversion to Christ.[46] Therefore it would appear that although many of those interested in the return of the Jews to the land of Palestine were involved with the LSPCJ, the organisation as a whole did not take a clear stand in that direction in the early nineteenth century. However, as Wilkinson notes, the 1881/2 Russian pogroms led the LSPCJ to issue a statement that they believed that this was part of a move of God to bring Jews back into their ancient lands.[47]

Edward Irving

The Scottish Presbyterian Edward Irving was partly influenced by a number of Jesuit theologians, having translated into English the work of the Chilean Jesuit Manuel de Lacunza. This was entitled *The Coming of Messiah into Glory and Majesty*, and published in a two-volume edition in 1826 and 1827. Lacunza, who died in 1801, wrote in 1790 under the pseudonym of Ben Ezra, a supposed converted Jew. Although Lacunza rejected the historicist view of eschatology in favour of a futurist interpretation, he considered that the antichrist would be a person, or confederacy of people opposed to God and believed that the antichrist would be defeated before and during the period of the return of Christ. Lacunza did not teach the pre-tribulation rapture envisaged by

---

[46] Wilkinson, *For Zion's Sake*, pp. 167-169.
[47] Wilkinson, *For Zion's Sake*, p. 169.

Irving and Darby, although he did believe that Christians would be caught up into the air with Christ at the final conflagration, and return with him to the earth in the 'day of the Lord's coming.' A 'day' that was thought to last for up to 45 earth days.[48] However, Lacunza in his eschatological scheme had believers returning to the earth during that 45-day period as messengers sent from God.[49]

The Jesuits had previously discussed both futurist and historicist views of the end times. The sixteenth century Jesuit Riberia had supported futurist eschatology where the antichrist would come and build a new temple in Jerusalem and outlaw Christianity. On the other hand the Jesuit Cuninghame, writing in 1813, believed Christ would return before the millennium reign mentioned in Revelation, while Alcazar (who died in 1613) and his followers interpreted Revelation in terms of fulfilment through the first century Roman Empire. So, although Irving found some influence in Jesuit theology, this influence is far from the complete picture. As part of his translation of Lacunza's work, Irving also wrote a 126 page *Preliminary Discourse* for these volumes in which he set out his own views on the end times and support for a new State of Israel. Incidentally, this preliminary discourse was dated as being written during Christmas 1826, and it may be noted that Irving reached different conclusions to those drawn by Lacunza.

In 1826 Irving freely spoke in terms of dispensations and argued that the wickedness of the Gentile nations was such that God would bring judgement upon them and remove them from their place. Only the elect would be saved and caught up into heaven; Irving quoted from Isaiah 24 and applied it to the Gentiles.[50] Secondly, Irving argued, once God had judged the Gentiles for unfaithfulness, God would restore a remnant of Jews. He commented that "The restoration of the Jewish nation, to be again the Church of God, and their re-establishment in their own land, to be the head of the nations, and the centre of the earth's unity."[51]

Another theme of Irving's theology was the restoration of spiritual gifts to the Church prior to Christ's return, and there was some excitement at the house of James and George MacDonald, and sister Margaret, in Port Glasgow. Manifestations of the Spirit were believed to be taking place. In March or April of 1830 Margaret believed she had a

---

[48] Lacunza, M. *The Coming of Messiah into Glory and Majesty*, (Trans. Irving, E.), (2 Vols.), Vol. II, 1826/27, p. 250.

[49] Lacunza, Op. cit., pp. 262-263.

[50] Irving, E. 'Preliminary Discourse,' in Lacunza, M. *The Coming of Messiah into Glory and Majesty*, (Trans. Irving, E.), (2 Vols.), Vol. I, 1826, p. iv.

[51] Irving, E., Preliminary Discourse, Op.cit., pp. iv & viii.

vision of a rapture where 'Spirit filled' Christians would be taken up into Christ before the antichrist was to be revealed, while the rest would go through the tribulation. This greatly impacted on Irving's beliefs, although a careful reading of the vision, if accepted as a valid prophecy, might suggest that it should be read to mean that Spirit filled Christians would be protected through the tribulation that was to come, and that it was not speaking of a physical rapture prior to the second coming of Christ. She related the spiritual coming to the parable of the wise virgins who kept their lamps burning so that we '…may discern that which cometh not with observation to the natural eye.'[52] What is interesting about the vision of Margaret MacDonald is that it warns of a false-Christ to come who will test the true Spirit filled believers who are to go through the tribulation, and not be taken out of it. Only those filled with the Holy Spirit would have the enlightened discernment once they had been brought into Christ afresh through a 'spiritual renewal.' Thus they would be able to recognise the antichrist through the time of tribulation. She commented that there '…will be outward trial, …but [it is] principally temptation.' And the 'trial of the Church is from Antichrist. It is by being filled with the Spirit that we shall be kept.'[53]

Incidentally similar prophetic promises were given in the New Testament period to encourage the believers to persevere through suffering and deception. In this sense then the great tribulation should not be seen as simply a time of physical suffering, but a time also of testing and deception in the Church; and this has been the nature of threats to Christianity through history. Danger comes from external violence and internal false teaching. In the prophecy she further warns that some people were 'turning from Jesus' and thus 'not entering in by the door', but 'passing the cross.'[54]

While it is possible to read Margaret MacDonald's prophecy in terms of the ongoing work of the Holy Spirit in the present Christian age, others read it to imply that there would be a secret physical rapture to come that would mark a new dispensation for Jews apart from the Gentile Church. Drummond and Irving's quarterly journal, *The Morning Watch*, (also known as *The Quarterly Journal of Prophecy and Theological Review*) published a commentary under a pseudonym 'Fidus,' which argued in the September 1830 edition that there would be a partial pre-tribulation rapture. In the June 1831 edition of *The Morning Watch* Irving made his own pre-tribulation teaching more explicit.

---

[52] In Norton, R., *Memoirs of James and George Macdonald of Port-Glasgow*, 1840, pp. 171-176. Based on her hand written account of 1830.

[53] Norton, *Memoirs*, pp. 171-176.

[54] Norton, *Memoirs*, pp. 171-176.

Interestingly then it may be seen that Margaret's words had the same effect as some of Jesus' parables in that it blinded some eyes while opening the eyes of others (Matt. 13: 10-17).

According to Irving Jerusalem was to be established as the centre of God's plan for the re-emergent Jewish nation and the world. Jesus was to come back, not in power and glory at first, but to take the Gentile saints away in a secret rapture. Believers, both the dead and those still living, would be caught up to meet him in the air. Therefore it would allow people to escape the great tribulation that was to come upon the earth.[55]

As noted, Edward Irving, as well as being influenced by the Jesuits, was also closely associated with Henry Drummond. Drummond was a descendent of an aristocratic Scottish banking family with Hungarian ancestry and also with links to well known Jewish banking families in Europe. Both Drummond and Irving helped to establish the Catholic Apostolic Church through a number of conferences on prophecy. These were held in 1826 and 1830 in Drummond's stately home at Albury, Surrey. Drummond was closely associated with the LSPCJ, as was the prominent Joseph Wolff who was also present at the Albury meetings. Wolff was also of European origin and a Christian convert from Judaism who later named his own son after Henry Drummond. Drummond also wrote articles for *The Morning Watch* that he controlled with Irving and a few others. This journal often discussed ideas along the lines of dispensationalism and support for a new Jewish state, as well as discussions on such things as cabalism and reports of the various utterances from Christian prophetesses as noted above. Henry Drummond for instance had a letter published in *The Morning Watch* of the 1st September 1829 in which he enclosed a Jewish prophecy from a learned Rabbi by the name of Rabbi Samson of Oster Poli, whom he described as a 'great Cabalist.' He placed great credence on the word of this Rabbi who foretold judgement on France, Spain and Russia followed by the calling of the Jews and the coming of 'David.' Drummond further criticised the amount of effort the Church used in preaching the gospel, considered the '...bustle for the circulation of Bibles and Tracts, sending out missionaries, and emancipating the oppressed of mankind' to be a '...tremendous delusion.'[56] Instead, Drummond believed that the Church should be primarily engaged in

---

[55] See for instance, MacPherson, D., *The Real Manuel Lacunza*, (nd).

[56] Drummond, H., *Dialogues on Prophecy*, Vol I, London: James Nisbet, 1827, pp. 6, vi-vii; in Wilkinson, Op. cit., pp. 179-180.

supporting the national restoration of Jews to their ancestral lands, and that this should be a central doctrine.[57]

There was great expectation and enthusiasm that God was doing a new thing through subsequent meetings of the Catholic Apostolic Church. But another developing stream, that was to become known as the Plymouth Brethren, was shaped by conferences held at Powerscourt in Ireland between the years 1831 to 1834. Although it should be noted that Brethren assemblies were developing prior to these conferences through the work of a number of travelling preachers such as George Muller, Henry Craik and Benjamin Wills Newton, especially in Southwest England and Ireland A number of small Brethren assemblies were also developing in Dublin during the late 1820s with members including the Catholic Edward Cronin, Church of Ireland Minister J.N. Darby, Edward Wilson of the Bible Society, and the Brethren missionary pioneer Anthony Norris Groves, amongst others.[58]

John Nelson Darby

Darby first came into contact with the idea of a national conversion and return of the Jews to Israel through Richard Graves, his tutor at Dublin's Trinity College. Darby studied theology and the classics at Trinity College, and later acknowledged that Graves had been an influence on him. Graves was notably involved with the Dublin branch of the LSPCJ, and as early as 1811 was interested in the return of the Jews to the land, as was another of Darby's tutors, Richard Elrington.[59] According to Wilkinson, Darby was probably also influenced by some of the prophetic millennial writing and teaching of the Irish Catholics who he came into contact with in Ireland, such as the works of Charles Walmesley and Barney McHaighery.[60]

Darby was at first interested in converting Roman Catholics through preaching along with other like-minded Protestants, and with some success with 600 to 800 conversions claimed per week across Ireland. But he became disillusioned by the actions of the Church of Ireland's Archbishop Magee. Magee wanted Catholic converts to recognise the supremacy of the Protestant faith and give their allegiance to the British Crown. A petition was organised and submitted to the

---

[57] Drummond, H., *Dialogues on Prophecy,* Vol. I., p. 100; and Drummond, H., *Tracts for the Last Days*, Vol I, 1844, p. 344; in Wilkinson, *For Zion's Sake*, p. 179.
[58] See Wilkinson, *For Zion's Sake*, p. 76.
[59] Wilkinson, *For Zion's Sake*, pp. 73-75.
[60] Wilkinson, *For Zion's Sake*, p. 72.

British Parliament by the Church of Ireland authorities on the 1st February 1827 that sought protection against Rome, but it only put back the work of the Church with entrenchment on both sides. As a result the flow of Catholic converts dried up. This led Darby to reject political activism in the Church on the basis that God's kingdom was heavenly not earthly. He likened the action of the Church of Ireland authorities to the Roman Church's authority they were opposed to.[61] This action by the Church of Ireland was perhaps a major catalyst that led him to fellowship in newly formed assemblies in Dublin. These were to form the basis for the Brethren movement, and thus lead to a break with clerical authority. There is though some irony that while Darby wanted Christian faith to be free from political influence and non-conformist as part of a heavenly kingdom, his teachings helped to enable the formation of Christian and political Zionism, this on the basis that a national, political, and earthly State of Israel was sanctioned by God, once the Church had been removed at the rapture.

At the Powerscourt conferences Darby was influential and the theology of dispensationalism was later to become more important to Darby than the apparent exercise of charismatic gifts that were becoming evident in Catholic Apostolic Churches. Benjamin Wills Newton, the Oxford Secretary for the LSPCJ chose not to attend the 12th annual meeting of that organisation, but instead decided to attend the Powerscourt meetings. Incidentally, other members listed in the 1827 annual report of the Irish branch of the LSPCJ included Lady Powerscourt as a patroness.[62]

In 1829 Darby was still apparently arguing in favour of a historicist view of prophecy, with prophecies relating to Israel considered fulfilled within the Christian Church.[63] Although Darby did address the 11th annual meeting of LSPCJ meeting in Plymouth in October 1830, it wasn't until later in the 1830s that Darby fully accepted and developed the theology of dispensationalism. The second Powerscourt meeting in September 1832 further discussed the question of the status of a Jewish nation before God, and Darby wrote to the editor of the Christian Herald on the 15th October 1832 commenting that the delegates at the conference were concerned with questions such as 'by what covenant did the Jews, and shall the Jews, hold the land [of Israel]?'[64]

---

[61] Wilkinson, *For Zion's Sake*, p. 75-76.
[62] Wilkinson, *For Zion's Sake*, pp. 80-81.
[63] Darby, J.N., 'Reflections' *The Prophetic Inquiry,* No.1 1829, pp. 1-31
[64] In Wilkinson, *For Zion's Sake*, p. 81.

Darby denied that Irving influenced him in his dispensationalist theology and it is likely that a number of factors were responsible for his change of mind during the 1830s. But some influence must have come through Irving and Drummond's publication The Morning Watch.

This quarterly journal sprang out of the Albury conference of 1828 and was financed by Henry Drummond, with John Tudor acting as editor. It was to last for only four years.[65] Later, under the influence of the increasingly independent minded Irving, the Catholic Apostolic Church began praying earnestly for revival and an outpouring of the Holy Spirit, with claims for utterances of tongues at his Regent Square Church occurring in London in 1831. This perhaps did not fit well with those who had a stronger interest in the Jewish cause, and the accident-prone Irving died at the young age of 42. Walker comments that the writing of Drummond (and perhaps others) in this journal was a more likely source of Darby's developing dispensationalism through the 1830s,[66] although it is questionable from Darby's outward character how much credence he would (or should) have paid to prophetic utterances from cabalists. Darby had visited the MacDonald's house in 1830 to inquire about Margaret's prophecy, although he didn't seem too impressed with the words of prophecy from Margaret. Having said that it is also odd why Darby would have continued reading the journal that was apparently flirting with cabalism, when Darby was seemingly leading his Church grouping into greater outward purity and exclusivity. Although it would seem that Darby was captivated by an interest in the new ideas relating to a Jewish nation that were being presented and discussed in that journal.

Darby's Theology

It would I think be a mistake to believe that Darby's theology was simplistic, and that he was not well educated and well read in theology. As noted he was trained at the leading Dublin Trinity College. The evidence would suggest that his thinking developed out of ideas that were already present in Protestant theology. Wilkinson gives some further clues as to the inspiration for Darby's beliefs pointing out that there was a general interest in the re-emergence of the place of Jews in Christian thinking through the rise of the Puritan movement. Although the Reformers such as Calvin and Luther had broken with Rome they

---

[65] Wilkinson, *For Zion's Sake*, pp. 197-199.
[66] See for instance: Walker, A, *Restoring the Kingdom*, London: Hodder and Stoughton, 1985, pp. 218-222. Walker relies on a work by Rowdon, H. *The Origins of the Brethren*, Pickering and Inglis, 1967

were still influenced by Augustine's beliefs that were essentially a-millennial. However, Calvin's successor Theodore Beza for instance was more accommodating of the place of Jews within a future restored kingdom of God.[67] There was also a gradual rejection and move away from a-millennialism towards pre-millennialism during this period. Wilkinson doesn't though give many further pointers to the origin of Darby's beliefs.

The dispensationalism that Darby adopted and developed is a division of history into periods of divine grace whereby God deals with people through divinely established covenants. In that sense I believe it may be seen as deriving some influence from Calvin's covenantal theology and also has some commonality with the preparatory dispensational theology of Irenaeus. Use of the concept of different historic dispensations of grace by Darby may suggest that his dispensationalism is an outgrowth and arguably a corruption of Calvin's covenantal theology. But instead of the unity between the Church and Israel that Calvin had taught, there was instead division under a dual-covenant system within Darby's developing theology. Under Calvin's scheme Christ's work of grace upon the cross was the means of salvation for all who lived before and after the cross. To Calvin, the cross was considered central to history, but Calvin believed that God has only ever had one lineage of people, one congregation upon the earth. That is a line that passed from Adam to Noah and to Abraham, Isaac and Jacob. Then it passed to the Israelites before the tabernacle in the wilderness, and to the remnant of Jews who came back from Babylon, and finally to Jesus the promised Jewish Messiah, and also by extension through Jesus to the Gentile people of the world as well as Jews.

If this type of covenantal dispensationalism were all there was to Darby's theology it would be no more controversial than Calvin's developed theology. But Darby, following Irving and Drummond, primarily associated dispensations of grace with a particular form of eschatology. This involved a pre-tribulation rapture for the Gentiles together with the restoration of ethnic Jews to the land of Israel where they would again be able to approach God through the old covenant given to the Israelites at Mount Sinai. In other words, Darby's dual-covenant theology offered a separate dispensation of grace for Jews from that given to Gentiles. In the form that Darby envisaged, the theology of dispensationalism is then associated with belief that God would restore the old covenant practices of worship. And if taken to its logical conclusion it also involved the rebuilding of the temple in Jerusalem following, or perhaps immediately prior to, a secret rapture.

---

[67] Wilkinson, *For Zion's Sake*, p. 140

In this scenario there was considered to be a spiritual dispensation of grace for Gentiles under the new covenant, but that there remains another earthly dispensation of grace under the old covenant that will be re-established in fullness in the end-times. However, this theology in effect develops a false dualism between Israel and Christ, and between Jews and Gentiles. It divides Israel from the Messiah, and it also divides Jews from Gentiles. However, as I hope to show in later chapters, the prophets were emphatic that the promised Messiah was to come for Israel and Judah as well as the Gentile converts, thus bringing all people together in Christ within the framework of a single covenant.

Wilkinson though seeks to clarify Darby's theology with the belief that Darby has suffered from misunderstandings in the past, partly because of difficulty reading him. What I think is also the case is that Darby was developing his theology throughout his life, and some of his earlier thoughts may not be consistent with later thinking. Wilkinson though firstly notes that Darby saw the Christian Church and Israel as two separate and distinct groups of people. Darby for instance, preaching from Romans 9-11, urged Christians to recognise that they have been grafted into the Jewish olive root, but Darby did not believe it necessary for Jews to be re-grafted onto their own root because he believed their initial calling as a nation was irrevocable.[68] For Darby, Israel had a national irrevocable calling, but Christianity was a gathering of saints.[69] In fact Darby further distinguished between the Church, the Gentile nations and Israel.[70] Darby believed that the Church, consisting of Jewish and Gentile believers, exists because of a spiritual dispensation, or parenthesis. For Darby God's timeframe as it relates to Israel is suspended until the rapture, therefore the Church is presently receiving heavenly promises and will soon be caught up with Christ into a heavenly place at the rapture. The Christian believers will govern the earth with Christ in heaven during the period of the millennium. However, Israel's calling was national and earthly, and would form the seat for Christ's earthly rule. Christians then were considered by Darby to be in union with Christ, but Israel belongs to God as an earthly nation having superior spiritual promises to those of Israel.[71]

This does however give the appearance of the type of Gnosticism that the early Church was concerned with challenging, being

---

[68] Darby, *Romans*, 'Synopsis of the Books of The Bible,' Vol. 4, pp. 222-223; in Wilkinson, Op. cit., p. 97.
[69] Darby, *The Claims of the Church of Eng*land, 'The Collect Writings of J.N. Darby', Vol. 14, (1870) p. 197; in Wilkinson, *For Zion's Sake*, p.102
[70] Wilkinson, *For Zion's Sake,* pp. 98-99
[71] Wilkinson, *For Zion's Sake*, pp. 114-115

derived from forms of Greek philosophy. Such pagan philosophy, especially that of neo-Platonism, tended to divide the material from the spiritual, and it led to a dualism that was often characteristic of the Gnostic teachings. Darby's system then falsely separated the 'earthly' carnal Jewish people from the 'spiritual' Church and the Messiah, in effect denying God's full revelation of Christ to Jews. So Darby's theology, in separating spiritual Israel from carnal Israel in this manner, appears to perpetuate a form of Gnosticism. This also has similarities with the type of semi-Gnosticism that Soulen believes to be present in the supercessionist teaching of the Church Fathers such as Justin Martyr and Irenaeus. In other words, if there really is a problem with structural supersessionism in the standard model as Soulen suggests then Darby's theology seems to perpetuate it instead of addressing it adequately. This is because Darby's teaching implies that the Jewish people today remain separate from the spiritual blessing that Christian people enjoy in Christ through the new covenant.

The earthly bound Israel is also to be the centre of physical battles within Darby's thinking. According to Darby, during the seven-year period of the tribulation many of the events recorded in the book of Revelation are to take place with Satan and the antichrist struggling for control of the Jewish people for a time. And in the end only a remnant of Jews would be saved when Christ comes back to his earthly throne at the end of the great tribulation period. Although Darby believed in a national salvation for Israel outside of the Church, only a remnant would be left alive at the end of the great tribulation. Many Christian Zionists generally fail to see the sad irony in this theology, in that while they claim to love Jews, in reality the teaching involves the destruction of a majority of re-gathered Jews in another Holocaust.

Darby further believed that the third temple would be rebuilt during this period and Old Testament sacrificial practices reinstated. But only as symbols of Christ's great sacrifice that was to be the actual, but unrecognised means of salvation for Jews post-rapture. If this was Darby's thinking, it could be seen as an extension of another aspect of Calvin's covenantal theology. Calvin believed that prior to Christ's work on the cross the Israelites materially approached God with animal sacrifices, but ultimately they were being saved through the blood of Christ where God's grace was at work before the actual redemptive event of the cross. It is possible then that Darby envisaged a similar situation where the work of Christ will remain hidden from Jews, even though effective. The temple was necessary, Darby thought, because the antichrist would one day seek to take it over, thus committing the prophesised abomination that causes desolation.[72] Under this theological scheme then the Christian Church would be spared the terrors of the great tribulation, but the Jews as a nation would not be spared with only a remnant surviving until the end.

The problem as I see it for the dispensationalist theology of Darby is that it seeks to hide the gospel from the Jewish people when it has been revealed to them in Scripture openly. It seeks to deny Jews the opportunity for a heavenly blessing that Scripture clearly teaches is their inheritance through Abraham, and this for the reason of offering Jews a lesser earthly blessing and great earthly suffering. By seeking to deny the full blessing of Abraham to Jews, it teaches that Jews are to go through another great tribulation alone, and this following the terrors of the Holocaust in the twentieth century and two thousand years of Jewish suffering. It also seeks to divide Jews from Israelites and Gentiles, when Scripture clearly teaches that God seeks to bring unity to all as part of a common plan for humanity through Christ and in his Church. Calvin's theology instead involved unity for Jews and Gentiles in Christ, and God's plan is to bring blessing and unity to all people through the promise given to Abraham.[73]

Benjamin Wills Newton and the Open Brethren

Sadly, the dispensationalist theology of Darby was partly responsible for the split between the early Brethren movement into Open and Exclusive groupings, although questions over Brethren governance and a power struggle were also seemingly to blame. At face value though divisions caused by disagreement over the timing of the rapture, whether pre or post, seem remarkably trivial and quite perverse, but it really involved a fundamental question relating to the extent of Christ's sacrificial work of grace. In other words, it seemed to involve a different gospel for Israel than the gospel for Christians, and thus it

---

[72] Wilkinson, *For Zion's Sake*, pp. 128-131 (Although I believe this event took place between AD 67-70 in fulfilment of Daniel's prophecy).

[73] Pawson also rejects the dispensationalist theology of Darby in favour of classic Zionism, which he believes is the traditional view of evangelical Christians' pre-Darby. There is also a question about the misappropriation of language. Those opposed to Darby's position have nothing against the broad concept of covenantal dispensationalism. The same with Zionism; many prophecies about Jesus (Isa. 35: 1-10) speak of Zion as spiritual Israel. One of my favourite hymns as a child was Isaac Watts' 'We are marching to Zion,' which many found uplifting in celebrating the beauty of the New Jerusalem without it being considered an earthly state of Israel separately from Christ.

downplayed the centrality of the message for Jews. The gospel was then increasingly seen as being necessary for Gentiles only.

Oxford graduate and influential Brethren preacher Benjamin Wills Newton openly questioned Darby's eschatology and did not attend the 1834 Powerscourt meeting as a result, apparently disagreeing with Darby over the timing and purpose of the rapture. As noted, Darby believed the Christian Church could be taken up in the rapture at any moment with the unconverted Jews then left to fulfil God's purposes on earth. The Jews would go through the great tribulation alone, together with a newly constructed temple and the re-introduction of old covenant practices. Newton though was coming to see that the return of Christ and the rapture could not happen until after the conversion of Jews and restoration of the Israelite nation as part of the Christian Church, and that both Jewish and Gentile believers would go through the tribulation together under the new covenant. As such, certain things had to happen first before Christ would return. Both men wrote an increasingly acrimonious series of pamphlets. In the early 1840s Newton considered Darby's theology of dispensationalism to be a serious departure from sound theology because it implied that Jews could be reconciled to God apart from Christ's sacrificial work on the cross, and claimed that Darby was practically giving up on Christianity. Other leading Brethren such as George Muller of the Bristol based Bethesda fellowship and Henry Craik also rejected dispensationalist theology on similar grounds, even though Muller had at one time been an enthusiastic supporter of the work of the LSPCJ. He had come to Britain to train as an evangelist to Jews with the organisation. Samuel Tregelles, a notable Brethren teacher also opposed the dispensationalism of Darby, commenting in *The Christian Annotator* in 1855 that Christians should be looking for the final advent, not a secret rapture accusing those who proposed such notions of being 'Judaisers.'[74]

While in Switzerland, Darby was concerned about the growing influence that Newton had within the Brethren movement and accused him of clericalism, a charge that was heard by a council of thirteen in April 1845. Newton was acquitted of this charge, but the actual cause of the split between Darby's exclusive Plymouth grouping and the more open Bethesda assembly was to do with an erroneous pamphlet that Newton had written concerning the humanity of Christ in 1847. Although Newton quickly admitted and repented of his error, Darby rejected Newton's apology and used it to destroy Newton's reputation and also attempted to isolate Bethesda by putting the whole Church out

---

[74] Tregelles, S.P., 'Premillennial Advent' *The Christian Annotator*, June 16, 1855, p. 190.

of fellowship with his own grouping; this for allegedly accepting Newton's heresy and refusing to deal with Newton's errors. The fact that Muller and Bethesda had rejected Newton's theological musing from the beginning and accepted Newton's quick repentant apology meant that Darby's continued attack was a cause of further division. Thus, while the repentant Newton was ostracised, and Bethesda considered heretical by Darby's group, Darby continued to promote widely his own theology that Newton had considered to be a partial denial of Christ's work on the cross.[75] It does not take too much imagination to wonder whether these side issues that were raised against Newton by Darby and friends were because of Newton's disagreement with Darby's theology, and because his growing influence was seen as a threat. Incidentally, it may be noted that the Open Brethren prospered more than the Exclusive group because of their greater openness with a devolved authority amongst the assemblies providing local autonomy, although Christian Zionist' teaching persisted in parts of the Open Brethren movement as well.

In more recent years many in the charismatic House Church movement (that largely grew out of the Open Brethren in the 1960s) rejected Darby's theology because it was leading to a sort of dispiriting 'holy huddle' mentality in the Church. Christians were not encouraged to see the Church as the Kingdom of God on earth, but only as a disparate community of saints called out of the world, waiting for the second coming. However, many today in the House Church movement follow a Reformed Covenantal theology and see the Church as God's kingdom on earth, even though not yet having arrived in fullness.[76] It is true that this can lead to a triumphal theology if taken to excess, but that need be the case.

Cyrus Scofield

The new framework of dispensationalism was later popularised by Cyrus Scofield, particularly through his *Scofield Reference Bible* that was first published in the early twentieth century. The associated biblical commentary identified seven dispensations of grace. At this time the Anglican LSPCJ was also developing as a vehicle for

---

[75] This account comes from; Steer, R. *George Muller*, Christian Focus Publications, 1997, pp. 104-111

[76] Terry Virgo for instance endorses Stephen Sizer's book, *Zion's Christian Soldiers* on his website as a positive review. See:
[http://www.terryvirgo.org/Articles/266632/Terry_Virgo/Resources/Books/Zions_Christian_Soldiers.aspx]

promoting Zionism, rather than seeking to provide a platform for converting Jews to Christ. In fact, it is noteworthy that the development of Christian Zionism has been closely associated with this organisation from the beginning of the nineteenth century, even though at first it did not take an official line on such matters. Now, the difficulty for those who have been taught the dispensationalist theology comes in trying to marry-up this view with the teaching of the New Testament, especially in Paul's letters to the Galatians and Ephesians. However, it must be said in response to this that not all supporters of Christian Zionism hold to the dispensationalist views of Darby and Scofield. Many Christian Zionists hold to a classical approach believing that God has restored a Jewish state so that, in time, there will be a mass revival and conversion of Jews to Christ before he returns. This is for instance seems to be the view of David Pawson.[77]

Development of Political Zionism

The first Zionist Congress was held in 1897 in Basel in Switzerland. The leader of the Zionist movement, Theodor Herzl, later commented in his diary (on the 29th August) that this meeting would prove influential in the future establishment of the Jewish State. Furthermore, he thought that within fifty years everyone will see it take place. Exactly fifty years later in 1947, on the same date of 29th August, the United Nations General Assembly passed a resolution by 33 votes to 13 in favour of the partition of Palestine. Within a year the State of Israel was born in May 1948.[78] *The Balfour Declaration* of the 2nd November 1917 had also promised that 'His Majesty's Government views with favour the establishment in Palestine of a national home for Jewish people…'

These sorts of events encourage Christian proponents of Zionism to believe that God is re-establishing Israel in fulfilment of Old Testament prophecies. Further supportive evidence is given from various biblical passages such as Ezekiel 36 to 38. Here the dry bones are said to come back to life as pre-signifying Israel's re-settlement in the land of Canaan. Another favourite passage is Isaiah 49:22 where even the Gentiles are said to carry the scattered Israelites back to the land.

---

[77] See for instance: Pawson, D, *Defending Christian Zionism*, Bradford on Avon, Terra Nova Publ. 2008; and Pawson, D, *Israel in the New Testament*, Bradford on Avon, Terra Nova Publ. 2009

[78] See: Pearce, T., *The Omega Files*, New Wine Press, 2002, pp. 80-81

This is what the Sovereign LORD says: 'See, I will beckon to the Gentiles, I will lift up my banner to the peoples; they will bring your sons in their arms and carry your daughters on their shoulders.' (Isaiah 49:22).

It is events and passages such as these that encourage Christians today to support the modern State of Israel politically. There is less concern to put developments in the context of our prime Christian calling to make disciples of all nations. In later chapters I will argue that these passages from Ezekiel and Isaiah should be interpreted in terms of their fulfilment in the Messiah and applicable to the northern exile of the house of Israel, not to the present dispersion of Jews.

Hal Lindsey and Friends

Hal Lindsey in *The Late Great Planet Earth*, argued that Israel was being re-established by God, but that it would then be attacked by communist Russia as representatives of Gog and Magog (his interpretation of Ezekiel 38 & 39).[79] Wolvoord and Wolvoord develop a similar eschatology in their book *Armageddon*.[80] But the end of the Cold War led many to belief that Hal Lindsey and friends were probably wrong, and others have looked elsewhere for the antichrist; contenders included various rulers of Islamic countries as Islam is considered the main threat to Israel in the present day. Further interest in Christian Zionism has come through Tim La Haye's *Left Behind* series of books.

As noted previously, what is often overlooked is that some forms of Christian Zionism require the State of Israel to be re-established because it is believed that Israel is central to the end-time battle of Armageddon. In this interpretation only 144,000 Jews will survive the battle, implying that the Jews of Israel will experience another Holocaust. Of course most Christians are powerless to stop the unfolding of history (in human terms) with little political influence, but it is highly questionable whether Christians with greater political influence should engage in activity that places Jews in great danger. Regrettably, they seek to bring about a series of events based upon an incomplete understanding of eschatology. Instead, I would suggest that Christian political activity should be focused on the two great commissions; firstly to be good stewards of the earth, and secondly to spread the gospel message of God's love to all nations and people

---

[79] Lindsey, H. *The Late Great Planet Earth*, Zondervan, 1974, p.152
[80] Wolvoord J.F. and Wolvoord J.E. *Armageddon: Oil and the Middle East Crisis,* Zondervan Press, 1974

irrespective of their ethnic identity. To try and make prophecy happen through human endeavour, apart from God's grace, is really to manipulate God and is a form of unbelief. Some Jewish leaders have also expressed concern that extreme Christian Zionism is hindering the peace process with Palestinians. And further concern relates to the entrainment of Jews into another Holocaust.

The growth of Christian Zionism is also causing concern amongst Palestinian Christians. In recent times, the leading clergy in Jerusalem released the *Jerusalem Declaration on Christian Zionism* on the 22nd August 2006 in order to counter Christian Zionism. In this statement the Patriarch and local heads of the churches in Jerusalem called for an end to militarism and for Christians to work towards peace and for the healing of the nations. They further noted that God has reconciled himself to the world through Christ (2 Cor. 5:19) and observed that Christian Zionism is a 'modern theological and political movement' that is really an ideology containing false teaching. This new doctrine they claim corrupts the gospel of God's 'love, justice and reconciliation' and replaces it with a worldview based on 'empire, colonialism and militarism.' (The full text is given in Appendix 1).

But why is there such interest and excitement in this for Christians? It may be that the appeal of Zionism, and the attraction of the restoration of a state called Israel, has something to do with it being an extension of the apologetic value of the continuation of the Jews. This was a position held for instance by Augustine. Some Christians are excited by Israel because they see it as a fulfilment of prophecy and a confirmation of their own faith prior to the second coming. History is seen to be playing out according to a divine plan. The existence of Israel then fills a confirmatory need in some Christians. However, the Bible teaches that faith comes as a gift of the Holy Spirit who provides revelation of the person of Jesus Christ to the believer. The problem is though that in this excitement it is possible to fall into error if beliefs are not properly evaluated against Scripture. The New Testament writers noted on a number of occasions not to get carried away with whims of doctrine, and warned against false teachers who were trying to get into the flock. The two main concerns were from those who wanted to take the Christian community back to legalistic Judaism, and the other threat came from pagan sources such as neo-Platonism and Gnosticism.

Now, it is worth noting that there are different views amongst Christian Zionists. So what are the basic teachings? While the more extreme views are often not stated, and clearly not held by all, it is worth noting and reviewing the most basic beliefs here. In February 1996 the *Third International Christian Zionist Congress* held in Jerusalem issued a declaration with five main points that may be seen as representative of the bulk of views in this area; as follows:

> God the Father, Almighty, chose the ancient nation and people of Israel, the descendants of Abraham, Isaac and Jacob, to reveal His plan of redemption for the world. They remain elect of God, and without the Jewish nation His redemptive purposes for the world will not be completed.

> Jesus of Nazareth is the Messiah and has promised to return to Jerusalem, to Israel and to the world.

> It is reprehensible that generations of Jewish peoples have been killed and persecuted in the name of our Lord, and we challenge the Church to repent of any sins of commission or omission against them.

> The modern ingathering of the Jewish People to Eretz Israel and the rebirth of the nation of Israel are in fulfillment of biblical prophecies, as written in both Old and New Testaments.

> Christian believers are instructed by Scripture to acknowledge the Hebraic roots of their faith and to actively assist and participate in the plan of God for the ingathering of the Jewish People and the Restoration of the nation of Israel in our day.

These claims will be considered in some detail as we go through subsequent chapters, although it may be noted that there are some points of agreement here between both sides. The main points of disagreement here relate to the question of election for Jews who reside outside of Christ, the correct interpretation of Old Testament prophecy, the purpose of the State of Israel today, and the related question of the identity of Israel.

The Teachings of John Hagee

Another main protagonist at the present time for Christian Zionism is John Hagee, who has written many books on the subject and often appears on Christian TV promoting his views. Hagee is one of the foremost Christian supporters of the State of Israel. He believes strongly that God has called the nation to fulfil a divine plan today, and amongst his writing is the recent *In Defense of Israel* that takes his pro-Israel theology a stage further. He has also more recently established a group called Christians United For Israel (CUFI) in America to gather further support for Israel.[81] He also expresses concern over the injustices carried out against the Jews by Christians through history.

Hagee is a controversial figure, and seems to follow Darby's theology quite closely, although his beliefs sometimes seem to go beyond even what Darby taught. For instance he continues to maintain that people and nations must bless Israel in order to be blessed by applying the seven-fold blessing given to Abraham (Gen. 12:1-3) to the modern State of Israel. This claim is repeated in this latest book where he comments that those who curse Israel will also be cursed.[82] This claim does however overlook Paul's statement that Abraham's blessing has come upon the Gentiles by faith because of what Christ has done upon the cross (Gal. 3:14). Instead, through Christ the curse of the Law has been removed because Christ became a curse for all, but Hagee seems to argue that Christians can only partake of the blessing of Abraham by blessing the State of Israel or the Jewish people as a whole. Of course as Christians we are called to love the Jewish people because of what Christ has done, but this claim of Hagee's seems to go beyond the straightforward gospel message of the New Testament. The misappropriation of the blessing of Abraham in effect encourages Christian compliance to his views through fear instead of engendering a loving attitude towards the Jewish people.[83] Such assertions invite further comment. The question is really asking whether we have fear towards the State of Israel because the Jewish state is seen as God's chosen agent and still in covenant relationship with God. But we need to be careful in asking who Israel is today. Should Christians be fearful of the State of Israel, or the Jews, because they still have Abraham's blessing and Christians don't? As noted Paul asserted in his letter to the Galatians (Gal. 3:14) that those who have faith in Christ - the seed of Abraham - have become partakers of the blessing of Abraham. So, it is the Christian believer, whether Jew or Gentile, who now possess this blessing. Of course out of this blessing we should now love and respect God, and people of all races and nationality including the Jews, but not live under an unhealthy fear that is not godly.

---

[81] Hagee, J., *In Defense of Israel*, Zondervan, 2008. He is the senior pastor of Cornerstone Church in San Antonio, Texas, which has 19,000 members. The stated goals of CUFI are to build support for Israel in America, and to communicate and educate the pro-Israel perspective to American politicians.
[82] Hagee, *In Defense of Israel*, 2008, pp. 111-119
[83] David Pawson follows a similar line of reasoning in his own book, *Defending Christian Zionism* (p.156) asking whether we fear the God of Israel. Of course it is right to have a respectful and reverent awe towards God, but that doesn't seem to be the point Pawson is making.

Understanding Israel

Hagee follows Darby quite closely in arguing for a dual-covenant theology where the Church is considered to be spiritual Israel and the continuing Jewish community and state form the earthly or physical Israel. It is noteworthy though that he does consider the Church to be spiritual Israel. But this further shows that his claim, that we need to bless the State of Israel in order to receive the blessings of Abraham, to be out of place.[84]

Hagee is also very critical of replacement theology believing that it is anti-Semitic. He thinks this stretches back to the time of the Church Fathers. The inference that he leaves from this is that modern adherents who question the place of the State of Israel today are equally guilty of anti-Semitism.[85] Hagee's polemical language and description of replacement theology is though a poor characterisation of historical understandings of theology. And although some anti-Semitic theology may have existed in history it need not represent the core of Christian teaching. I will return to discuss this at length in subsequent chapters, but use of such inflammatory language and accusations of anti-Semitism against anything that is not liked does not help build respectful dialogue and understanding.

He does though make some valid criticisms of Christian persecution of Jews through history. And those opposed to political Zionism need to recognise and acknowledge the suffering of Jews through history, and also demonstrate love for Jews today, even if expansionist Zionism is rejected as an ideology. But Hagee really takes his argument too far, especially when he comments that Hitler's deeds were motivated by his Christian faith. Hitler was far from holding to any recognisable form of Christian belief. He believed in a nationalistic 'Positive Christianity;' a faith devoid of any substance, and in fact closer to atheism or pantheism than the New Testament faith. Many

---

[84] Hagee believes further that the stars mentioned in God's discourse with Abraham are representative of the Church as spiritual Israel while the sand on the seashore is representative of the earthly nation of Israel with Jerusalem reserved as its capital city. The two entities he believes exist side by side and neither can cancel the other out. Sizer though rightly points out that Nehemiah saw the numerous stars in the night sky as representing the fulfilment of God's promise to Abraham in and through the Jewish people (Neh. 9:23). In other words the blessing continued through the Jewish people in the time of Nehemiah and it is wrong to divide God's blessing in the way Hagee does into dual covenants. See: Hagee, J. *Final Dawn and Jerusalem*, Nashville: Thomas Nelson, 1998, pp. 108-109. Sizer, *Christian Zionism, Road Map to Armageddon*, Leicester: IVP, 2004 p. 139. Nehemiah was writing around 430 BC.
[85] Hagee, *In Defense of Israel*, 2008, p.145

The Roots of Christian Zionism

Christians were opposed to Hitler's fascism, and paid with their lives, although many gave in for a quiet life. They stayed within the nationalistic German Evangelical Church accepting political control of the clergy.

Regrettably, it would seem that this type of pro-Israel teaching is leading some Christians today to turn away from the redemptive sacrifice of Jesus and seek to embrace Judaism. Instead they look to re-establish the Old Testament system of worship and even campaign for the rebuilding of the temple in Jerusalem. In his most recent book Hagee takes another step in this direction by arguing that the Old Covenant is not dead, and by claiming that Jesus did not intend to be the Messiah to the Jews.[86] It would seem that in making such a case Hagee has in fact taken a step away from the traditional gospel message as given in the New Testament. In this section of his book he comments that Jesus was not offered as the Messiah to the Jews, and that he was not authorised by God to use supernatural signs to prove he was the Messiah of Israel. Hagee's case is based upon his belief that Jesus repeatedly told his disciples to tell no one of the miraculous works that he was doing, thus refusing to even claim to be the Messiah. According to Hagee, Jesus only intended to be the saviour of the world, and refused to be the Jewish Messiah, commenting that Jesus rejected the role of Messiah in both word and deed (although Hagee has perhaps softened his views a little in a recent revised copy of his book). But for Hagee, if Jesus were openly proclaiming himself as the Jewish Messiah he would have been a conquering ruler who would have sought to gain the support of the general public for the purpose of the overthrowing the might of Rome.[87] For Hagee, Jesus' comment that 'My kingdom is not of this world' as recorded in John's Gospel (John 18:36), rules him out as the Jewish Messiah.

Hagee uses Scripture very selectively taking passages out of their proper context. At one point he makes use of a passage in Matthew (Matt. 12:39-40) to build his case, in which Jesus compared the sign of Jonah to his own ministry where it is written that the 'Son of Man [will be] three days and three nights in the heart of the earth.'[88] Leaving aside the given sign of the crucifixion and resurrection in this passage, Hagee simply makes the point that Jonah went and preached to the Gentiles in Nineveh. Jesus was simply comparing himself to Jonah's ministry by becoming the saviour and preacher of righteousness to the Gentile world. However, looking at this passage in context shows Jesus

---

[86] Hagee, *In Defense of Israel*, 2008, pp. 121-169; 158
[87] Hagee, *In Defense of Israel*, 2008, pp. 137, 139-140, 143, 145
[88] Hagee, *In Defense of Israel*, 2008, pp. 137-138

condemning the Pharisees as 'an evil and adulterous generation' for seeking a sign, and that the repentant Gentile men of Nineveh will stand in judgement over the unrepentant Pharisees, and their generation (Matt. 12:38-41).

So what evidence does Scripture give that Jesus was the Messiah to Jews as well as Gentiles? Firstly, in Jesus' prolonged discourses with the Pharisees and Teachers of the Law he concluded by commenting that their house will be left to them desolate (Matt. 23:1-38). Then he used a Messianic phrase '...I tell you, you will not see me again until you say, 'Blessed is he who comes in the name of the Lord.' (Matt. 23:39) In Hebrew this statement is *Baruch ha ba be shem adonai*, which is recognised as a Messianic greeting by Jews. Jesus was saying very clearly to the Jewish leaders that he was the promised Messiah, and that they should accept him.

Furthermore, the apostle John in his letters warns against those who downplay the place of Jesus as the Messiah calling them deceivers and antichrist (1 John 2:22-23; 2 John 1:7). If the State of Israel is being raised to such a level by some Christian leaders that it comes to stand in the place of Christ, and if some Christians are teaching that Jews do not need to come to Christ, then isn't that the type of deception that John warned against? Those strong supporters of Christian Zionism need to be aware of these dangers and consider whether they are deceiving or being deceived in their excessive love for the State of Israel.[89] In any other context this sort of teaching would be seen as a move towards liberalism.

The Old Testament prophecies show the promised Messiah was to come through Judah and David, and to be a blessing to all nations. The wonderful blessing that Jacob spoke over Judah (Gen. 49:8-12) was that the sceptre would not depart from him and that a ruler would come who would bring obedience to the nations. Later we find in the prophets that this ruler was to sit on David's throne establishing righteousness forever, (Isa. 9:7) and that his purpose was to bring salvation to Judah and Israel as both King and Priest (Jer. 23:5-6 & Jer. 33:15-18). In the account of Jesus' birth, for instance in the *Magnificat* (*Mary's Song*) it is revealed that in Jesus there is help for Israel according to the promise given to Abraham (Luke 1:54-55). And in Zechariah's song there is also the expression of joy that Israel is to have a saviour and redeemer from the line of David, according to the promises given to Abraham and the prophets (Luke 1:67-79). In other words, the Gospel writers highlight

---

[89] It is noteworthy that Pawson in fact rightly criticises this aspect of Hagee's theology and rejects this form of dispensationalist Zionism in favour of classical Zionism. Pawson, 2004, pp. 84-5

the fact that Jesus was to be the saviour and promised Messiah; first to the Jews, but also that his kingdom rule on the throne of David would extend to the Gentiles and be an everlasting kingdom. I will return to discuss the text of Scripture in more depth later, but it is regrettable that Hagee ignores these prophetic words and only refers to Simeon's comments (Luke 2:27-32) that Jesus was to be a light to the Gentiles; thus wrongly dividing the word of God.[90]

It is equally clear that for the first few years the early Christian community consisted mainly of the remnant part of Judah, Levi and Benjamin, together with some other Israelites. Initially the Apostles focused on the Jewish nature of their new way in the Messiah, only later did more and more Gentiles join. And with this global challenge the leaders had to come to terms with how the Law of Moses should be applied to Gentiles. But what happened to the Jewish ethnicity of Christianity? In Orthodox Jewish tradition a person could be considered Jewish through birth, marriage or conversion and there is still no clearly accepted view of what constitutes 'Jewishness.'[91] The early Christian Jews did not straight away forget their Jewish identity as the history of first and second century Christianity records.[92] Jesus was the Messiah to the Jews first, and many Jews accepted him as the fulfilment of their faith, but many others did not. Newly converted Gentiles then took their place in the natural olive tree.

It is apparent that the Apostles were concerned with the degree to which Jewish practices should be followed in the early Church. There were those within it who favoured maintaining a strong link with the older traditions of Judaism, but Paul argued strongly that the Old Covenant system of worship has passed away for good and had been replaced by the promised New Covenant work of Christ (Gal 4:21-31). He goes so far as to compare the old city of Jerusalem and its temple worship to Hagar. This is because her son was not born of the promise of God. According to Paul, those who continue to follow the Old Covenant temple practices are in fact in slavery, while the New Jerusalem is above and free according to God's promises to Abraham. Therefore, through Christ's perfect sacrificial death, the old Mosaic

---

[90] Hagee, *In Defense of Israel*, 2008, p. 133

[91] Hagee rejects this traditional Jewish view. Hagee, *In Defense of Israel*, 2008, pp. 49-56. But it is noteworthy that when the Israelites left Egypt many foreigners joined with the people of God.

[92] James, Jesus' half brother, for instance continued to pray in the temple for several decades after the ascension of Jesus, even gaining the name 'camel knees' according to *Eusebius' Ecclesiastical History* (1:XXIII). There was also a large contingent of Pharisees who joined the Jerusalem Church.

system of sacrifices and worship has been superseded and thus rendered redundant.

So in summary of Hagee's position, I would suggest that it is a danger to take one or two Scriptures out of context without understanding the wider message. When Jesus came to the Holy Land as the Messiah many Jews missed his coming because they were looking for a physical conquering king who would overthrow the Roman Empire, not realising that God was looking for humility and spiritual renewal first. Hagee is seemingly repeating these errors in his teaching and appears to be arguing that Jews today do not need to come to their own Messiah. Perhaps Hagee is following Darby's theology in believing that Jesus' work of redemption is the actual means of salvation even though presently hidden from Jews, but this is not clear. But even so, that is a rather odd theology to hold for those who claim to love the Jews so much. Must Jews be denied access to the good news in Jesus? Instead, in their zeal for Jews and Zionism they only offer Jews an earthly and carnal hope. I find this odd.

There are also political considerations concerning the suffering of Palestinians and Jews. Jesus condemned the Pharisees for their exploitation and brutality (Matt 23) and the discourse between Jesus and the Pharisees is I believe of profound political significance for this discussion. As such, if we turn a blind eye to the suffering of Palestinians believing that God will bless Israel whatever they do, we are mistaken. But while it is of utmost importance to call for the rights of Palestinians to be respected, and Jews too, I do not believe that it is right for Christians to call into question the State of Israel's existence as a political entity, an entity that is legally established in human terms. That question should be left to God who has allowed Israel to exist according to his permissive will. Political activity, I would argue, should be focussed on being a prayerful, prophetic witness to the Jewish state. Hagee does though make some valid points about the suffering of Jews in history, and Jewish people should be able to see the love of Christ in Christians as we live out our faith. However, love for Jews doesn't mean an uncritical support for Israel and its political and military activity. Love towards Jews, as a people, shouldn't now be turned into suffering and hatred for the Palestinians. God's plan now should not to be made out to exclude Palestinians from their own historical lands, as Christian support for the expansionist policies of the State of Israel appear to be aiming at. I think that Hagee means well in his love for Jews, but it is a love and theology that is not properly thought through in terms of its impact for both Jews and Palestinians.

The Roots of Christian Zionism

Other Denominations and Theologians

It would be mistaken though to think that these questions only arise amongst Fundamentalists such as Darby and Hagee. With the horrors of the Holocaust fresh in people's minds more mainstream theologians and denominations have also moved to change their approach towards the Jewish people. The idea that the Church has replaced Israel has therefore been set in focus and challenged by some Christians in recent decades. Karl Barth for instance believed that Israel has remained 'elect' even in rebellion from God. In this sense God has preserved the Jewish people through their continued rejection of Christ, and that this provides a testimony of the truthfulness of God's existence, and to his faithfulness. Barth does though see the Church as a union of Jews and Gentiles who are obedient to Jesus. But Israel's continued disobedience is itself seen as part of God's predestination and plan. Therefore the final conversion of Jews will only be enabled by a direct move of God's Spirit that will eventually bring Jewish Israel to Christ. In light of this, Barth believed that direct evangelism or missionary activity to them is almost futile and the Christian community should instead live out the gospel message in loving Jews today.[93] Barth helpfully distinguishes between a covenant of obedience for Jews and Gentiles in Christ, and a continued 'election' for Jews even in disobedience. Soulen's view is that the distinction between Israel and the nations remains, with the Church representing a provisional fellowship consisting of the two people groups of Jews and Gentiles. In this light he doesn't see the Church as the present reign of God, but merely a fellowship of believers. Neither does he believe that the Church should seek to convert the Jews to Christ; instead Christians should live godly lives before Jews and express the love of God to them. While I would agree that we ought to show Christ's love to Jews, we should not seek to withhold the Messianic message from them; that would not be an expression of love in my view, and is arguably anti-Semitic. Whether they accept it is another matter, but we should not forget than many Jews have found Christ through history.

In terms of an example of the denominational position changing to be more accommodating of Jews, the 1987 statement by the American based General Assembly of the Presbyterian Church asserted that replacement theology is 'harmful' and needs to be thought through with greater clarity. Instead, they believe that God's covenant to the Jewish people remains in force and that God has not rejected his people

---

[93] Barth, K *Church Dogmatics*, Edinburgh: Clark, (1956-75) II/2 pp. 199-209 from Holwerda. *Jesus and Israel*, p. 11-13. See also Soulen chapter 4.

completely (from Rom. 11:2). Therefore the statement asserts that the Jewish people remain in that covenant relationship with God.[94]

It would seem then that there has been a trend to play down the importance and significance of the gospel message for Jews amongst some mainstream Christian believers and denominations. Barth argued that Jews are still the 'elect' even in disobedience, but it would seem that others are moving further to legitimise the continuation of Judaism more completely, and it is being increasingly argued that the Jewish faith provides a valid path to God apart from Christ; a teaching that the apostle Paul would have challenged vigorously. As noted, there would seem to be little difference now between the positions of some theologians in the main denominations, perhaps with a tendency towards multi-faith liberalism, and the writing of some of the more fundamentalist Christian Zionists such as Hagee.

Summary

In the previous two chapters I have summarised the beliefs of both sides in this debate. I believe that Calvin's covenantal theology forms the basis for a correct understanding of God's purposes in the world today through the Church that is the faithful part of Israel. While there is truth in Soulen's claim that some theologians taught a form of replacement theology historically, this was not universal. There were varying approaches to the relationship between the Church and Israel. Tom Wright also wants to place Israel at the centre of God's plan; a plan that is being worked out through the New Covenant and manifest in the Christian Church. This also seems to be the view of Motyer, Holwerda and Robertson.

There has also been a great deal of tolerance shown towards Jewish exiles in many periods of time, despite other regrettable periods of antagonism and animosity. It is true as well that some Christian teaching has ignored the Church's Jewish roots and is therefore wrongly focussed. But an increasing number of Christians do not believe that the type of replacement theology that Soulen characterises really captures the full purpose of God. This purpose is being worked out in the Christian Church and the world today. I believe then that Soulen makes some valid points concerning the loss of the Church's Israelite identity and is right to point out the problem of structural supersessionism and a semi-Gnostic approach to Israel that divides it into a spiritual and carnal

---

[94] Reported by Brockway, A. et al. (1988) *The Theology of the Churches and the Jewish People*, Geneva: WCC Publ. 1988, pp. 111-113. (The statement quotes from Romans 11:2). See also Soulen, *The God of Israel*, pp. 2-3

entity. However, I don't believe we should accept Soulen's wider conclusions because they do not tie in with the New Testament teachings of Paul. And Soulen doesn't really resolve the semi-Gnosticism that is still present in the dual covenant theology of Darby and Hagee that divides Israel into a spiritual and earthly part.

In light of the problem of semi-Gnosticism in some forms of Christian theology I believe it is important to accept that the New Covenant is in fact the fulfilment and continuation of the covenantal promise given to Abraham - a theology that is in accord with Calvin's teachings about the Church and Israel. From this, it follows that the Christian Church should be identified as spiritual Israel. But I believe we should go further than this by examining closely the Old and New Testament writings afresh and consider how the Christian Church relates to ethnic Israel as well as spiritual Israel. In order to do this it is necessary to look at the legal and ethnic dimension of Israel and the Church, and question how Christianity is ethnically and legally linked to the descendants of both Judah and Israel. As I hope to show later, the Church should be seen as possessing both the ethnic birthright of Israel from Joseph's line, and being under the authority of the ruling Messianic king who was to come through the Judaic line of David; that is Jesus Christ. In other words, I am going to argue that Christians should accept the Jewish nature and origin of Christianity more strongly, and we should identify more closely with the Hebraic heritage as a people coexisting with the natural children of Abraham. That is the *one-new-man* union in Christ that comes through faith. For this reason I believe that it is correct to speak in terms of Judeo-Christian continuity because Christianity exists in unity and continuity with the remnant of the Judaic-Israelite nation that was called out by God in the Old Testament. It is a remnant that is now united with Gentiles in the Messiah. This is a remnant of Jews and Israelites consecrated to God and brought into union with Gentiles, this according to God's promises in the Old Testament.

So I think there can be agreement that the standard historical Christian meta-narrative[95] needs to include Israel, as both Soulen and Wright suggest. For theologians such as Wright, Robertson, Holwerda and Motyer, Israel is at the heart of this meta-narrative as part of a single covenantal plan of grace that includes Jews, but also extends to Gentiles. For Soulen, Hagee and Darby Israel has a place alongside the Church in a continuing separate covenantal relationship with God, but I think we need to avoid this type of dual-covenant theology.

---

[95] That involves Creation, Fall, Redemption in Christ, and the final Consummation of all things in Christ.

Understanding Israel

So, in the rest of this book I am going to conduct a detailed study of the history and theology relating to Israel. If it is important to place Israel within the Christian meta-narrative then it is necessary to look at this question in some depth. So questions I want to ask include consideration of the history of Israel, whether in the land or in exile; consideration of what the prophets said about Israel, and how the New Testament writers read and understood the Old Testament. But we may also observe that the name *Israel* first appears as a spiritual title given to Jacob when he learnt to come into submission to God.

PART II – UNDERSTANDING ISRAEL

Chapter 4

Israel and Biblical interpretations

In the last two chapters both positions have been considered and various difficulties identified. In the next few chapters the question of Israel will be considered in further depth, but before moving into fresh study the question of hermeneutics needs to be considered first. That is, what interpretive framework should be applied in order to answer the question of Israel's identity, and its place in relationship with God and the Church today?

As discussed already Soulen has argued that there is a failure to engage with history in the structural supercessionism that he believes exists in Christian theology. I believe that Soulen does make some important points in relation to the need to address the historical questions concerning Israel, even though I would question his understanding of who Israel is under the New Covenant - and therefore question his conclusions. But I am going to take seriously Soulen's claim that there is a partial flight from history in the standard model of biblical interpretation concerning the place of Israel in God's plan; particularly the final consummation of all things in Christ. This failure to take seriously the historical role and place of Israel in Church history Soulen calls semi-Gnosticism, and is therefore identified as a form of supercessionism. However, while Soulen does make some useful points I believe this claim is not universally valid. For instance, Calvin's type of covenantal theology does take seriously the continuity of Israel within the Church framework - both literally and spiritually.

There are some further important points that ought to be made in relation to developing a correct interpretive framework of the Old and New Testaments.[96] Firstly, Christian hermeneutics developed into two differing positions during the patristic period. On one side, Origen was one of the main proponents of a theology that tended to emphasise the symbolic reading of Scripture at the expense of the historical. This more dominant Alexandrian School emphasised the spiritual interpretation at

---

[96] Prasch, J 'Apostolic Jewish-Christian Hermeneutics and Supercessionism,' in Smith, C.L (ed.) *The Jews, Modern Israel and the New Supercessionism*, Lampeter: King's Divinity Press, (2009) pp. 47-62

the cost of considering the importance of the literal. Scripture was then allegorised and spiritualised. The desire was to seek out the hidden symbolic meaning of the text, and influence for this came from both Philo and Plato. There is though a form of Gnosticism in this approach because it strongly separates the spiritual meaning of Scripture from the more earthly plainer account. In response to this, Jacob Prasch believes that through Christian history the development of replacement theology has been driven by the practice of over spiritualising theology, and therefore he believes wrongly applies the promises meant for Israel to the Church.

The other approach from the early Church period was the Antiochene School. This approach was much more literalistic, but for many centuries it was overshadowed by the Alexandrian School that tended to read Scripture symbolically. Although there is a lot of merit and advantage in this more literalistic approach of the Antiochene school it doesn't fully take into account the way the New Testament authors were thinking and writing.[97] A proper balance is needed between the literal and spiritual readings, as Augustine for instance tried to do. With the coming of the Reformation there was a much greater desire to read Scripture literally within a grammatico-historical interpretation. That is to give proper regard to the intention of the authors, to take into account the literally style, and to read the text literally where appropriate.

Prasch believes that the style of New Testament literature was in fact typical of Rabbinical thinking of the second temple period, and sits within the history of Jewish writing that included for instance the Qumran Dead Sea Scrolls.[98] This he believes means the text should be treated as typical Jewish Midrash. He argues that because the early followers of Jesus were primarily Jewish, their writing should be interpreted in the Jewish context. He points also to the German biblical critics who believed that the Scriptural writings should be understood within the cultural setting of the living community, what they called *Sitz im Leben*. But unlike the liberal German critics, Prasch's approach is to take the New Testament writings at face value. He believes the *Sitz im Leben* should be applied in the thoroughly first century Jewish context;

---

[97] Prasch, *Apostolic Jewish-Christian Hermeneutics*, pp. 47-50
[98] Prasch, *Apostolic Jewish-Christian Hermeneutics*, p. 51-52. He sources his argument from the Jewish scholar Jacob Neusner although without supplying a further source reference.

such context includes the history, culture and theological grounding of the writers.[99]

Prasch also believes that the interpretation of the Old Testament used by the New Testament authors is that of *pesher*; an approach that seeks to read the text's spiritual symbolism to expound doctrine. The more literal approach to reading texts is known as *peshat*. Within the *peshat–pesher* reading the symbolism sheds light on the theological doctrine, but the literal reading is not undermined. Neither is the doctrine based upon the textual symbolism with the literal reading entirely allegorised, as would be the case with Gnostic thinking.[100] Prasch uses as an example the text of Hosea 11:1 (that is quoted in Matthew 2:15) which reads 'When Israel was a child, I loved him, and out of Egypt I called my son.' Hosea is here referring back to the historical event of the Exodus (the *peshat*), but as a Messianic prophecy it speaks symbolically of a future truth (the *pesher*). Matthew therefore takes the writing of Hosea and applies it Christ.

However, others are not so convinced that the New Testament writers such as Matthew were using the *pesher* approach found in the Dead Sea Scrolls. Lee Campbell for instance highlights some of the research in this area and believes that there are important differences between the Gospels and the writing of the Qumran community who tended to interpret the prophets symbolically line by line.[101] He therefore believes that if Matthew had used *pesher* it would have been far too subjective and eisegetical an approach to make the New Testament writing reliable. He notes that there are other approaches in first century Jewish thinking that could have been used.

Whilst the exact nature of the New Testament writer's approach may not accord as closely to the Qumran writing as some may wish, it is evident that Matthew was reading the historical account of the Old Testament symbolically. This is in terms of it pointing forward to theological truths concerning the person and work of Jesus, particularly

---

[99] The need for consideration of context is also important in Tom Wright's new perspective on Paul, where he calls for a hermeneutic of doctrine in a more holistic sense, that is taking account of how the historical Jewish community with all its social, political and cultural understanding approached doctrinal and theological beliefs and statements. Wright, N.T. *Justification: God's plan and Paul's Vision*, London: SPCK, 2009, pp. 28-29. Wright references this idea from Thistelton A.C. *The Hermeneutics of Doctrine*, Grand Rapids: Eerdsman, 2007

[100] Prasch, *Apostolic Jewish-Christian Hermeneutics,* pp. 52-62

[101] Campbell, L., 'Matthew's Use of the Old Testament: A preliminary Analysis,' *Xenos Online Journal'*, Issue 3, 2000.

in relation to Israel. In this light, Matthew showed that Jesus fulfilled and completed the work that Israel had failed to do. Matthew does highlight the theological symbolism in the historical events of Israel, but it is a symbolism that is focussed upon fulfilment in Christ. David Holwerda further shows that Matthew's Gospel was written to bring out the symbolism of the historical events of Jesus' life to show that Jesus succeeded where Israel had not. Just as Jesus was called out of Egypt, so too was he baptised in the Jordan, and then sent into the desert for forty days to overcome temptation. Whereas the Israelites had grumbled and resisted the Word of God in their forty-year wanderings, Jesus overcame the devil by quoting and upholding Scripture.[102] So Matthew does seem to read symbolism in events, and uses it to expound theological doctrines. If his approach was a form of *peshat-pesher* then it was in a different, more focussed, way than the methodology of the Qumran community; that is an approach where the symbolism is focussed upon Jesus.

It is clear I think that there is a developing theology in the New Testament that does spiritualise the promises made about Israel in the Old Testament, and applies them to the person and work of the Jewish Messiah, and what this means for the first century congregation of believers. This teaching is not dualistic Gnosticism because it is concerned with the Holy Spirit being poured out upon a multitude of people, but firstly upon the Messiah who came in flesh. So there is a very strong sense in the New Testament that the promises relating to Israel have been fulfilled in and through Jesus Christ. The early Church did not reject Israel or believe they had replaced it, but instead they believed that Christ's work embraced and fulfilled Israel, even if only as a remnant. This Israel now exists and is being built up in the body of Christ - that is the Church. The Christian community is now filled with God's Holy Spirit who brings the life of the Messiah into each one of us.

There was indeed a problem with the Old Covenant in that the nation of Israel was weakened by an unavoidable reliance upon flesh. This is because of the fallen human nature. Israel was made subject to the carnal nature, and it was this weakness that Christ overcame through his life, death and resurrection. The symbolic meaning found in the theology of the New Testament doesn't negate the material, but brings the carnal and spiritual into a more appropriate balance, although it is not yet brought to the perfection that will be evident at the final consummation of creation. So I believe that it is right to take the

---

[102] Holwerda, D.E (1995) *Jesus and Israel: One Covenant or Two?* Grand Rapids: Wm B Eerdsman Publ. Co. 1995, pp. 40-58

spiritual aspect of Christ's work in fulfilling Israel's calling seriously. On the other side it is possible to overemphasise the spiritual aspect of New Covenant theology in relation to Israel by widening the dualism between the Church and Israel of the Old Testament until it can have no place in Christ. That is something to be avoided.

However, I believe there remains a case for considering the history of fleshly Israel in more depth, but within the proper context. In order to do this it is necessary to conduct an historical analysis through the Old and New Testaments alongside the careful theological study. That is, it is necessary to look at the history of Israel in the Old Testament within the context of what the text actually reveals, and not assume that the matter is already settled. Many today apply Old Testament prophecy to the modern State of Israel without considering the context. I believe that many Christian Zionists have a weak grasp of the historical narrative of Israel in the Old Testament. There would seem to be a tendency to apply prophecies relating to Israel in a very literal sense in the present day, but there is less concern to study in depth the actual context of the narrative. Soulen, and many Christian Zionists, do not consider the question of Israel's modern identity in light of Scripture in sufficient depth, believing the question is obvious and settled, and therefore needs to no further consideration. This question is though I believe much more complex than generally believed.

I intend then to consider these more literal questions in relation to the identity of Israel. That is to ask, who is really Israel today, spiritually, ethnically and legally? The legal questions arise when it is asked who was given possession of the priesthood, the sceptre and the birthright of Jacob's sons? So I want to consider these questions alongside the question of Israel's ethnic and spiritual identity.

So, the hermeneutic I am working with here is one that takes seriously the need for a proper balance between the spiritual, fleshly and earthly aspects of the place of Israel. We need to establish a proper balance between the literal and symbolic reading of Scripture, and not mix them up inappropriately. I also accept Soulen's point that the standard framework of the meta-narrative of Christian theology needs to include the place of Israel, but I would argue that this ought to be in relation to the person and work of Jesus. And I believe this is something Calvin's covenantal theology seeks to do, as does Tom Wright for instance in the present time. So towards the goal of understanding the proper balance for Christian theology between ethnic Israel and spiritual Israel I will look in depth at both historical and theological issues; that is to examine the theology and prophetic writings of the Old Testament authors within the historical setting and context.

Chapter 5

The People of Israel in the Old Testament

The calling of Abraham begins the long-term scriptural narrative of God's overarching plan of redemption for mankind and the world; this includes restoration and consummation of the whole of creation with the return of Christ. The events of Abraham's life followed several hundred years after the Flood, a catastrophe that had wiped the slate clean following the Fall of Adam. Abraham received several promises from God over a period of time. He was told to leave his land and settle in a place of God's choosing, and God promised to bless him and his family. The first seven-fold blessing is recorded in Genesis 12.

> 'I will make you into a great nation and I will bless you;
> I will make your name great, and you will be a blessing.
> I will bless those who bless you and whoever curses you I will curse;
> And all the peoples on earth will be blessed through you.' (Gen 12:2-3).

The second blessing is in the form of a covenant that God promised to Abraham relating to a great multitude of descendents, and the possession of land. Abraham had pointed out to God that he had no offspring, and that his inheritance would pass to a distant relative. God responded by reminding him that he is Abraham's shield and reward, and then makes this covenantal promise relating to the promise of land.

> 'To your descendents I give this land, from the river of Egypt to the great river, the Euphrates...' (Gen.15:19).

The third promise is found in Genesis 17 and relates to an everlasting covenant in which Abraham is told he will become the father of many nations. The land of Canaan was said to become an everlasting possession for descendents who would come from his seed (Gen. 17:5-8). Circumcision of the flesh was required as a sign of this covenant. The further promise was that this blessing would come through his wife Sarah who was at the time barren, but that she would give birth to a son who was to be called Isaac. We are told in the account that both Sarah and Abraham were old and they had little hope left that a child would be born to them at that time (Gen. 17:15-22). But a child was born to Sarah. The account in Genesis then continues with the birth of Isaac, and an account of his life together with that of his brother Ishmael. Genesis then provides an account of Isaac's children Esau and Jacob.

So there are a number of themes that come out of the covenantal promises given to Abraham and his family that I want to focus on in the rest of this book. Later I will discuss this in relation to the way they are interpreted in the New Testament. The promises of Abraham include the land of Canaan, the promise relating to the 'seed' of Abraham, and the promise to fill the earth with descendents through Sarah. It is interesting that according to the Genesis account the requirement for circumcision pre-dated the Mosaic covenant and is instead part of the earlier Abrahamic covenant. It is also noteworthy that Paul interpreted the 'seed' of Abraham as a single person. And this is a separate blessing to the promise of God to make Abraham's descendents as numerous as the sand or stars. There are of course several other questions that arise, such as the temple and the place of Jerusalem within the new covenant, but I will leave discussion of these for now.

But firstly, there is the question of the history of the numerous people of Israel as the collective offspring of Abraham. That includes ethnic Israel and the house of Israel, but extends to spiritual aspects in the New Testament. Consideration needs to be given to the meaning of the 'seed' of Abraham that is interpreted by Paul as being fulfilled in Jesus Christ. Also is the question of the promise of the land of Canaan to the descendents of Abraham, and what this means for us today.

So, in this chapter I am going to trace the history of Israel through the Old Testament up until the time of Zechariah. In doing this study some interesting points arise. It first becomes apparent that the name 'Israel' was given to Jacob as a spiritual title once he had finally learnt to trust in God's provision. Previously Jacob had used deception to steal the birthright of Abraham and Isaac from the older brother Esau. This birthright had belonged by right to his twin brother Esau who was the first-born. The fact that God had planned to give it to Jacob anyway because of God's sovereign choice did not initially register in Jacob's mind. So we first encounter Israel as a spiritual title bestowed upon Jacob for his eventual submission to God.

But to whom did Jacob-Israel pass the birthright? The Bible records that he gave it to Joseph's line; that is to Joseph and his son Ephraim, and not to Judah who had the wonderful promise that the Messiah would come through his line (1 Chron. 5:1-2; Gen. 48-49). In other words, the coming ruler and the national birthright were separated in the Israelite tribes, as was the priestly line separated in Levi. Judah's tribe was chosen to provide kingship over Israel, and eventually to the

Messiah. Today Judah's line forms the main populace of the State of Israel, but significantly they did not possess Israel's birthright because it had passed to Joseph's lineage.

As noted, the first mention of Israel in the Bible relates to the account of the tension and family feud between the twin brothers Jacob and Esau (Gen. 32). Jacob had stolen Esau's birthright even though God had planned to give it to Jacob lawfully. In fact Jacob was cunning and adept at gaining blessing through illegitimate means. Esau on the other hand had a fearsome reputation as a hunter, and Jacob was in fear of his life for tricking his brother, and as the story unfolds he runs away to his uncle Laban. Jacob then is in a state of trepidation and seeks protection from God, acknowledging he has done wrong. As Jacob later prepares to meet his brother once more the account reveals that he first had to wrestle with God in the guise of the angel Peniel all night. Jacob in his determination and turmoil refused to let go until he received God's blessing. So God blessed Jacob for his perseverance and gives him the new title *Israel* because he struggled with God for blessing and overcame.[103]

But what effectively happened in the story is that Jacob at last realised that he needed God for his protection and blessing, and he could no longer fix his own blessing as he had done in the past and get away with it. Israel then was a spiritual title that was conferred upon Jacob once he finally realised his need for salvation and submission to God, and that God reigns over the affairs of mankind. But that is really only the start of the story of Jacob-Israel. The story of Jacob continues to unfold with the activities of his children, who for instance sold Jacob's beloved son Joseph into slavery. And then Joseph after his release from captivity and rapid promotion brings them all to settle in Egypt, thus rescuing the whole of Jacob's family from famine. At the end of his life Jacob blesses his children, including Ephraim and Manasseh, the two sons born to Joseph and his Egyptian wife.

Israel and the Birthright

So we can see firstly that Israel was a spiritual title given to Jacob. It needs to be noted at this point that there is further confusion over use of the name Israel in the Bible. Sometimes Israel refers to the northern tribes, especially Joseph and Ephraim in exile, at other times it refers to the united kingdom of Judah and Israel, at other times it refers to the remnant of Jews; that is those of the tribe of Judah who lived in

---

[103] The title can also mean that God saved him. From the Hebrew *ye* = he; *sra* = struggle or save; *el* = God.

Palestine at the time of Christ. Other times, particularly for instance in Acts 2:5, the Jewish label may refer to Israelites who adhere to the religious practices of first century Judaism. Today people often use the name Israel for the State of Israel, or the Jews as a people, without considering that the majority in the state today are identifiable as ethnic Jews in the main, and not those more widely considered to be Israelites in the Old Testament; that is, the twelve tribes.

Furthermore, we often fail to notice those Israelites of the exiled ten northern tribes who did not return to the land, prior to the coming of Christ. Pawson seems to make this mistake suggesting that the first exile experienced by the Israelites was the Babylonian captivity, with the second exile occurring following the rejection of Christ. Thus he seems to overlook the exile of the northern ten tribes by the Assyrians around 721BC, and misses the scriptural promises of restoration for the majority of ethnic Israelites in the Old Testament. So there is often confusion over use of names and titles in the Bible because we don't take the time to consider context and ask which group is being referred to in a particular passage.[104]

Before we get into the chapter fully it is worth looking at the promises relating to Joseph and Ephraim, and also the prophetic blessing that Jacob–Israel spoke over them.[105] Jacob especially blessed Joseph, and also his sons Ephraim and Manasseh. Jacob's desire was that they would be known after Abraham, Isaac and Jacob-Israel and that their offspring would spread across the earth (Gen. 48:15-16). The longer blessing for Joseph is found in Genesis 49:22-26. According to this passage Joseph was blessed to become a fruitful vine planted by a spring (fruitfulness being an important part of God's blessing) and his branches would spread over a wall. The implication being that his line would extend into other nations. Joseph's arm was said to be steady in the face of battle, and Jacob-Israel said that all of his blessings would rest upon Joseph who would be the prince amongst brothers. In other words, Joseph and his sons were to possess the birthright of Jacob-Israel. However, the sceptre, the promised ruler, was to come through Judah (Gen. 49:10). Reuben was in fact the firstborn, but was stripped of his right because of his sin in defiling his father's bed with the concubine Bilhah (Gen. 35:22). This is clarified more clearly in the book of Chronicles.

---

[104] See Pawson, *Defending Christian Zionism*, pp. 97-99

[105] It is worth noting that Ephraim and Manasseh were born to an Egyptian mother Asenath, and Ephraim was named because God had made Joseph fruitful (Gen. 41:42,52). Incidentally, Ephraim was Joseph's second born son, but his blessing would exceed that of his older brother.

Israel in the Old Testament

'[Reuben's] right as firstborn were given to the sons of Joseph son of Israel...and though Judah was the strongest of his brothers and a ruler came from him, the rights of the firstborn belong to Joseph.' (1 Chron. 5:1-2).

The Old Testament carefully records the history of Israel as a united nation that reached a peak under David and Solomon, but later was divided into an Israelite faction of ten tribes, and a smaller Jewish faction largely consisting of the tribes of Judah and Benjamin. The Assyrians later carried the larger faction of Israel into exile, and their history becomes more obscure, but as we will see the Prophets did not forget them, nor did the Apostles - as I will show later. So when we come to read the Old Testament care needs to be taken in order to understand which Israelite group were being referred to, and therefore avoid incorrect interpretations. The danger is that we might apply prophecies that relate to the northern tribes of Israel to the tribe of Judah, or to the present day State of Israel if we ignore the context. I would urge readers then to consider the following discussion regarding the Old Testament and prophetic writings carefully in what I believe to be the correct context; that is by considering which Israel the Prophets were referring to. Although it is true that occasionally Judah is considered a remnant of Israel in the Bible, the Prophets are clear that God had not forgotten the northern tribes of Israel. Therefore they had a continued place in God's heart even in exile, often being identified after Ephraim and Joseph. In fact, as I hope to show, this northern Israel was promised reunification with Judah, under the New Covenant, and under the coming Judaic Messiah. This is part of the promised consolation of Israel that Simeon had hoped for, and saw coming to fruition in the birth of Jesus (Luke 2:25-26).

I believe that Scripture teaches that the Church, the ecclesia that is the body of Christ, exists as the legitimate continuation and reunion of the congregation of Israel and Judah, in a spiritual, ethnic and legal sense, but now under the Messiah. This understanding I believe comes out of the Old Testament Prophets. There is of course a danger in over emphasising the spiritual dimension of Israel at the expense of the literal or carnal Israel. Some of those who teach against Christian Zionism fail to fully appreciate an interpretive framework where significant theology is interwoven with real people, history and events. If we fail to recognise this we are in danger of creating a false dualism where everything is spiritualised until it has no meaning in the physical world. There is a need therefore to address the Scriptures that speak of a return of Israel to the land of Palestine, both in a literal as well as a spiritual sense. However, on the other side of the fence there is the danger of applying a false literalism to Scripture where the words of the text are fitted into an interpretative framework that doesn't respect the historical and cultural context.

So, I believe that Christian Zionists are right to argue that the Old Testament Scriptures, which speak of a return of Israel to the land, need a literal interpretation, but they are wrong in their interpretation because of a failure to understand who Israel is in the proper historical and theological context. What I think is evident, and I hope to show it in subsequent chapters, is that the Old Testament Prophets were speaking of a return of the ten northern tribes of Israel to the land in both a literal and a spiritual sense, being united together with Judah's tribe, but under the promised Messiah, Jesus. This union also extends to the Gentile people and nations who come to Christ. And with such a vast number of people coming to faith in the new way that Jesus established, the land that united Israel had been given, has now been extended to include the whole earth. And of course the whole earth belongs to the Lord by order of creation (Exod. 19:5-6).

Furthermore, we may note that the disciples were Jews and formed a legitimate, lawfully established Jewish community. However, what I think can be shown is that these Jewish disciples took the message of the kingdom to the scattered Israelites. This took place both during, and after Christ's ministry on earth, thus fulfilling the prophesied reunion of Judah and Israel according to God's promises in the Old Testament. Gentiles joined as well. It follows therefore that Gentile converts were assimilated into an essentially Jewish and Israelite ethnic mix and identity through their conversion. Later intermarriage diluted the outward Jewish appearance of Christianity. Gradually the Jewish culture and identity became more and more foreign in outward appearance, although I believe the Church remains Jewish and Israelite in terms of its heritage and ethnic root, and in terms of its legal status.

Another aspect that ought to be considered as well is the influence of Greek speaking Jews on the culture of Christianity. We can see for instance the tension between Greek speaking and Hebrew speaking Jewish Christians in the decision to appoint seven deacons in the early Messianic community (Acts 6:1-7). Many Jews had already adopted Greek modes of thought and culture prior to the coming of Jesus, as exampled by the translation into Greek of the Old Testament books (the Septuagint (LXX)) a couple of hundred years before Christ. We may note then that the developing culture of the emerging Christian Church was shaped in part by Greek speaking Jews and Israelites of the Diaspora, as well as Gentiles. It wasn't then just about Gentiles overlooking the Jewish roots of the faith, but Hellenistic Jews putting their own stamp on the growing and maturing Church.

The early Church was also related to Abraham's children through the spiritual reality of faith. It is important therefore to remember that the true children of Abraham, the true Israelites, are those who have faith in Christ because of the promises of God to the Patriarchs. It is not simply a matter of birth. Remember that Israel is primarily a spiritual title conferred upon those who rely upon God to save, direct and protect them. Paul noted in the letter to the Roman Christians that 'not all who are descended from Israel are Israel,' but only those born again according to God's promise that comes by faith (Rom. 9:6-9).

Before getting too far off track I will now look at the Old Testament Prophets in greater depth and examine what their preaching and message entailed. I will go through their writing in a broadly chronological order. What I hope to show is that a clear and consistent message emerges that is in harmony with the later teachings of the New Testament writers. This message is that the northern exiled Israelites too would be restored and reunited with the house of Judah under the authority of the coming Messiah.[106] This promise of God would also extend to the Gentiles, and the small land of Palestine would be too small to contain the full spiritual blessings of Abraham to be worked out through the coming Messiah.

Amos

Amos was one of the earlier writers of the divided kingdom period, ministering during the early and mid part of the eighth century BC; that is around 760 to 750 BC during the reign of King Uzziah of Judah and Jeroboam II of Israel. Although he was a shepherd from Tekoa in Judah (Amos 1:1) he was called to speak to the northern Israelite kingdom.[107] Through a series of visions God spoke through Amos that the prosperity of the northern kingdom of Israel would be laid waste because of unrighteousness, especially because of the oppression of the poor, immorality and idolatry (Amos 2-8). God's desire instead was that the 'house of Joseph' should allow '...justice [to] roll on like a river, righteousness like a never-failing stream' (Amos 5:

---

[106] The southern tribes also contained those of the priestly tribe Levi, and some from the tribe of Simeon who were assimilated into Judah along with the tribe of Benjamin.

[107] I am primarily relying upon the notes in the *NIV Study Bible* for the historical background of the Prophets.

6, 24). The Israelites however rejected this message and ignored the warning that Israel and the house of Jeroboam would be destroyed. Amaziah, who was the priest of Bethel, in fact told Jeroboam to send Amos back to Judah (Amos 7: 7-17). As it turns out Amos' prophecy was fulfilled around 721 BC with the Israelites exiled to Assyria. The first Christian martyr Stephen also alluded to Amos and noted that the passage accuses the people of taking up the idolatry of Molek and finding affinity for the star of Rephan, even as they persecuted the prophets (Amos 5:26; Acts 7:43).

However, even in this harsh judgment there was hope for the future. There is in this passage a remnant theology. Although the Israelites would be decimated, even so, a tenth would survive (Amos 5:3). The house of Israel would not be totally destroyed, but Israel would be shaken among the nations (Amos 9: 8-9). Later God would come and rebuild Israel, after this period of judgment and exile, and 'David's fallen tent' would be rebuilt and repaired to its former glory. Israel would possess the remnant of Edom and the nations that bear the name of God (Amos 9: 11-12).[108] The significance of this is that James, like Stephen, appeals to Amos (Acts 15: 16-17) when the Apostles bring news to the Jerusalem Church that the Gentiles are converting to Christ. Amos further asserts that the 'reaper will be overtaken by the ploughman,' and new wine will drip from the mountains. God promised that he will one day bring back the exiled people of Israel, and they will once more be planted in their own land never again to be uprooted; this at the same time as the Gentiles will be brought in (Amos 9: 13-15). The Jerusalem Church under the authority of James then saw the fulfillment of this prophecy, that concerns the restoration of the house of Israel from exile, as beginning to take place in their own time.

Hosea

The book of Hosea is one of the more significant in this discussion, particularly as passages are quoted with reference to the re-gathering of Israel in Romans and in 1 Peter. Hosea was from the northern part of Israel and prophesied in the latter part of the eighth century BC, during the reign of Jeroboam who was king over the house of Israel. He was therefore a contemporary of Amos, but went further in identifying Assyria as God's instrument to judge Israel. His ministry continued during the Judaic reign of Uzziah, Jotham, Ahaz and Hezekiah. As noted already, the exile of the northern house of Israel took place in 721 BC. This is recorded in 2 Kings 17: 6; 'The King of

---

[108] The Edomites forefather was Esau, Jacob's twin brother.

Assyria captured Samaria, and deported the Israelites to Assyria. He settled them in Halah, in Gozan on the Habor River, and in the towns of the Medes.'

Paul later quotes from Hosea in his letter to the Romans (Romans 9: 25-27), and notes that the promise of God was that a remnant of Israelites would be saved. God would call a people who were not his people, 'sons of the living God' (Hosea 1: 10; 2: 23). The writing of Hosea needs to be considered in depth in order to correctly understand what the Apostle was saying in Romans 9-11. I will return to the letter to the Romans later. But from the Old Testament Prophets it can be seen that it was God's plan to graft Gentile believers onto the root of Israel, but also to re-graft the nations of exiled northern Israel back into the natural olive rootstock as well. According to Hosea, God would make the Israelites as numerous as the sand on the seashore and therefore beyond measure (Hosea 1: 10). The land of Canaan could never hold such a number of people and it was always God's plan for the seed of Abraham to be sown, or scattered, into the world, and through conversion in the Messiah become a blessing to all nations.

Hosea, writing during the time just prior to the northern exile, is commanded by God to take an adulterous woman called Gomer to be his wife; this is symbolic of the adultery of Israel (Hosea 1: 2-3). Hosea is then told to name his children according to the prophetic plan of God. The first son was called Jezreel, meaning God scatters, because God planned to break the kingdom of Israel and bring it to an end, thus scattering, or sowing, the northern Israelites amongst the nations. The second was named Lo-Ruhamah because God would no longer show love to Israel. However, Judah would find love and be saved as a nation according to God's sovereign choice and power, and not because of the works of man. Their preservation was because of the necessity to appoint the Messiah who was to come through Judah. The third son was named Lo-Ammi to indicate the rejection of the Israelites, where God says to them that '...you not my people and I am not their God' (Hosea 1: 4-9). However, reunion is later promised between Judah and Israel under one ruler, and the Israelites will again be called 'sons of the living God,' and Hosea writes that the 'day of Jezreel' will be great. But in their exile the Israelites will have become as numerous as the sand on the seashore (Hosea 1: 10-11).

In the next chapter we find Hosea elaborate further on how God would deal with the people of Israel. First of all God says that he would divorce Israel and then send her away because of her sin (Hosea 2: 2-7). However, in Israel's wanderings she would fail to find satisfaction with foreign lovers (that is foreign deities) and thus she would desire to be reunited with God. God then promised to 'allure' Israel again and show love to her, bringing her through the desert and removing the worship and invocation of Baal from her lips. Israel was promised that she would again call upon God as 'my husband' and not 'my master' (Hosea 2: 14-17). God further promised to betroth or remarry Israel through a new covenant that would last forever based upon righteousness and justice, love and compassion. God said that the people would find peace and safety again (Hosea 2: 14-20).

This covenant will also impact upon the birds and animals as well, and Hosea writes that the skies will respond to the earth and together they will bring forth grain, oil and new wine and thus respond to those who have been scattered.[109] So fruitfulness and prosperity are promised, as is the promise of restoration. The Israelites who were rejected and unloved by God would again be called 'my people' and they would identify themselves as God's people (Hosea 2: 21-23). There is the promise of reunification between Judah and Israel within a new covenant, and thus remarriage to God is foreseen on a new basis. God had sent Israel away and divided Judah from Israel, but in the end there would be reunion, restoration and reconciliation.

The blessings and promises of God had always included the prosperity and fruitfulness of the land to those who walk before God, thus confirming the promises to Abraham. Moses too is told that God would bring the Israelites out of their slavery in Egypt into a land flowing with milk and honey (Exodus 3: 8). It is interesting to note that Paul refers to this aspect of the earthly blessings of God in Romans (8: 21) where the whole creation is to be redeemed from frustration and decay and brought into glorious liberty through God's children.

The same theme continues through the third chapter where Hosea is told to remarry Gomer and show love to her, even though she had lived for many days in disgrace and adultery. Through this God showed that he still loved the people of Israel. Although the Israelites would live without a king or prince for many days, in the end they would return and seek God and 'David' (that is Jesus) their king. Because of this they are told to abandon their sin as they come trembling to God in the last days (Hosea 3: 1-5).

Much of the rest of the book of Hosea is taken up with describing the immediate judgment that is to come upon Israel (Israel here is often identified as Ephraim (Hosea 6: 10; 8: 11; 9: 3: 9: 16 etc), but Judah too will not escape from judgment in the end and a 'harvest' of judgment is appointed for them also (Hosea 6: 11). However, the promise remains that in the end the people of Ephraim will return to

---

[109] In Isaiah a young wife who had been divorced was also to be brought back with deep compassion (Isaiah 54:5-10).

God and be healed from their sin and wandering as God will again 'love them freely.' Israel, that is Ephraim, will blossom like the lily and the cedar of Lebanon, they will flourish like corn and God himself will provide their fruitfulness (Hosea 14: 1-8). The message of Hosea, like Amos, is directed primarily to the northern house of Israel and to Ephraim. Although they were to be judged for their idolatry and sin in the end they will be restored in righteousness and God will provide for their fruitfulness. According to Hosea, Judah would be saved initially in order to bring forth the leader, that is the coming Messiah, but in the end they too will be judged for their sin.

Isaiah

The book of Isaiah too is significant. Isaiah's ministry began in 740 BC, before the northern Israelite exile and also therefore before the Judean exile, but he continued to minister through the period of the northern exile until around 681 BC. He was therefore a contemporary of Micah, Amos and Hosea, and prophesied to Israel. Although with the hope that Israel would again be reconciled and restored in the future.

In the text, Isaiah sees that a fruitful branch would come from the stump of Jesse and rule with wisdom and understanding as given by God's Spirit (Isa. 11: 1-2). This root and tender shoot will become a banner for the nations, and bring a remnant of the exiles of Israel and Judah into God's rest from the four corners of the earth (Isa. 11: 10-12). These people will be gathered out of the nations, including those who are in Assyria, and there will then be unity between the remnant of Judah and Ephraim.[110] In this text God promised to make a highway for the remnant of his people who were in Assyria, but under the leadership of the shoot of Jesse (the Messiah) as a banner to the nations (Isa. 11: 12-16).

The promise of God had always been to bless the nations of the earth through the offspring of Abraham, and Isaiah commented that God would 'enlarge' the nation of Israel and 'increase' the government of the Messiah who would sit on David's throne forever (Isa. 9: 3, 7). Jacob is further promised compassion and resettlement in the land according to God's word. But also the Gentile nations would join with the Israelites in unity, and together they would possess the nations (Isa. 14: 1-2). They would bring their former captor, the king of Babylon under their feet; even the morning star (often considered to be Lucifer) would be brought down because of his pride (Isa. 14: 3-16). With the sins of God's people atoned for, they would then fill the world with fruit

---

[110] Ephraim – the Assyrian Israelite exiles.

(spiritual fruit) and the pagan stones would be smashed and the Asherite poles removed from their place (Isa. 27: 6-9).

Isaiah 49 is often used in support of Christian Zionism, but it is addressed to the 'islands' and 'distant nations' (Isa. 49: 1). The first section of this chapter considers the coming Messiah, the servant of the Lord who is described as a polished arrow concealed in God's quiver, called from before his birth (Isa. 49: 1-2). His mouth is said to be like a sharpened sword and he is hidden in the palm of God's hand. Although God says, through Isaiah, that; 'You are my servant, Israel, in whom I will display my splendour' (Isa. 49: 3) this passage is not referring to Israel as being God's servant at this point because it is also stated that he (the Messiah) was born for the purpose of bringing 'Jacob back to him and [to] gather Israel to himself' (Isa. 49: 5). The passage is then asserting that God will display the servant's splendour through Israel and through reconciliation between Judah and Israel. However, according to the passage the gathering of Jacob and Israel on its own is considered too small a thing for the servant because he is also to be a 'light for the Gentiles' so that he 'may bring [God's] salvation to the ends of the earth' (Isa. 49: 6).

> "This is what the LORD says - the Redeemer and Holy One of Israel - to him who was despised and abhorred by the nation, to the servant of rulers: "Kings will see you and rise up, princes will see and bow down, because of the LORD, who is faithful, the Holy One of Israel, who has chosen you." (Isa. 49: 7).

The Lord further promises to make the servant to be a 'covenant for the people' to 'restore the land' to bring the captives out and set them free.

> "In the time of my favour I will answer you, and in the day of salvation I will help you; I will keep you and will make you to be a covenant for the people, to restore the land and to reassign its desolate inheritances, to say to the captives, 'Come out,' and to those in darkness, 'Be free!'" They will feed beside the roads and find pasture on every barren hill. They will neither hunger nor thirst, nor will the desert heat or the sun beat upon them. He who has compassion on them will guide them and lead them beside springs of water (Isa. 49: 8-10).

God further says that he will turn the 'mountains into roads,' and the 'highways will be raised up' (Isa. 49: 11). This levelling of the ground will allow the exiles to return, coming 'from afar - some from the north, some from the west, some from the region of Aswan' (Isa. 49: 12).

> Shout for joy, O heavens; rejoice, O earth; burst into song, O mountains! For the LORD comforts his people and will have compassion on his afflicted ones (Isa. 49: 13).

In this passage, God promises to remember Zion as a mother remembers her baby, and claims that he has engraved Israel in the palms of his hands and will therefore bring the sons of Israel back to the land (Isa. 49: 14-18). But the land will be too small for the people and they will ask God for more land (Isa. 49: 19-20). In other words under the New Covenant the Israelites would be brought back into the land, but the land will be extended beyond the borders often considered the possession of Abraham's offspring. It would therefore be wrong to apply this passage to the modern situation to justify the confiscation and annexation of Palestinian homes and villages. The Lord further promises to '...beckon to the Gentiles, I will lift up my banner to the peoples; they will bring your sons in their arms and carry your daughters on their shoulders. Kings will be your foster fathers, and their queens your nursing mothers...' (Isa. 49: 22-23). The captives will even be rescued as plunder from fierce warriors and the children brought to safety (Isa. 49: 24-25).

> Then all mankind will know that I, the LORD, am your Saviour, your Redeemer, the Mighty One of Jacob." (Isa. 49: 26).

The passage is really talking about the ingathering of the sons of Israel back into the land as a result of the work of the Messiah in the first century, but like other Old Testament prophecies, the land is stated as being too small for them. Gentiles will help in that ingathering, but the blessing that Israel receives will extend to the Gentiles and to the ends of the earth for the glory and splendour of the servant; that is Jesus. Although this promise included the land of Palestine, or the 'Holy Land,' it had become too small to contain the full blessings of God, and even Gentiles are to take the gospel to the scattered Israelites.

God further promises that foreigners who bind themselves to the Lord will not be excluded from his people (Isa. 56:3,6). God declares that as he gathers the exiles of Israel, so others will be gathered as well (Isa. 56: 8), but the blind watchmen of Israel saddened God for their lack of faithfulness, the careless shepherds who lacked knowledge and understanding (Isa. 56: 9-12). However, God said that he was going to give Zion a new name, and the nations of the earth will see the glory that is given, where Zion's righteousness will 'shine like the dawn', and her salvation 'like a blazing torch' (Isa. 62: 1-2). No longer will Israel be deserted, but God's delight will cause him to remarry her, and she will become a banner to the nations (Isa. 62: 3-11). In Isaiah 65 a people that had not sought God will be called and found by him, but the obstinate people of God will be rejected (Isa. 65: 1-2). However not all the people of Jacob and Judah would be rejected, as some good fruit would be found amongst the grapes of God's people. He will allow them to inherit the mountains of Israel in God's land. But those who had forsaken God would be rejected.

Isaiah then is consistent with other passages such as Jeremiah 31 and Hosea 1 (particularly Hosea) where God says that he will restore Israel, but the land will be too small to hold them all. The blessing will also extend to the Gentiles according to Hosea (and as interpreted by Paul in Romans (Rom. 9-11)). The land in these passages should be seen in light of Jesus' teaching about the kingdom of heaven spreading across the whole earth, and not simply be seen as a narrow strip of land in the Middle East. No longer is God restricting his work to a single nation and small piece of land, as he did in the time of the judges and kings, but he is now fulfilling his plan to bring salvation to the ends of the earth, which was always part of God's promise given to Abraham.

Isaiah then ought to be interpreted to read that the global Church under the New Covenant would become a union between the Gentile believers as well as a reunion of Judah and Israel. This is also in fulfilment of the prophecies of Hosea and the other Prophets. Unlike Judah, the northern tribes of Israel did not appear to return to the land after their period of exile in any real sense. They had settled in the surrounding nations, but later they received the gospel preached by the Apostles. In this way Israel was reunited. This reunion was legitimately Israel in a spiritual and legal sense because it brought Joseph's birthright blessing and the promised Sceptre of Judah (Jesus) together. Although this is not yet the full story as will be discussed further.

Micah

Micah also prophesied during the second half of the eighth century BC as a contemporary of Isaiah and Hosea. He predicted the fall of Israel to the Assyrians, and condemned the leaders of Judah and Israel for their sin; those 'who build Zion with bloodshed, and Jerusalem with wickedness' (Mic. 3:10). However, after a period of judgement, deliverance and restoration to the land are promised. Micah tells us that God promised to gather the remnant of Israel and bring them together as a flock of sheep, for instance where 'their king will pass through before them, the Lord at their head' (Mic. 2:12-13). In the last days we are informed that the mountain of God's temple will be established and become a place of hope and teaching for the nations, and the 'law will go out from Zion' (Mic. 4: 1-2). As a result of this there will be peace amongst the nations. Swords will be beaten into ploughshares, and 'nation will not take up sword against nation' neither will they 'train for war any more' (Mic. 4: 3).

Despite a temporary judgement against Israel, God promises to gather the exiles, and the lame will be turned into a strong nation and the Lord will rule over them in Mount Zion (Mic. 4: 6-7). Israel will be ruled over by a king who will come out of Bethlehem 'whose origins are from of old, from ancient times' (Mic. 5: 2). Although Micah asserts that Israel will be temporarily abandoned, a time will come when Israel will return and be restored, and the ruler will 'shepherd the flock in the strength of the Lord' (Mic. 5: 3-4). Israel will then live in security, and the greatness of the shepherd 'will reach to the ends of the earth, and he will be their peace' (Mic. 5: 4-5). It is noteworthy then that the new nation of Israel under the shepherd Jesus Christ will be concerned with establishing peace across the whole world, and not seek to expand secular-political borders in a small part of the Middle East. At the right time Israel will be in submission to the Messiah; the one who came from Bethlehem.

Jeremiah

Jeremiah's writing is also of importance to this discussion. He was from a priestly line and his ministry covered a period from 626 BC to around 586 BC. This ministry was undertaken after the Assyrians had taken the northern tribes into captivity, and it overlapped with the beginning of the southern exile of Judah in Babylon. Jeremiah was then primarily writing against the sins of Judah and warning of God's judgment. However, Jeremiah also speaks of future restoration for both Judah and Israel under the righteous messianic shepherd.

'The days are coming declares the Lord, when I will raise up to David a righteous branch, a King who will reign wisely and do what is just and right in the land.

In his day Judah will be saved and Israel will live in safety.

This is the name by which he will be called: The Lord Our Righteousness' (Jer. 23: 5-6).

Understanding Israel

Jeremiah then asserts that at a future point in history people will no longer say 'As surely as the Lord lives who brought the descendents up out of Egypt,' but they will say, 'As surely as the Lord lives who brought the descendents up out of the land of the north, and out of all the countries where he had banished them.' The people will then live in their own land (Jer. 23: 7-8). In other words, the promised shepherd king of David's line will gather both Judah and Israel, with Israel gathered out of the north. These are places where the Israelites had been exiled and scattered by the Assyrians. Christian Zionists sometimes use this passage to point to the gathering of East European and Russian Jews to the Holy Land in the present day as fulfillment, but I believe the context points in another direction; that is to the restoration of the Assyrian exiles.

Jeremiah further expands on the restoration of Israel and Judah in a lengthy discourse (Jer. 30-33). Both Judah and Israel are promised restoration to the land of their forefathers (Jer. 30: 1-4). No longer will Jacob or Israel be enslaved, but they will be brought out of a distance land and be given peace and security where they will serve the 'Lord their God and David their king' (Jer. 30: 8-10). God will 'restore the fortunes of Jacob's tents' and have compassion on them; the city will be rebuilt with songs of rejoicing and thanksgiving heard as God 'adds to their numbers' (Jer. 30: 17-19).

Jeremiah further notes that God loves the clans of Israel with an everlasting love and that they will be built up again. Therefore he will allow the people to rejoice and plant vineyards on the hills of Samaria (Jer. 31: 1-6). Samaria was, importantly, the area where the northern tribes (not Judah) had lived prior to their exile; the capital city also had the same name. Jeremiah says further that the people of Israel will be brought out of the land of the north and from the ends of the earth to settle in their own land (Jer. 31: 8). God will make the paths level alongside streams of water for 'Ephraim...my first born son [the birthright holder],' and they will come with weeping and prayer as they return, and God promises that he will be like a shepherd to the scattered flock of Israel (Jer. 31: 9-10). They will then rejoice in the bounty of Zion as they settle in the land (Jer. 31: 12). God says that he will hear the cries of distress of Ephraim, and acknowledge the people's repentance. And Jeremiah, in a dream, hears God call for road signs to be set up for Israel's return (Jer. 31: 18-21). Both the house of Judah and the house of Israel will be planted in the land (Jer. 31: 27). God then promises to make a new covenant with the house of Israel and Judah, a prophecy that is quoted by the writer to the Hebrews (Heb. 8: 8-12; Jer. 31: 31-34).

"The time is coming," declares the LORD, "when I will make a new covenant with the house of Israel and with the house of Judah.

It will not be like the covenant I made with their forefathers when I took them by the hand to lead them out of Egypt, because they broke my covenant, though I was a husband to them," declares the LORD.

"This is the covenant I will make with the house of Israel after that time," declares the LORD. "I will put my law in their minds and write it on their hearts. I will be their God, and they will be my people.

No longer will a man teach his neighbour, or a man his brother, saying, 'Know the LORD,' because they will all know me, from the least of them to the greatest," declares the LORD. "For I will forgive their wickedness and will remember their sins no more."

God further says that the descendents of Israel will never cease to be a nation before him, as long as the sun, moon and stars endure (Jer. 31: 35-37). Jeremiah further prophesies that Israel will be re-gathered to a place where they can live in safety. God will give them a heart to fear and serve him faithfully, this through an everlasting covenant that God will put in place (Jer. 32: 37-41). The promise given in chapter 23 (Jer. 23: 5-6) is repeated in chapter 33 (Jer. 33: 15-16) with the addition that David will never cease to have a man sit on the throne of Israel (Jer. 33: 17). God's covenant with Jesus can never be broken, and earthly priests will minister continually before God.

Ezekiel

According to Ezekiel God had not forgotten the exiled Israelites in the subsequent centuries of the Old Testament period. In his writing there are a number of prophecies relating specifically to the northern tribes of Israel, and not to Judah, although these prophecies are found in some of the less colourful parts of the Old Testament and therefore often overlooked. Ezekiel had much to say about these northern tribes of Israel and was writing more than one hundred and twenty years after their exile. Ezekiel's prophetic ministry was carried out under the exile of the southern tribes of Judah in Babylon and he began his ministry after 597 BC, lasting some twenty years.

According to Ezekiel, Israel as a nation was to remain subject to the Assyrian authorities for several hundred years. During his ministry, Ezekiel is told by God to perform a rather odd symbolic act whereby he is commanded to lie on his left side for 390 days in order to bear the sin of the house of Israel (Ezek. 4: 1-5). Under this act the days were symbolic of years (Eze. 4: 5). The reason this is specifically a sign for Israel is because Ezekiel is next told to lie on his right side for 40 days to bear the sins of the house of Judah (Ezek. 1: 4-6). What is of further interest is that the house of Israel went into exile under the Assyrians in 721 BC, and they were slaves in Assyria for 390 years until the forces of Alexander the Great finally destroyed the power of their captors in 331 BC. Assyria generally lay to the north and northeast of Israel in what is today Lebanon and Syria. The Babylonians later conqueror Assyria in 609 BC, driving the Assyrians and their captives further north and east, and 70 years later the Persians took over in 539 BC, but the northern tribes were not released at that time from their captivity. Following their final release in 331 BC, the Assyrian Israelite captives scattered to the northwest to Asia Minor and to the east. What is clear though is that God had not forgotten the northern tribes of Israel that were in exile.

Ezekiel had further prophecies regarding the house of Israel, where for instance the lost tribes were considered as a flock of neglected sheep without a shepherd (Ezek. 34: 1-31). In this prophecy, God lamented the lack of faithful shepherds over the flock of Israel and noted that as a result they had been scattered over the hills and mountains of the whole earth with no one to search for them (Ezek. 34: 1-6). So God himself promised to search for the lost sheep that had been scattered (Ezek. 34: 11-12) and bring them back into the land, pasturing them on the mountains of Israel (Ezek. 34: 13-16). God also promised to protect them from plunder and judge fairly between the sheep, placing over them the faithful shepherd 'David' (Ezek. 34: 17-24). The prophecy goes on to assert that God would make a covenant of peace with the house of Israel and bless their land with fruitful abundance (Ezek. 34: 25-31).

Prophecies concerning the house of Israel, and the promise of the reunion of Judah and Israel continue through Ezekiel 36 and 37. God promised to bless Israel by removing them from the surrounding nations and therefore to bring them back into their own land, this for the sake of his own holy name in spite of their unfaithfulness (Ezek. 36: 23-24). God then promised to cleanse the people from their impurities with the sprinkling of clean water and by giving them a 'new heart' and a 'new spirit' (Ezek. 36: 25-26). In this regard God said that his Spirit would be in them and they would then be moved to obedience (Ezek. 36: 27), with the further promise of fruitfulness and great increase in number.

In Ezekiel 37: 1-10 the dry bones are seen to come back to life where tendons, skin and muscles are added, then God breathes life into the body. These bones are representative of the 'whole house of Israel' where God promises to place his Spirit within them as they are settled in their own land (Ezek. 37: 11-14). This I believes needs to be read in the context of the work of the Messiah as the passage goes on to relate.

In the second part of Ezekiel 37 (Ezek. 37: 15-28) both Israel and Judah are promised reunification under one king. Ezekiel is told to take a stick and write on it 'Belonging to Judah and the Israelites associated with him' and then to take another stick and write 'Ephraim's stick, belonging to Joseph and all the house of Israel associated with him.' Then Ezekiel is told to join the two together in his hand (Ezek. 37: 15-17). The promise here is that God is going to bring back into the land of Israel all his people, both the people of Judah and the northern tribes of Israel, and join them together so that they will never be divided again, and also to save them from their sin (Ezek. 37: 18-23). The promise is further given that they will then dwell in the land of Jacob under the great shepherd-king David forever, with a great increase in number. And God further promised to make a covenant of peace with them that will be an everlasting covenant, so that the nations will see that it is the Lord who makes Israel holy (Ezek. 37: 24-28). I believe this was fulfilled in the time of Christ and the apostles. As noted, there are other prophecies in the Old Testament that speak of God making a covenant under one ruler with a reunited Israel and Judah (Hos. 1: 11; Jer. 31: 31; Jer. 50: 4-6).

God further desired to have compassion on all the people of Israel bringing Jacob back from captivity, where God will pour out his Spirit upon the house of Israel (Ezek. 39: 23-29).[111] In the following chapters (Ezek. 40-46), Ezekiel sees a new temple being built where God will live amongst the Israelites forever (Ezek. 43: 7). The writer to the Hebrews later identifies the body of Christ as the temple. Ezekiel (Ezek. 47) then sees a river flowing out of the east gate of the temple towards the Dead Sea. This will be a life-giving blessing to all it touches, and it was said to be too deep to cross. Trees will grow along the banks of the river, and fish will live in the Dead Sea.[112]

---

[111] In Ezekiel chapters 38 and the first part of 39, after a period of 'many days' and in 'future years' Gog and Magog will be summoned against a people who live in safety on the mountains of Israel, a people gathered out of the nations, but God will bring judgement against Gog.

[112] The apostle John also saw a vision of the New Jerusalem coming down from heaven where the Lord Almighty and the Lamb are the temple together with a river flowing out from the throne of the lamb to be a blessing to all nations (*Rev. 21-22*).

Zechariah

Zechariah was a contemporary of Haggai and his ministry continued from around 520 BC to around 480 BC. From a priestly line he had returned with the exiles from Babylon in 538 BC, and thus his ministry covered a period just before, and immediately after the restoration of Judah, but prior to the foreseen restoration of the house of Israel. Zechariah begins by speaking about the return of Judah to the land, but also mentions that those scattered in the north will be brought back, that is the exiles forced out by the Assyrians (Zech. 2: 6), together with many nations joining with the Lord to become God's people (Zech. 2: 11). It is this Zion that is described as the apple of God's eye (Zech. 2: 8).

With Judah restored Zechariah then sees God 'saving the house of Joseph' and restoring them in his compassion (Zech. 10: 6). The Ephraimites will be gathered back to the land, and become as numerous as before, being brought out of Egypt and Assyria (Zech. 10: 6-12). God promised to save Judah and Israel and make them a blessing (Zech. 8: 13). Then Zechariah sees the coming king bringing righteousness and salvation, but in gentleness and humility even riding on 'the foal of a donkey' (Zech. 9: 9). In his grace and might God will take away the 'chariots from Ephraim' and the 'war horses from Jerusalem' (Zech. 9: 10). He will further proclaim peace to the nations, extending his rule to the ends of the earth, and through his covenant of blood he will set the prisoners free. Judah will become as a bow with Ephraim the arrows in God's quiver (Zech. 9: 11-13). God in his meekness and majesty will rule over the whole earth through a union of Judah and Israel where his arrows will flash like the lightning (Zech. 9: 10-14). Zechariah further hears God say that he will become a shepherd to Judah where the ruler will be the cornerstone of his people empowering them to overcome their enemies (Zech. 10: 1-5). God promises to strengthen and save the house of Joseph as well as the house of Judah with the people gathered back into the land. There will be a great increase in number as the Israelites are brought back from Egypt and Assyria (Zech. 10: 6-12).

However, just as Zechariah sees reunion between Judah and Israel and resettlement under the good shepherd, he also sees further division for rebellion, and observes that one flock will be marked for slaughter because of unfaithfulness towards God. In their rebellion they paid the shepherd the price of thirty pieces of silver and God revoked his Old Covenant with them (Zech. 11: 4-17). God will thus break his two staffs marked Favour and Union. The shepherd who is close to the Lord would be struck by the sword and taken away from them because they had turned against him and as a result the sheep would be scattered.

Two-thirds, that is the greater part, will fall into judgement and be lost (Zech. 13: 7-8).

However, one-third of the united Judah and Israel, the smaller remnant, would be strengthened at the hands of the shepherd. They would be refined by fire as silver and gold and as a result the people would acknowledge God, and God would hear their prayers (Zech. 13: 8-9). It was therefore to be through God's Spirit that he would pour out on the house of David a new spirit of 'grace and supplication.' This new spirit within them would then lead them to mourn for the one 'they [had] pierced' (Zech. 12: 10-14), and thus cleanse them from their sin (Zech. 13: 1-2). At least in part this was fulfilled on the day of Pentecost.

Zechariah notes as well that Jerusalem would become a cup that sends nations reeling, or a rock on which those who come against the city will be injured (Zech. 12: 2-3). While Christian Zionists find appeal in this passage for their particular interpretation I think instead that these verses should be interpreted in terms of the New Jerusalem; that is the Jewish Christian community of the first century AD. It is this heavenly city that is a reference to the Jewish apostles being raised up as the leaders of Judah. In the passage they are described as braziers in a woodpile and God says that he will save the dwellings of Judah first, and the feeblest amongst them would become like David (Zech. 12: 6-8). See for instance how Peter, the small pebble, was transformed by the Pentecost experience to become a powerful preacher. The rock is however symbolic of Jesus, and the Church as the body of Christ full of the Holy Spirit will grow from that small stone and bring to an end the idolatrous kingdoms of the world (as recorded in the prophecy of Daniel (Dan. 2: 31-35)). But we should note that this passage in Zechariah is in the context of God pouring out the Holy Spirit upon the house of David with subsequent weeping for the one who was pierced; this is Jesus. 'On that day' a fountain would be opened to cleanse the people from their sin, and the idols would be banished from the land (Zech. 13: 1-2).

God also says through Zechariah that he will be jealous for Zion, and return to dwell in Jerusalem, where Jerusalem will be called a 'City of Truth' and God's mountain will be considered 'Holy' (Zech. 8: 1-3). God will bring back a remnant of his people from the east and west (Zech. 8: 7-8) where both Judah and Israel will be a blessing, bearing fruit for God according to his righteous judgements (Zech. 8: 12-14). Powerful nations and people of different languages will seek the Lord in Jerusalem, taking hold of the righteous Jews and asking to go with them because they have heard that God is with them (Zech. 8: 20-23).

So in summary, I believe the book of Zechariah should be interpreted in the same way as the other prophets as being a reference to the work of Jesus the Messiah in restoring the house of Israel alongside the house of Judah. The good news of God's New Covenant then extends to the Gentile nations who are able to share in the gospel message. The Jewish apostles preached first to Jews, but later Gentiles gladly joined with them. However, there was betrayal from those who should have been the Messiah's closest friends, and the greater part of Judah fell away from God. It was however the righteous remnant of Judah, the Jewish disciples and their friends, who took the new way of grace forward as part of the Church's mission to reach out to the house of Israel and to the nations.

There are then a number of points that come out of this study of the Old Testament prophets. The restoration of Israel was to be centred on the promised Messiah, the son of David and a king born in the line of Judah. The Prophets, when read in context, were evidently concerned about the restoration of the ten tribes of the house of Israel, often denoted by the names of Joseph and Ephraim. This represents the northern Assyrian Israelite exiles, and should not be applied to the present day State of Israel. There was to be reunion between the house of Israel and the house of Judah. The land considered holy in the New Covenant was to be extended to cover the whole earth, and the way of salvation in the Messiah was to go to the Gentile nations as well as the scattered Jews and Israelites. There would be one flock. However, those who would rebel against the Messiah would not find rest in God. I have set this out as a table in Appendix 3.

Chapter 6

Restoring Israel to the Land

The Old Testament then speaks of the restoration of the northern Israelite exiles through the Messiah. In recent times some have tried to trace these lost tribes of Israel in Asia and Europe, with a number of theories given. However, much of this is speculative and only the basis for such arguments is given in Appendix 4. Instead, a much simpler case can be made for the unification of Judah and Israel in the early Christian period, one that is in accord with the Old Testament prophecies and New Testament letters. It is evident that when the early Christian apostles travelled and preached many of their converts were from the northern tribes of Israel. And this work was by God's design. It was a deliberate action on the part of the apostles who believed they were acting under Jesus' direct commission. At the time of Christ, and soon after, the scattered Israelites were not considered lost at all. But following conversion to Christianity their identity became linked more closely with the Christian Church, and this was becoming increasingly non-Jewish in outlook and culture; that is a Greek characteristic. Therefore their separate Hebraic identity gradually disappeared. As the Christian Church re-settled Palestine in the early centuries, with communities and churches built, Jews and Israelites re-entered and settled in the land as part of the united Messianic community. But Christianity was spreading far beyond the borders of Palestine. Israel therefore did resettle the land according to God's promises in a literal sense, but not in the way Christian Zionists recognise today.

The important and interesting question here then concerns the place of settlement of the northern tribes of Israel following their Assyrian exile. What happened to them and where did they go? Although it is widely assumed today that once the Israelites had gone into exile their separate identity slowly diminished to the point where they were subsumed into the surrounding cultures and effectively disappeared as a people and nation. This is certainly the view of the *Encyclopaedia Britannica*[113] and of the *Interpreter's Dictionary* of the Bible.[114] The text notes of the *New International Version Study Bible* also for instance have very little to say on this matter, and largely

---

[113] Encyclopaedia .Britannica. 'Ten Lost Tribes of Israel.' Vol. 11, 1991.
[114] Sanders, J.A. 'Exile' in Buttrick, G.A. et al (eds.) *I.D.B.* New York: Abingdon, 1962, Vol. 2, p. 187

interpret comments relating to Israel, following the northern exile, in terms of its application to the tribe of Judah. Some Jews today recognise the problem believing that there are many unfulfilled promises in the Old Testament that speak of the reunion of Judah and Israel under the Messiah, but many believe the Israelite tribes have simply disappeared from history. This problem is for instance recognised in the *Jewish Encyclopaedia*.[115] But how can Scripture be fulfilled if the northern Israelite tribes have disappeared? As has been shown in the previous chapters the prophets spoke of reunion under the Messiah.

The prophets then are clear that the new covenant would be with both the house of Judah and the house of Israel under one shepherd who is the promised ruler of Judah; that is 'David' the Messiah. But only a part of Judah and Israel would be saved at this time. However, it can be shown that this was fulfilled in the person of Jesus Christ?

The New Testament writers were not silent on this subject, although again the text notes of the *NIV Study Bible* overlook the significance of what was being said by Jesus and the apostles. Matthew records that Jesus sent out the twelve disciples with authority to heal the sick and drive out evil spirits (Matt. 10: 1-5). The disciples are commanded at this time not to go to the Samaritans or the Gentiles, but to the 'lost sheep of the house of Israel' (Matt. 10: 6).[116] This phrase is pointing to the fact that Jesus was acting in fulfilment of prophecy (for instance Ezek. 34: 1-12 and Jer. 50: 4-6), because God had promised through these prophets to be a shepherd to the scattered sheep of the house of Israel. It also implies then that the disciples were sent out of the land of Palestine to the surrounding nations where the Israelites were then scattered by the Assyrians. That is towards the lands south of the Black Sea, the Zagros Mountain region and south of the Caspian Sea, although Jesus further commented that the disciples' ministry to the cities of Israel would not in fact be complete until he returns (Matt. 10: 23). It becomes clear then that the fulfilment of the Old Testament prophecies relating to Israel's restoration took place in the time of Christ and shortly afterwards, although this fulfilment would not be complete until Christ returns. While the disciples were sent away for a short time during Jesus earthly ministry, Jesus taught and preached in the towns of Galilee (Matt. 11: 1).

Another significant passage is found in Acts 2: 5-12, where Luke records that there were God fearing Jews from every nation in

---

[115] Jacobs, J, 'Tribes, Lost Ten,' *Jewish Encyclopaedia*, ed. Singer, I., and Adler, C., New York: Funk and Wagnalls, 1925, Vol. 12: p. 249

[116] The NIV states only 'lost sheep of Israel', but the Greek is 'lost sheep of the house [Gk oikos] of Israel' (also *Matt. 15: 24*).

Jerusalem for the Pentecost celebrations (Acts 2: 5). They witnessed the disciples speaking in their own languages on that day, and then listened to Peter's preaching. Although Luke comments that they were Jews, the list of nations he gives is of interest because it includes the areas where the northern tribes of Israel had been scattered. Although clearly the 3,000 people converted on that day did not represent all the people of Judah and Israel it was a significant first step (and importantly correlates with the 3,000 who died at the giving of the Mosiac Law in Sinai).

It is recorded that there were 'Parthians and Medes' in Jerusalem (Acts 2: 9-10). According to the passage in 2 Kings 17: 6 the Israelites were exiled and placed in 'Halah, in Gozan on the Habor River, and in the towns of the Medes.' The later Parthian empire included areas of Media, and the Jewish historian Josephus commented that the ten tribes remained beyond the Euphrates, (in the region of Media and Parthia) even until the time of Josephus, and had become an immense multitude too numerous to count.

> '...but then the entire body of the people of Israel remained in that country; wherefore there are but two tribes in Asia and Europe subject to the Romans, while the ten tribes are beyond Euphrates till now, and are an immense multitude, and not to be estimated by numbers.'[117]

Josephus in the same passage also comments that Esdras (Ezra) sent a copy of an epistle he had received from God to '...all those of his own nation that were in Media.' Josephus was writing for the Roman authorities and it is interesting to note that for many years the Parthian Empire was often at war with Rome. The historian George Rawlinson argued that the Parthian name might actually derive from a word meaning 'exile,'[118] although the root of the word is similar to the Hebrew word for 'covenant' (BRT, literally 'to fetter,' if the B is mutated into a P). The Hebrew for covenant is similar in form in the Assyrian language.[119]

Other names of places recorded in Acts 2: 9-10 include Cappadocia, Pontus, Asia, Phrygia and Pamphylia. The area of Pontus

---

[117] *Antiquities of the Jews*, (11.5.2), The Works of Josephus, translated by Whiston, W., Hendrickson Publishers. 1987. 13th Printing. p. 294.

[118] Rawlinson, G. *The Sixth Great Oriental Monarchy or the Geography History and Antiquities of Parthia*, New York: Dodd, Mead & Co. 1882, p.19

[119] Vine, W.E., Unger, M.F., and White W. Jr, Vine's Complete Expository Dictionary of Old and New Testament Words, Nashville: Thomas Nelson, Publ., 1985, pp. 50-51.

and Cappadocia are geographically north and west of 'Halah, Gozan and the Habor River' (from 2 Kings 17: 6). Interestingly the Greek historian Diodorus of Sicily noted that a part of the Assyrian empire was later forced northwards settling between Pontus and Paphlagonia on the southern Black Sea coast.[120] (Other parts of the Assyrian empire later extended to the northern coast of the Black Sea). It may be noted then that the people groups represented in Acts 2: 9-10 were from areas where the Assyrians had migrated with the captive northern Israelite tribes. Peter, having preached to these exiled believers on the day of Pentecost, had not forgotten them. He later wrote his first epistle to the 'chosen sojourners of the dispersion' [Gk. *diasporas*] of Pontus, Galatia, Cappadocia, Asia and Bithynia, chosen according to God's foreknowledge' (1 Pet. 1: 1-2). In other words, Peter was acting as God's chosen apostle to the Israelite Diaspora, which was settled in much of what is now modern Turkey. Undoubtedly this group of people included Jewish and Gentile believers as well. With so many converts on the day of Pentecost, the apostles would have taken records of names and addresses, and then followed up with apostolic visits. In fact they would have been negligent if they had not done so, and the fact that the book of Acts records the number of converts, and their places of origin, suggests they kept records.

In fact all of the disciples were chosen to be missionaries to the people of Judah and Israel first, and they preached in the lands where the 'lost' tribes dwelt. According to Acts, the disciples asked Jesus if he was going to restore the nation of Israel at that time, but Jesus' response was that they were not to know the times of such events. Instead they were to go and preach the gospel in Jerusalem, Judea and Samaria and to the ends of the earth through the power of God's Spirit (Acts 1: 6-8). William Cave for instance noted that Thomas took the gospel of Christ to Parthia, then to the Medes, Persians, Carmians and nations further east.[121] There is also a strong tradition that Thomas went as well to a Jewish community in Kerala, southern India. Bartholomew went to Armenia and Asia Minor, Thaddeus to Assyria and Mesopotamia, with Philip going to the Scythians and Upper Asia.[122]

In Acts 2 (Acts 2: 14-39) Peter also addressed the crowd calling them by three different titles. First of all he addressed the 'Jewish men' and the 'inhabitants of Jerusalem' and quotes from Joel (Acts 2: 14).

---

[120] Diodorus Siculus, 'Histories,' 2:43, In *Diodorus of Sicily*, Trans. Oldfather, C.H. et al. 12 Vols. London: William Heinemann, 1933

[121] Cave, W., *A Complete History of the Lives, Acts and Martyrdom of the Holy Apostles*, Philadelphia: Solomon Wiatt, 1810, Vol. 2 p. 331

[122] Cave, *Complete History*, pp. 168, 203

Then he addresses the crowd as 'men of Israel' (Acts 2: 22) and quoted from David, asserting that 'all the house of Israel' should now know that Jesus is the Christ (Acts 2: 36). Finally, Peter commented that repentance and the promise of the Holy Spirit is for 'you,' 'your children' and all those who are 'far off' (Acts 2: 38-39). It is noteworthy as well that the hearers of Peter's message were cut to the heart in fulfilment of Zechariah's prophecy.

James (James 1: 1) also mentions that he is writing as a servant in Christ to the 'twelve tribes in the dispersion' (Gk. *diaspora*). This is significant because of James' status as the leader of the Jerusalem church and half-brother of the Lord. James shows his leadership in the Council of Jerusalem (Acts 15). A dispute arose between a group of converted Pharisees, and the apostles Peter, Paul and Barnabas. James is left to make a concluding remark and quoted from the prophet Amos. God promised, through Amos, to return and rebuild David's fallen tent so that a remnant of men may seek the Lord, together with all the Gentiles who bear God's name (Acts 15: 16-17; Amos 9: 11-12). This is said to be at a time when God would bring back the exiles of Israel into the land (Amos 9: 13-15).

The Apostle John in Revelation also sees the full measure of Judah and Israel coming into God's kingdom with the symbolic 12,000 from each tribe (144,000) (Rev. 7: 1-8). Clearly the leaders of the Church desired to reach out to all the people of Israel in fulfilment of Old Testament prophecy, and according to the command of Christ. The Church then became a union of Judah and Israel, and eventually as united Israel it re-settled in Palestine establishing communities and building churches in fulfilment of those prophecies.

One possible argument against this might be the question of Paul's teachings, and whether he taught that Judah was to be reunited with the northern tribes of Israel under the Messiah. I think Paul does touch upon this, although it is not so strong in his teachings for a number of reasons. It was Paul who was primarily chosen as the apostle to the Gentiles, to their kings, but also to the sons of Israel (Acts 9: 15). Primarily then his ministry was to Gentiles, and his area of responsibility mainly covered regions around the Mediterranean Sea where Jewish traders had settled and lived side by side with the local Gentile population. The Holy Spirit had prevented Paul from entering Asia where many of the scattered Israelites had settled, that was Peter's area of responsibility. Also Paul was not one of the twelve sent out by Jesus to the lost sheep of the house of Israel as the other apostles had been (Matt. 10). Thus the question is not so important in Paul's teachings. But I think he does address the question, especially in

Romans 9-11 where he references Hosea, and he does take the gospel to some of the scattered Israelites through his ministry.

For Paul, the new Israel though is the kingdom of heaven where faith is of importance, not simply birthright or possession of land (Romans 9: 6). This kingdom is to spread through the whole earth as yeast spreads through dough, or a mustard seed produces a tree that grows across the whole garden (Matt. 13). The king of this kingdom is the promised Messiah from the line of David, and the domain is the Church that exists across the whole earth. We are informed that the wheat will grow amongst the weeds until the time of the end. As noted in the prophetic writings, the land of Israel would become too small to contain the full promise of God, where the descendants of Abraham were promised to be as numerous as the 'sand on the seashore' and Abraham's blessing was ultimately for all nations across the world. The gospel then extended to the Gentile nations according to the promise to Abraham, as Isaiah reminded his readers (Isa. 49: 6), but the kingdom of God exists as primarily a spiritual kingdom upon the face of the whole earth where entry is by faith in Christ.

It may be argued as well that failure to recognise the place of the northern tribes of Israel, who were taken into exile under the Assyrians, is itself a form of replacement theology. If it is believed that they disappeared for good and were replaced by Judah and Benjamin as representative of Israel, then all the promises to those tribes, especially the birthright promise to Joseph and Ephraim, become null and void. As noted at the start of the previous chapter, Jacob-Israel blessed Joseph, saying that all of his blessings would be upon the head of Joseph and by extension also upon his offspring Ephraim and Manasseh (Gen 49: 26). Both Ephraim and Manasseh were promised that they would be called by the name of Abraham, Isaac and Jacob-Israel, and that they would extend across the earth. Locating the ten tribes across the world is though a speculative exercise, and not one of immediate interest to this study. What I hope to have presented in this book is the more simple exercise; that is to show that the ten tribes were not lost during the first century AD, but that their separate Jewish-Israelite identity became obscured following their conversion to Christ. This loss is because the Christian Church adopted more Greek ways of thinking and lost sight of its Hebrew heritage. There is a place for recovering a more Hebrew mindset in Christian circles, although without getting carried away by those who would take away from God's grace, as Paul warned against in Galatians. It is finding that narrow path between the Gnosticism of ancient Greece and the Jewish tradition-of-the-elders that seeks to impose heavy and unnecessary loads upon mankind.

Chapter 7

Israel in Matthew's Gospel

In this chapter I will examine the teachings of Jesus in the Gospel of Matthew, and how the Gospel writer understood Jesus' purpose in terms of the fulfilment of prophecies relating to Israel. The main focus will be on Matthew's Gospel and some discussion of the other Gospels, together with reference to the teachings of the prophets, especially Zechariah. This is though only a brief look at the Gospels.

Matthew 1. Jesus' birth

Matthew starts by giving the genealogy of Jesus through the line of Joseph, a son of David, but emphasizes the virgin birth quoting Isaiah (Isa. 7: 14). He notes that the Messiah will be called Immanuel, meaning 'God with us' (Matt. 1: 23). Matthew also records that the angel instructed Joseph to call his son Jesus, the Greek form of Joshua, which means 'to save' because he will save his people from their sins (Matt. 1: 21). With the coming of the Magi to Jerusalem it is recorded that the chief priests and teachers of the Law replied to Herod that the Messianic Judaic ruler was to be born in Bethlehem, and he would be a shepherd to Israel (Matt. 2: 6; Mic. 5: 2). However, king Herod wanted to kill the promised Messiah.

Luke offers greater depth in both the events that led to the birth of the prophet John, and the events that led to the birth of Jesus. Mary is recorded as having had a vision of an angel who informed her of the forthcoming birth, and is told that her son Jesus will rule on the throne of David according to God's promise, thus ruling over the house of Jacob forever (that is over both Judah and Israel (Luke 1: 33)). Mary gives thanks and praise to God and states that Jesus is to be a help to Israel, as God has now remembered to be merciful to Abraham and his descendents according to the promises to the Patriarchs. With the birth of John the Baptist, Zechariah, John's father, offers praise to the God of Israel asserting that a 'horn of salvation' has been raised up in the house of David, thus remembering the covenant of promise to Abraham, and that John would be a prophet preparing the way for the Lord (Luke 1: 67-72, 76). So we should note that the fulfillment of the blessing of Abraham would be through the Messiah. Later, when Jesus was presented to the temple, Simeon also spoke. He had been told that he would see the coming Messiah who would be the 'consolation of Israel.'

He prophesied that Jesus would be a light to the Gentiles, and would bring glory to the people of Israel. God's salvation would be revealed to all people (Luke 2: 25-32). But he warned Mary and Joseph that the child would cause some to fall, and some to rise in Israel with the thoughts of many hearts exposed (Luke 2: 34-35). Anna, the prophetess from the Israelite tribe of Asher, also spoke about Jesus to all she met in the temple area.

Matthew 10. Shepherding the Lost Sheep of Israel

As noted already in the previous chapter, in Matthew 10 Jesus is recorded as sending out the twelve disciples to preach abroad the kingdom of God as they were commanded to go to the 'lost sheep of the house of Israel' (Matt. 10: 6). This is a reference to the biblical prophecy that God would be a faithful shepherd to the exiled people of Israel (especially Ezek. 34: 1-12 and Jer. 50: 4-6). In these passages then God himself promised to be a shepherd to the scattered lost sheep of the house of Israel, and this was fulfilled in Jesus.

Matthew 13. Kingdom Parables

Jesus also had much to say about the 'kingdom of Heaven' or the 'kingdom of God,' especially in his many parables, for instance Matt. 13. The Scribes and Pharisees saw the nation of Israel ideally as a single kingdom within a particular land with one king, but Jesus taught that the new kingdom of God was to have a different structure, commenting that the new kingdom would go beyond the limitations of that which had gone before. Jesus was to be the eternal Messianic king from David's line, and Zion was to have a new name (from Isa. 62: 1-2). I believe that we need to read Jesus' parables in light of Old Testament prophecies, and in the context of the situation of first century Judea. If we scratch beneath the surface the parables are often seen alluding to the prophetic writing.

In these parables, Jesus said that the wheat and weeds would grow up together in the world and only be separated at the end of the age so that the good crop would not be damaged (Matt. 13: 24-30). No longer would there be a single nation in a single land, an entity that the religious Jews were looking for, instead the new kingdom would be scattered amongst the nations.

The kingdom of heaven was also compared to a mustard seed, in that although it is the smallest of garden seeds, it grows into the largest garden tree, spreading beyond its borders. But in doing so it allows the birds of the air to shelter and perch on its branches.[123] Incidentally, Joseph's blessing was that his line would spread over a wall and outside of their borders. Also Jesus said that the kingdom of heaven is like yeast that spreads through the whole dough (Matt. 13: 31-33). In these parables Jesus was saying that the kingdom of heaven would be in the whole world, and not limited to a single state, as had been the case in the past. This kingdom would then spread throughout the world and transform it according to God's government of grace and peace. Merchants would see such great value in the new kingdom that they would be willing to sell all they had in order to enter in. Jesus was not thinking then of setting up a single nation in a single land, but one spread across the whole earth in fulfilment of the promise given to Abraham. His descendants would be a blessing to all nations on earth. However, Jesus also told his disciples that he spoke in parables so that those with callous hearts would not understand his message (Matt. 13: 10-15).

Matthew 21. Jerusalem and the Fig Tree

In chapter 21 Matthew records the triumphal entry into Jerusalem of Jesus. He chose to ride on a colt, the foal of a donkey (Matt. 21: 1-6). In doing this Jesus was fulfilling the prophecy of Zech. 9: 9 as a sign of the king, coming in deliberate humility and gentleness. This was a message to the offspring of Zion. Jesus then identified himself with the prophecies of Zechariah. As noted, Zechariah prophesied reunion between Judah and Israel, but also God warned of further division for those in rebellion against him. As Jesus entered Jerusalem the people cried out the Messianic greetings, 'Hosanna to the Son of David' and 'Blessed is he who comes in the name of the Lord' (Matt. 21: 9). Jesus then entered the temple area and cleared it of the corrupt money-changers, but also he spent time healing those who came to him (Matt. 21: 12-14).

Jesus later performed a symbolic act by cursing a fig tree that was not bearing fruit, but only lovely green leaves (Matt. 21: 18-22 & Mark 11: 12-21). Jesus did this because the fig tree had no fruit, even though it was not the season for figs; commenting further that it would

---

[123] The mustard tree caused problems for the Pharisees and teachers of the law because it spread outside of clearly marked borders, thus breaking the Mosaic Law. Because it became a tree its fruit could not be harvested until the fifth year, but its life span was only a few years and the tree might then have died before its fruit could be used (see *Lev. 19: 19, 23*).

never bear fruit again. This took place shortly after Jesus had cleared the temple, accusing the religious authorities of turning the temple into a den of robbers (with reference to Jer. 7: 11). Thus the cursed fig tree should be seen as a reference to the corrupt temple authorities and leaders as representatives of apostate Israel. The prophet Micah commented that God would be unhappy when, at harvest time, he couldn't find any of the grapes or 'early figs' that he desired, noting the wickedness of the people (Mic. 7: 1-7). There also appears to be a symbolic reference in this act to Jeremiah 24 (Jer. 24: 1-10). The prophet sees God placing two baskets of figs, one good and one bad, in front of the temple. According to Jeremiah, the figs represented the division of Judah into a basket that was bearing fruit according to God's righteousness, and those who were not. God's promise to the basket of good figs was to give them a heart to seek after him, while the basket of bad fruit would receive nothing. In other words, the only way the Jewish nation could bear fruit in the future was through the Messiah, as the old system of worship and temple authority would be totally replaced by the new sacrifice of Christ. It may be seen then that the intention of Jesus was to separate out the 'good figs' of the tribe of Judah from the 'bad figs.'

Jesus went on to say that the kingdom of God would be taken away from the chief priests and Pharisees and given to those who would produce the fruit of the kingdom. Through a parable Jesus said that even though they knew he was the heir of the vineyard, they planned to kill him anyway, along with the servants the prophets who had gone before, and therefore they planned to steal the inheritance from the Son (Matt. 21: 33-42).

But although they were condemned by Jesus and told that they would lose their position, we need to remember that the first Christians were almost entirely Jewish. In other words, according to Zechariah a remnant of one third of Judah would remain and continue according to God's promise, while it was the rebellious two thirds that were to be cut off (Zech. 13: 7-9). Although the Church gradually lost its Jewish identity as more and more Gentiles joined, the Church ought to be seen as a legitimate continuation of the tribe of Judah today with Jesus as the Messiah seated on David's throne.

Matthew 23. A Desolate House

In Matthew 23 Jesus spoke seven woes over the Pharisees and teachers of the Law, which I would suggest is significant in light of the seven fold blessing of Abraham. In other words, in this declaration Jesus was revoking his covenant of Favour and Union with the existing order that was resisting the blessing of the Messiah (see Zechariah 11). Jesus concluded his statement by commenting that the sins of their forefathers would come upon their generation, all the way from the guilt of the shed blood of Abel to Zechariah the priest who was murdered in the temple.[124] Jesus further commented that their house would be left to them desolate (Matt. 23: 1-38). Then he says; 'For I tell you, you will not see me again until you say, 'Blessed is he who comes in the name of the Lord'' (Matt. 23: 39). In Hebrew this last statement is *Baruch ha ba be shem adonai,* a greeting recognised by Jews as being Messianic. This was the greeting the people shouted when Jesus entered Jerusalem on the young donkey. In other words, Jesus was saying to the Pharisees and teachers of the Law that he was the Messiah, and that there would be no one else; as such the only way to find the Messiah was to recognise and accept him. The old ways of temple sacrifice were then brought to nothing, and their 'house' was to suffer desolation. However, even in this harsh judgement there was, and is, mercy to the Jews, in that a way back to God is still open through Jesus for those who repent and turn back to him.

There is also a warning in Jesus' words, teaching his followers to beware of the leaven, or yeast, of the Pharisees and Sadducees (Matt. 16: 6). But were these comments overly rhetorical and just figures of speech on the part of Jesus? Most Christians ignore the significance of what is said in the passage viewing the Pharisees as mere legalistic religious ideologues. However, there is, I would suggest, some evidence that the Sadducees and Pharisees had already embraced, or been influenced by, pagan political philosophy, working it into their own theology. By the third century BC, Jewish philosophers such as Artapanus and Aristobulus were already sympathetic to the works of Plato believing that Moses had taught Orpheus, and Aristobulus believed that the writing of Moses had heavily influenced both Plato and Pythagoras. However, both Plato and Pythagoras may have been involved in the esotericism of Egyptian and Babylonian paganism. Plato also influenced Philo, and the unconverted Saul, who was a rising and zealous star in the Sanhedrin. Saul had been trained in Greek philosophy as well as studying under Gamaliel. In other words, in first century Palestine the beliefs of the Greek thinkers, and therefore also perhaps that of Babylon and Egypt, had some influence upon the leadership of the Jewish state, more especially through the political beliefs of the

---

[124] The apostle John also records Jesus' criticisms of the Pharisees where he accuses them of being children of the devil because of their lies and desire to murder him (John 8: 42-47, also see Rev. 2: 9).

Pharisees and ruling classes. This may be seen when it is considered in light of the political philosophy of Plato. The class divisions of Plato's Republic may also be evident in the practices of the Sadducees and Pharisees in the first century setting, as they were acting like Plato's philosopher-kings. In the Republic, Plato had set out his social order for the ideal city-state of Polis with a subservient population ruled over by philosopher-kings and a high class military. The majority of Jews lived in an impoverished and subservient position in first century Palestine, partially through Pharisaic exploitation, and were held in check by the Roman army.

Jesus criticised the Pharisees commenting that they should not be called 'Rabbis' because they were really 'brothers' with their fellow Jews (Matt. 23: 8). He therefore condemned them for their exploitation of the poor, an exploitation that was incidentally allowable in their interpretation of Moses (the Tradition of the Elders), but not allowed in the Torah. Jesus also commented that the Pharisees and teachers of the Law would fill up on the sins of their forefathers (sins that included murder and idolatry in the Old Testament history) even as their house would be left to them desolate (Matt. 23: 32).

Interestingly, in Revelation John sees a harlot riding the beast and the woman is identified as Mystery Babylon, a great city (Gk *polis*) who rules over the earth (Rev. 17: 5, 18), but the woman will eventually be brought to nothing, and her destruction will come in one hour (Rev. 18). In other words, Jesus' was harsh towards the Pharisees and teachers of the Law because he could see beyond the surface and see their hearts, as they were seemingly embracing the politics of mystery Babylon in their class-ridden politics. They were indeed being seduced and blinded by their privileged position, unable to see the Messiah and understand the full counsel of Old Testament teachings. However, it is important to stress that these prophesies were not given against all Jews, but against a corrupt and idolatrous leadership who were exploiting the poor in Jewish society. The poor of Jewish society were very much the victims of this type of political philosophy and Jesus reached to these Jews, his own people, first.

Matthew 24. End Time Prophecies

In Matthew 24 Jesus speaks prophesies about events to come. Firstly, he comments that the temple will be levelled with no stone left unturned (Matt. 24: 2). This was fulfilled in AD 68-70 when the Roman armies brought judgement against Jerusalem, destroying the temple and leaving no stone unturned in order to extract the gold. There are though I think two prophecies interwoven into this passage. One concerns the judgement against Judah in the first century; the second concerns the second coming of Jesus. The sign of the first judgement is the 'abomination that causes desolation' which was a sign for the Christians to flee to the hills and therefore escape the judgement that was to come upon Jerusalem (Matt. 24: 15-22). Eusebius[125] has a lot to say about this judgement upon Jerusalem in his Ecclesiastical History, and how the Christians escaped because of Jesus' prophecy, although a complete discussion of this will take us away from the theme of the book.

The sign of the second judgement is the sign of the fig tree producing more green leaves (Matt. 24: 32-33). While Jesus cursed the fig tree, he said that it will again appear bringing forth more green leaves in the future, noting that this will be a sign of the end of the age (Matt. 24: 32 & Mark 13: 28). Some Christian Zionists use this statement about the fig tree sprouting more green leaves in order to legitimise the modern State of Israel, but totally miss the point about the green leaves. Hal Lindsey for instance comments that this is an important sign of the restoration of the Jews to the land.[126] However, green leaves speak of outward glory, but no inner fruit. Jesus was looking for the inner fruit not the outward show. Therefore as a symbolic act Jesus cursed the tree because it was only bearing green leaves, and not fruit. The fruitless fig tree was thus representative of the Jewish ruling authorities and their lack of fruit. From this, I believe that Jesus' comments should be understood to mean that a Jewish nation called Israel will return bearing more green leaves, i.e. having the external appearance of Israel, but not bearing the required fruit that God desires. The prophecy of Jesus then may be interpreted to imply that a separate Jewish nation would arise again in the future bearing more green leaves before the end of the age, but lacking the fruit that God requires, thus having no part in the true Israel that is a union of Jews, Israelites and Gentiles in the Messiah.

The re-emergence of such a State of Israel then may be seen as a sign that the second coming is near. God has allowed the State of Israel to exist as part of his permissive will; that is he has permitted modern Israel to exist as a nation, but this Israel is not living according to God's directive will, which is to bear fruit by accepting the kingship of Jesus over Israel according to God's righteousness. Indeed the State of Israel is a secular republic and it is impossible for it to bring forth the

---

[125] Cruse, C.F. (trans.), *The Ecclesiastical History of Eusebius Pamphilus - Bishop of Caesarea, In Palestine*, 1850. Reprinted as *Eusebius' Ecclesiastical History*, Baker Book House, 1995.

[126] Lindsay, H, *The Late Great Planet Earth*, London: Lakeland / Zondervan, 1970, p. 53

fruit that God requires outside of Christ; instead the Church is the true Israel of God because it accepts Jesus as king of Israel.

Throughout Matthew's Gospel he highlights how Jesus fulfilled the Old Testament prophecies that spoke of the coming Messiah. Jesus was to be the Messianic king from David's line, the saviour for his people, and a shepherd to the Jews and lost people of the house of Israel. Jesus came to unite Judah and Israel, but he also condemned the faithless leaders, the chief priests and Pharisees who had corrupted God's people with exploitation and false teaching. Jesus then broke his covenant of *Union* and *Favour* with that two-thirds part of Judaism, according to Zechariah's prophecy, by pronouncing that their house would be left to them desolate. However, God remembered his promise to Abraham by making a New Covenant with those Jews who followed him and who heard his voice. The remnant of Judah was promised restoration under the Messiah, a promise that continues to this day. The next chapter will look at the New Testament letters of Paul to see how the early Church saw its position before God.

Chapter 8

Israel in Romans

In the next few chapters I will look at the apostolic writings of the New Testament, especially Paul's writing and influence, and see how he saw the fulfilment of Old Testament prophecy relating to Israel in the light of Christ. What I think is apparent is that Paul was presenting a message that he believed to have been given by revelation, although he was careful to ground his teaching in the Hebrew Scriptures, in fact more firmly than we sometimes think. As part of this message he worked to build unity between the Gentile converts and Jewish believers because he saw that through Jesus both were being brought together into God's new plan of salvation in Christ. Paul was keen for Jewish believers, particularly those from Jerusalem, to accept Gentiles, but also for Gentiles in the Greek and Roman world to accept Jews. There was then the need to challenge a growing replacement theology in Rome.

Letter to the Romans

The main passage from Romans that Christian Zionists appeal to in support of their particular interpretation of Scripture is that found in Romans 9, 10 and 11. These three chapters need to be taken as a single discussion, and in context with all of Paul's teaching, especially in the rest of Romans. I believe in this passage as well Paul was expounding the message of the Old Testament prophets, especially from Isaiah and Hosea, and this needs to be taken into account to really understand the message of Paul. So in this chapter section I want to look in depth at Paul's teaching in Romans. Steve Motyer has done a more extensive study of these passages in Romans and I will be referring to some of his work in this chapter.[127]

The letter to the Roman Christians was most probably written sometime around the late 50s to early 60s AD. The Church in Rome at the time consisted of Gentile and Jewish believers, and Paul was partly writing to encourage greater unity. Events and circumstances in Rome had led to the separation of believers; that is between the Gentiles who expressed their freedom in Christ and were allowed to remain in Rome, and Jewish Christian believers who were following certain of the Old

---

[127] Motyer, S, *Israel in the Plan of God*, Leicester: IVP, 1989

Testament practices, but had to endure a temporary expulsion. As a result of these events in Rome the Gentiles came to form the larger grouping. Some distrust between the two sides developed once the Jewish believers were allowed to return to Rome some years later. This distrust meant that difficulties arose as they tried to reintegrate into the Gentile Christian community.

David Pawson gives some further background to the problem that had arisen in Rome.[128] It would seem that Jews had been banished from Rome in the early to mid 50s AD by the Emperor Claudius because they were stirring up trouble against the Christians on account of 'Chrestus.'[129] Because of this the Jewish Christians were forced to leave along with the Jews. This expulsion appears to have lasted several years, but with the new Emperor Nero coming to power the Jews and Jewish Christians were allowed to return some years later.[130] However, by this time the Gentile Christians in Rome were reluctant to welcome the Jewish believers back into their fold and were developing a belief that God had now rejected the Jews and chosen the Gentiles. In other words, it was the development of a real replacement-type of theology that Paul was responding to, and in this context Paul was writing in order to encourage unity between Jews and Gentiles in the Roman Church.

However, Paul also set out his gospel and theology to a community that was living in the heart of the pagan world with its corruption and idolatry. Part of Paul's thinking then was to build and encourage Christian unity in the pagan city by explaining God's universal plan of salvation and righteousness that was to include Jews and Gentiles. In this context he rejected the Roman Christian belief that God had replaced the Jews and had now chosen the Gentiles. It is noteworthy as well I think that Paul wrote to the Christian community and expressed a belief in the continuity of Jews in God's plan shortly before his visit to Jerusalem (Romans 15: 23-29).[131] Paul's teaching

---

[128] Pawson, D, *Israel in the New Testament*, Bradford on Avon: Terra Nova Publ. pp. 96-99

[129] The text notes of the NIV Study Bible in Acts 18:2 gives further information. Suetonius in *Cluadius 25* records that the Jews had caused a great deal of trouble on account of 'Chrestus' (Jesus Christ).

[130] Luke in Acts 18:1-3 records that Aquila (who was originally from Pontus) and his wife Priscilla were among those who were forced to leave Italy and as a result they settled in Corinth where Paul was able to meet with them. By the time Paul writes Romans they are back in Rome (Romans 16:3-4).

[131] Paul planned to visit Rome, but he had aid to take money from the Greek Christians in Macedonia and Achaia to Jerusalem first. As events unfolded it was this visit that led to his capture and then to an appeal to Caesar in Rome.

amongst the Jews and Gentiles around the Mediterranean was causing problems with the leadership in Jerusalem who were trying to covert their fellow Jews. They apparently had a different belief than Paul about the significance for Jews of certain Old Testament practices.

The Elect of God and Israel

The question of the 'elect' in Paul's letter to the Romans has been problematic for Christians through many centuries. The central passage of Romans 9-11 asserts that a remnant of Jewish believers forms part of the elect of God and has therefore received divine grace (Rom. 9:11, 11:5, 11:7, 11:28).[132] But in what sense does Paul say the Jews are the elect of God? The Greek word for the elect or chosen of God is *ekloge* and is used to refer to the chosen people of God; those specially picked out as Abraham had been.[133] Paul points out that through the history of Israel it is evident that 'not all who are descended from Israel are Israel', (Rom. 9:6) but only those born according to the promise of God (Rom. 9:7-9). He uses the birth of Jacob and Esau as an example of this type of election where the younger brother Jacob was called forward for God's express purposes, even before either of the twins had the chance to do anything good or bad (Rom. 9:6-13). Election in the context here is concerned with God's divine calling to bring about his plan of salvation for mankind. Both were children of Isaac, but only one was selected to fulfill God's purposes and form the nation of Israel.

Furthermore, we may see that Jacob as a young man was also a manipulator who tried to work out his own blessing by deceiving his father Isaac. But later he had an opportunity to seek God's face for his blessing when he struggled with the heavenly, angelic visitor. He had come to the end of himself because of fear of his brother Esau and wanted God's blessing and protection. In doing this he placed himself in submission to God, and it was at this time that God called him *Israel* (Gen. 32:22-32). So, we may note that Israel is a spiritual title conferred upon those in submission to God, and originally it did not refer directly to ethnicity. Someone may then be a descendent of Jacob, but not be living as Israel. Paul wrote further in Romans that many of the people of Israel failed to accept Christ because they were living by the works of the law, and not by faith. They weren't seeking God in submission, but

---

[132] The question of God's election in general is though problematic with various opinions voiced, but questions about predestination and freewill, and the five points of Calvinism are beyond the scope of this present study.

[133] This is sourced from; *Vine's Dictionary of New Testament Words*, p. 196

in pride they were trying to show the outward form of their religion as a means of gaining approval before men and God. Jesus then became a stumbling block to them; as Paul noted, He has become 'a stone [in Zion] that causes people to stumble' (Romans 9: 30-33). We may note from this then, that today any form of Zionism that doesn't recognize the place of Jesus in relation to Israel is stumbling over the stone.

In terms of the election of a remnant of Israel in the first century, Paul in Romans refers back to the time of Elijah (Rom. 11:4) where God kept for himself seven thousand Israelites who had not bowed the knee to Baal. From this example Paul comments that '...at the present time there is a remnant [of Jews] chosen by grace' (Rom. 11:5), but he also notes that 'the others were hardened' (Rom. 11:7).[134] The first part of this statement is a reference to those Jews who accepted Jesus, and Paul in the letter sees them as the elect remnant of Israel. For Paul the Church was established by the election of those Israelites who were obedient to their calling in Christ. In other words, the Church, initially consisting of Jews and Israelites on the day of Pentecost, formed the legitimate remnant of ethnic and spiritual Israel. Compare, if you will, the specially chosen 120 priests appointed by Solomon to minister before God at the dedication of his temple (2 Chronicles 5-7), and the 120 in the upper room when the Holy Spirit came with tongues of fire (Acts 2). On the former occasion the cloud of the glory of the Lord filled the temple and fire burnt up the offering. The 120 present on the day of Pentecost then may be seen to represent the chosen priests of a new temple where God dwells directly with men. Solomon recognized from this that a temple of stone could not contain God, and that foreigners would find blessing in God as well. Gentiles were subsequently grafted into Israel; this is now the Church; the *ekklesia* of Israel. But from this passage in Romans we may discern that Paul is challenging replacement theology, and instead teaching a remnant theology that is in continuity with Israel, both spiritually and ethnically.

The second part of the passage is a reference to the other Jews who rejected Jesus in the time of the New Testament writing. In Romans 11 Paul asserts that these unbelieving Jews have been cut out of the olive tree with the Gentiles grafted in. But this does not give Gentiles the right to become proud; instead they should be humble and thankful and work for the restoration of the unbelieving Jews who may be grafted in again if they accept Christ. Gentile Christians are further called to make the Jews envious of their new faith through their faithfulness, love and good conduct (Rom. 11: 11). It is evident then that

---

[134] Paul quotes from Isaiah in Romans (Rom. 9:25-27) and notes from this that only a remnant of Israel will be saved (Isa. 10:20-25; Isa. 11:12-16).

in Paul's teaching the concept of a chosen people as the elect of God was directed towards those Israelites and Gentiles who were now obedient to Christ. Paul wrote further that there is now no difference between Jews and Gentiles in terms of their status before God, both must come to Christ to receive righteousness the same way; that is through faith (Rom. 10: 11-13). God will therefore justify both the Jews and the Gentiles through the same faith, and that righteousness from God has come to all apart from the Mosaic Law. And as Paul noted this is attested to by the prophets and the Law (Rom. 3: 21-31).

So Paul doesn't use the concept of a chosen people to refer to those Jews who turned away from Jesus as the promised Messiah, but to those Jews and Israelites who accepted Jesus. However, the message of Paul (Rom. 11:28) is that because of God's sovereign plan the disobedient Jews are still loved even in their time of rebellion (as for instance a man might still love his divorced unfaithful wife if we consider the Hosea metaphor), but that they are not presently chosen. The great hope of Paul, through the elective plan of God, is that they too may come back into the fold and become the elect of God once more.

In the first century then there was division amongst the Jewish community; that is between those Jews who were called out to Christ by God and those who were obstinate towards him. And it is evident that such division happened periodically through Israel's history, with God calling out a remnant to faithfulness.[135] This New Testament division was also predicted in the Old Testament writing of Zechariah, who saw that the good shepherd, the 'man who is close to [the Lord]', struck with the sword so that the sheep will be scattered (Zech. 13: 7). As a result of this two thirds of the sheep would be cut off, while the other one third would be tested and refined in the fire as silver or gold. This one-third remnant would then call on the Lord and become God's people (Zech. 13: 9).

As noted already, it is evident that Paul is presenting a teaching that comes out of the book of Hosea where the prophet saw the house of Israel divorced for idolatry, but God still loved them in divorce and wished to bring them back because of that love. This passage in Romans should therefore be read in the context of Hosea's message. However, it ought to be remembered that Hosea was speaking to the house of Israel in rebellion, while in the first century it was more evidently members of the house of Judah who were in rebellion for rejecting Christ, although the scattered Israelites were living amongst pagans. But the gospel was equally given to the house of Israel as well as the house of Judah. The

---

[135] As noted already the existence of division and rioting amongst the Jewish community in Rome was the reason Emperor Claudius expelled them all.

promise in the writing of Hosea was that the house of Israel would be restored to God as well. It would seem then that Paul is presenting a theological principle in the text here where he observes that God holds all over to disobedience for a season, so that he may have mercy on all in the end; that is to all the offspring of Jacob, as well as the Gentiles (Rom. 11:29-32).[136]

Paul has shown, with reference to the prophet Hosea, that God will call a people who are not his people 'sons of the living God' (Rom. 9:26; Hos. 1:10; 2:23). While some commentators think Paul's use of this passage is a reference to Gentile believers being grafted into Israel, Motyer believes that it should be read in the context of the book of Hosea and refers to the gathering of Israelites back into covenant relationship with God. Motyer notes though that other Old Testament passages refer to the Jews and Gentiles being grafted together into the new Israel and that Hosea may have had both Gentiles and Israelites in mind.[137] Paul also quotes from the book of Isaiah to make his point about the re-gathering of the people of Jacob through the coming redeemer who will turn godlessness away from Zion (Rom. 11:26-27; Isa. 59:20-21). This statement, and Paul's referencing of Hosea and Isaiah, should then be read as meaning that Paul looked forward to the conversion of the house of Israel as well as the eventual conversion of Jews because the gospel was spreading across the world where the Israelites had been scattered.

All Israel?

The phraseology of Romans 11:25-26 has caused some controversy in the past with a number of ideas put forward as to who or what 'all Israel' is referring to. The verse is translated in the NIV as follows.

> 'Israel has experienced a hardening in part until the full number of the Gentiles has come in. And so all Israel will be saved...' (Rom. 11:25-26)

---

[136] Incidentally Aquila (Acts 18:1-3) was originally from Pontus, a region where the northern Israelites had settled in exile. So Paul may have had both the house of Israel and the house of Judah in mind when writing this passage.
[137] Motyer, *Israel in the Plan of God*, pp. 75-78

Israel in Romans

Motyer offers various views that have arisen in Christian theology in the past in relation to the meaning of these verses.[138] Firstly, he points out that all Israel might mean the whole Church, and he recognizes that many, including Calvin, have interpreted it in this way in the past. Calvin believed that all Israel was referring to both Jews and Gentiles who were being brought together into Christ's kingdom as part of the ultimate consummation of the 'Israel of God' in the world.[139] However, Motyer doesn't find this entirely convincing because he believes it entails two different uses of the name Israel in one sentence; that is Israel as a racial group, and Israel as the Church. He thinks instead that the context is the historical nation of Israel being saved. Secondly, the idea of all Israel could mean the fullness of the remnant of Israel. But Motyer considers that there is a division of Israel into a remnant and the hardened people who are not yet saved, and it is the latter that are of special concern to Paul. The context is of God seeking to make these people jealous through the inclusion of Gentiles, and this seems to be an allusion to a theme in Deuteronomy where God says that 'I will make them envious by those who are not a people...' (Deut. 32:21). So for Paul, in this context, all Israel must include both the remnant and those presently hardened as a future hope of salvation.

The third interpretation of all Israel could be a reference to all the Jews of the last generation before the second coming. There are a number of different ways this has been understood by different groups. Dispensationalists see in this a dualistic approach with two streams of grace, one for Jews and another for Gentiles. One difficulty with the type of dispensationalism as expounded by Darby and Hagee is that it develops a dualistic theology with two olive trees, one dispensation for the Jews and Gentiles in Christ, and one for Jews outside of Christ. Motyer points out that in this type of approach dispensationalists are, with some irony, in agreement with those more liberal Christians who maintain that there is a continuation of the Old Covenant for Jews. However, in the message of Romans, Paul only saw one olive root for both Jew and Gentiles. His desire was that in the end all Israel would be re-grafted into the single olive tree and be saved (Rom. 11:23). He insists that Israel is loved on account of the Patriarchs because of God's election and will be saved as a people in the end as a result of God's promise to Abraham (Rom. 11:28). So, because of election, the

---

[138] Motyer, *Israel in the Plan of God*, pp. 145-162. The following discussion is based on this section of his book.

[139] Calvin, J. *The Epistle of Paul the Apostle to the Romans*, Edinburgh: St. Andrew's Press, 1961, p. 255

hardened Israelites are still loved even in divorce, but presently they are outside of God's covenant and not presently the elect.

Others who reject dispensationalism, but accept this third position, believe that it is a reference to an end time revival where all Jews of the last generation will come to Christ. But Motyer believes that the 'and so' of verse 26 is not a temporal reference, but one of method, meaning 'this is how all Israel will be saved.' Furthermore, the reference to 'all' should not be understood in numerical terms, but in terms of a full representation of Israel.[140] Moyter also believes that the passage should not be seen in the future, but in the ongoing present as a result of Christ's work of grace. It is in this context that Paul quotes from Isaiah where the redeemer will come and turn godlessness away from Jacob. Paul argues that Israel may now receive mercy on account of the Patriarchs (Rom. 11:31), so the tense should be seem as present continuous. In other words the Jews and Israelites are being saved through the entire Christian age as the gospel goes out to the world. So although this may include an end time revival amongst the Jews I would argue that it is not mandatory to a correct reading of the passage. Motyer's own position seems to be that the verse means that according to election both the remnant of Israel and those presently hardened will be brought together into the Church which is now the true Israel of God, and that there may be an end-time revival.[141] John Stott also reads the passage to suggest that it means that there will be an end time revival of Jews, but within the context of unity between Jews and Gentiles within the Church.[142]

Pawson offers another possibility. He doesn't believe that the passage refers to every Jew who has ever lived or will live in the future. Neither does he believe that all must mean literally every single Jew alive in the last days. He sees instead that all should be understood in a holistic sense to mean all representatives of Israel in the last days, and this he believes includes representatives from every one of the twelve tribes. Furthermore, Pawson alludes to Revelation (Rev. 7) where the apostle John sees the fullness of Israel brought together with 12,000 from each of the twelve tribes worshipping God in unity.[143]

---

[140] Motyer, *Israel in the Plan of God*, pp. 152-153

[141] Motyer, *Israel in the Plan of God*, pp. 156-157

[142] Stott, J. 'The Place of Israel', in, Sizer, S. *Zion's Christian Soldiers: The Bible Israel and the Church*, Leicester: IVP, (2007) pp. 164-172

[143] Pawson, *Israel in the New Testament*, Terra Nova Publ. (2009), pp. 180-193. Elsewhere (p.181) he seems to conflate his argument about Israel because he asserts that Israel must mean the Jews, even though Judah was only one tribe of the twelve.

So that is basically how Motyer, Pawson and Stott interpret the passage in Romans relating to the salvation of all Israel, and I think there are some important points raised in these positions. I want now to consider whether we can take this a little further. As I have already discussed in previous chapters concerning the writings of the prophets, the context of Paul's use of Hosea and Isaiah is I believe very relevant. According to the Old Testament prophets the northern ten tribes of the house of Israel had been scattered amongst the nations for their disobedience, but the promise of God to them as a nation was eventual restoration. Judah had been seen as a remnant of Israel for centuries and allowed to remain in the land to bring forth the Messiah, but now the larger part of Judah had become hardened as well with only a remnant of Judah becoming obedient to faith in Christ. And we can see also that in the time of Paul the tribes of Israel were scattered amongst the nations, but the gospel was going out to them as well and some (including Aquila from Pontus) were finding faith in Christ. Remember also that Paul was writing to bring unity between the Gentile believers and Jews in Rome. I would suggest then that all Israel must include those Israelites of the Assyrian dispersion.

There is another relevant point to highlight in relation to the wording of Romans 11:25-26. In the Greek language the word *ethnos* is translated as Gentiles, but it can refer to the nations, and that includes the Jewish and Israelite nations as well.[144] We therefore make a mistake if we think that *ethnos* cannot be used for Jews and Israelites. In fact in English the word ethnic is used in much the same way, where people of every nation have their own ethnic identity and that includes a Jewish ethnic identity as well. So when Paul is speaking of the fullness of the Gentiles, I would suggest that could include Jews and those from the other tribes of Israel who were scattered in the nations. In other words, as Paul rejoiced because the gospel was going out amongst the nations of the world, he saw that those coming to Christ were scattered Israelites and Jews as well as non-Jews, and in this way all Israel would eventually be saved because the Israelites were scattered in the nations. And this is why Paul is so keen to build unity in the Christian community.

In Romans 15 Paul returned to the place of Jews and Gentiles in the Church and pointed out that the promise of God to Abraham and the Patriarchs was that the Gentiles too would come to glorify God (Rom. 15:7-12). And Paul made similar comments earlier in the letter noting that Abraham's faith was credited to him as righteousness before his circumcision, and therefore he is the father of the uncircumcised as well

---

[144] In 1 Peter 2:9 the Church is called a holy nation (Gk *ethnos*).

as the circumcised. The promise of Abraham was that he would be a forefather of the whole world, a promise that was to come through faith (Rom. 4:1-25). The blessing of Abraham then cannot be limited to the modern State of Israel.

So in summary, the use of the word 'election' (Rom. 9-11) doesn't mean that the Jews can still be reconciled to God under the Old Covenant, but instead the passage may in part be a reference to an end time revival of Jews. This would mean then that Jews are to receive grace and mercy to believe in the work of Christ in the end. Under this scenario the Jewish people would finally come to place their faith in Christ because of grace given on account of the promise made to the Patriarchs. However, as Paul noted the gospel message *now* goes to Jews everywhere and the door to Christ is open to all. The tense in Romans 11:25-26 is present-continuous and indeed throughout history Jews have come to faith in their Messiah.

Election then is to do with God's global plan of salvation; first a remnant of faithful Jews and Israelites would be saved at the foundation of the Church, then over time the full measure of Gentiles would be brought in. But at the same time God is seeking to make the remaining Jews jealous of Christian faith, and so inspire a longing for restoration to God in the present time. We should pray that they might hear his voice once more so that all Israel will be saved. Completion of God's plan will be achieved when the remaining Jews accept Christ, and it will mean 'life from the dead' for all when that plan of salvation is complete (Rom. 11:15). The action of Christians today then should not be to seek to absolve Jews of their responsibility and need for the Messiah by proposing two streams of grace, but instead to love the Jews enough to bring them to the Messiah, back into their own natural olive tree. This olive tree is today identifiable as the Christian community consisting of Jews, Gentiles and Israelites grafted together into the Israelite olive root. While I believe and pray that God will bring the remaining Jews to faith in Christ in the end in this way, I do not believe that political or religious Zionism, which is outside of Christ, has any positive place in God's plan. The Jews today do not need to enter Palestine to receive God's mercy and grace; it is available across the whole world, but only through the Messiah. But Jesus has become a stumbling block to them as a rock placed in Zion. While we ought to follow Paul in rejecting replacement theology, we also need to challenge Christian Zionist' theology that holds the Church back from bringing the fullness of the gospel to Jews.

Chapter 9

Israel in Galatians and Ephesians

In the previous chapter it has been shown that Paul was responding in part to the Roman Christian belief that the Gentiles had replaced the Jews in God's plan. So Paul rejected replacement theology and believed instead that the Church was built on an ethnic, legal and spiritual Israelite root. At the eastern end of the Mediterranean the Jerusalem Church was coming under pressure from a number of Pharisees and Hebrew speaking Jews who were seemingly converting to Christ. They had a different belief about the place of the Mosaic Law in the life of Jews and Gentiles. As a result of this development a number of 'super-apostles' were being sent out to the Gentile congregations from Jerusalem and they were seeking to counter Paul's teaching. They thought Paul was going soft on the Law. Instead they wanted Gentiles to follow and accept Jewish practices beyond what Paul had taught. In failing to understand the gospel that Paul preached they were trying to instil a stricter adherence to the Law for the Greek speaking Jewish believers. In doing this it is clear that they had a different understanding of grace than Paul, evidently lacking his revelation and belief about what God had done through the work of Christ. Perhaps they were motivated by fear of the Zealots in Jerusalem, or perhaps they simply did not understand the full revelation of grace that Paul was teaching. This struggle over beliefs comes out strongly in several of the New Testament letters of Paul, and in the following discussion I will focus upon the letter to the Galatians and Ephesians.

Letter to the Galatians

Paul wrote the letter to the Galatians to counter the 'super-apostles'[145] who were seeking to impose certain Jewish legal practices upon the believers in the area of Galatia and surrounding districts. There is uncertainty though over the exact timing of the letter, with various dates given between AD 48-57, and whether it was written to believers in the northern or southern regions of Galatia. Perhaps Paul had believers from both regions in mind. However, Paul was writing to

---

[145] See also for instance 2 Corinthians 11:5 where Paul challenged the super-apostles who were undermining his previous work in preaching his gospel of grace.

challenge the imposition of Mosaic legal requirements, such as circumcision, upon the new believers by some Jewish individuals.[146] Paul believed that the Law of Moses, and the requirement for circumcision under the covenant of Abraham, had now been fulfilled through the work of Jesus Christ. He therefore accused the legalists of confusing and corrupting the gospel of grace (Gal. 1:7); a gospel that Paul himself had previously preached to the Galatians. However, as noted, this wasn't just a problem for the Galatians; it was part of a crisis for the growing Christian community as a whole. How should the old ways of Judaism be understood in the light of the new way that had been instigated by Jesus the Messiah?

Paul asserted in his letter to the Galatians that his gospel had not come through men, but had been given to him as a revelation from God (Gal. 1: 11-12). Paul had though submitted his message to the leadership present in Jerusalem, especially James, Peter and John (Gal. 2:9), and they had supported his work amongst the Gentiles. But a situation had later arisen in Jerusalem where the leadership of the Church had partly given in to pressure to impose more Jewish practices upon Gentile converts (Gal. 2:1-10). As a result of this even Peter and Barnabas were compromised (Gal. 2:11-13). However, Paul opposed them because of his strong belief that the work of Jesus Christ was sufficient for justification before God, a work that comes through faith. No one, Paul asserted, could be justified before God by observing the Law, or by working out one's own salvation, but it could only come through faith in Jesus Christ.

In the next few chapters of Galatians Paul builds his case using the example of Abraham. He points out that Abraham was the father of those who believe, because Abraham had believed God and that faith was credited to him as righteousness (Gal. 3:6). Therefore those who have put their faith in Christ have become children of Abraham, and this includes both Jews and Gentiles. It follows that those who do not have faith in Christ cannot be recognised as Abraham's children. The promise to Abraham was that 'All nations will be blessed through you,' (Gal. 3:8) and through faith the blessing given to Abraham has come upon the Gentile believers (Gal. 3:9,14). However, in contrast, those who rely on the Law of Moses for salvation are in fact under a curse, because according to Scripture those who do not completely fulfil the law are

---

[146] Along with Romans, this letter became an important document of the Protestant Reformation wherein salvation was believed to be by faith alone. In this regard it helped the reformers challenge the theology of the Roman Catholic Church that at the time required faith and works, although corrupted by indulgences.

cursed (Gal. 3:10; Deut. 27:26). Thankfully, Christ has now redeemed those who have faith in him from the curse of the Law by becoming a curse for us, because he was hung on a tree according to biblical prophecy (Gal. 3:13).

Paul further notes in this passage that Christ came to fulfil the promise given to Abraham because Jesus Christ is the 'seed' of Abraham (Gal. 3:16; Gen. 17:3-8). The everlasting covenant that God made with Abraham was to be confirmed in flesh with the sign of this being circumcision (Gen 17:9-16).[147] The promises given to Abraham are partly related to ethnicity with God making an everlasting covenant with Abraham and his offspring. For instance they would become as numerous as the stars in the heavens (Gen. 15:5).[148] It has been shown in previous chapters that Abraham's children of the flesh, the descendents of Isaac and Jacob, and especially those of Ephraim and Manasseh's line, grew in number as promised into the nation of Israel. However, that Israel became divided, and the larger faction was divorced for a season because of their sin. Later Israel would be restored.

For Paul the true Israel of the everlasting covenant could only be formed in a spiritual sense in the body of Jesus Christ, who was the promised fleshly 'seed' of Abraham. Thus the true Israel is made up of those who follow the Messiah, and are included in him. Today that is in the Christian Church because it is being built up into the heavenly tabernacle that is Christ's own body. And it includes Jews, Gentiles and the Israelites who are scattered in the nations. This is the reason why all, whether Jew, Israelite or Gentile must come to Christ in the same way to form the fullness of Israel. It is not replacement theology because all must come in through the same door, Jesus Christ. Instead it is about unity, continuity and fulfilment through God's promises to Abraham. A remnant saved first, but then reaching out to the lost, whether Jews or Gentiles.

But while the world was waiting for Christ, the Law of Moses was given because of transgression until the promise of the seed came (Gal. 3:19). Paul notes that the Law of Moses could not set aside the

---

[147] Significant theology that is spiritual in nature is often revealed in Scripture through material events and people, thus having both a material and a spiritual application. But while there are dual aspects, Judeo-Christian theology rejects dualistic theology, because the spiritual and material are being brought together in Christ.

[148] The promise also included the land of Canaan to Abraham's descendents, now I believe being fulfilled through the Palestinian and Messianic Christian communities living in the Holy Land as representative of the global Christian Church.

covenant previously given to Abraham. This is because Abraham's covenant was given as a promise solely from God as an inheritance to both Jews and Gentiles (Gal. 3:17-18). It was not mediated; it was a divine promise. The Mosaic Law on the other hand had been given with Moses acting as a mediator between Israel and God to prepare the people of God for Christ's coming. So those who seek to impose the Law of Moses today, because they consider it to be God's ongoing covenant, overlook the greater covenant that God had first promised through Abraham. This is now to be received by faith. And we are told in Galatians that Jesus Christ is the fulfilment of the Abrahamic covenant that had been made solely on the basis of God's promise. It could never be replaced by a separate mediated legal code (Gal. 3: 17-20).[149]

Through Christ, the promise of God to Abraham has now set Christians free from bondage to the Law because it is a greater covenant than the Law of Moses. Paul commented that the Law of Moses was an interim measure meant to eventually lead people to Christ when the time of Christ finally came (Gal. 3:21-24). Furthermore, under the new covenant there is now no difference between Jew and Greek, male and female, slave and free. All who are in Christ are children of God irrespective of their nationality, gender or social status. And all of this is the free gift of God given according to God's promise, to set free those who accept Christ's gift of grace (Gal. 3:26-29).

In chapter four Paul further urged his readers not to seek after the old city of Jerusalem and its form of temple worship, because that city was not the city of the promise. Instead, the new city of Jerusalem is free and above and she is our mother. Paul comments that Abraham had two sons, one by the free woman Sarah, and the other son by the slave woman Hagar. The son of the free woman was given as a result of the promise of God. The two women then also represent two covenants; the covenant of the slave woman, Hagar, represents Mount Sinai in Arabia and her children are in slavery under the Mosaic Law. Hagar then represents the old city of Jerusalem, whereas Sarah represents the New Jerusalem that is above and free (Gal. 4:21-26). As such, all Christians are urged to have nothing to do with the slavery that comes by the Law, but are instead urged to enter into the inheritance of the free woman and her promised son Isaac (Gal. 4:28-31).

Paul also challenged those who wanted the Gentile Galatians circumcised asserting that it no longer has any meaning; instead Christians are baptised into Christ who incidentally fulfilled the law of

---

[149] In fact it has always been by faith and Abraham is the father of faith because he believed God and it was accredited to him as righteousness.

circumcision on the eight day thanks to faithful parents (Gal. 5-6). What matters is the new creation, and Paul wishes peace and mercy on all in the 'Israel of God' who follow this rule (Gal. 6: 16). Paul elaborated on this theme a little more in Colossians where he asserted that Christians have now received Christ's circumcision through baptism into his death and resurrection. Through Christ's life he fulfilled the Law of Moses, including circumcision, and then nailed the Law to the cross nullifying it in his flesh. Subsequently, Christians have been raised to life in Christ with sins forgiven. Christians are now called to live as though dead to sin and alive in him having received Christ's circumcision. In this way Christians fulfil the requirement of the Abrahamic covenant for circumcision because of the work of Jesus Christ (Col. 2: 11-23). God sees us circumcised in Jesus.

Letter to the Ephesians

The letter to the Ephesians was partly written to explain the unity that God planned between Jews and Gentiles, and also to reveal the extent of God's grace in Christ. In the letter, Paul elaborates on the *mystery* of the gospel that had previously been hidden from earlier generations. He notes that God's desire is to bring everyone to unity and fullness in Christ; that is to bring Jews and Gentiles together as one new man, and 'to bring all things in heaven and on earth together under one head, even Christ' (Eph. 1:10). Paul asserts that Christ has been raised from the dead and is now seated in heavenly places where he has been given the highest authority and accolade. Now God is bringing everything under his feet, for Christ has been appointed the 'head over everything for the church [Gk: *Ekklesia*], which is his body, and the fullness of him who fills everything in every way' (Eph. 1:20-23). The Church then, consisting of a union of Jews and Gentiles, is described as representing Christ's body on the earth. Furthermore, Christian believers, both Jews and Gentiles, have been raised up with Christ and made alive in him (Eph. 2:4-6), this for the purpose of reigning on the earth.

Paul further expands on the message of unity asserting that the Gentiles have now been brought close to God alongside the Jews. Although Gentiles were once considered 'foreigners [Gk: *xenoi*] to the covenants of promise' and 'excluded from citizenship [Gk: *politeias*] in Israel' they have now been brought near through the blood of Christ (Eph. 2:11-13). The two groups of people have been made one, and the 'dividing wall of hostility' has been removed between the Israelites and Gentiles. God has now destroyed the legal barriers in his own flesh. It was God's purpose to make one new man out of the two, thus bringing peace and unity to both communities (Eph. 2:14-16). Further to this, God has made Gentile believers 'fellow-citizens [Gk: *sumpolitai*] with God's people' and equal members of 'God's household' in the commonwealth of Israel. Therefore Gentiles can no longer be considered 'foreigners and aliens' to the Jews. God's household is further being built into a holy temple where the prophets and apostles have provided foundations with Christ established as the chief cornerstone. Paul then asserts that this holy temple, the Church that is Christ's body, is rising up and being built together in unity - a unity that consists of both communities. This building then forms into a dwelling place for God's Spirit (Eph. 2:19-22).

Paul asserts that this message had previously been hidden from previous generations, but that now God has chosen to reveal this mystery. It is a message that reveals that God's intention is make Gentiles joint-heirs, part of a joint-body and joint-sharers [Gk: *sunkleronoma kai sussoma kai summetocha*] with the promises of God in Israel[150], 'members together of one body [of the one new man]' thus sharing in the promises of God in Jesus Christ (Eph. 3:1-6).

It is quite clear that Paul sees the Church, the *Ekklesia*, as a union of Jews and Gentiles in Christ, where Gentiles have been grafted in alongside a remnant of Jews to be fellow citizens of the commonwealth of Israel. Paul then is asserting in Ephesians that the *Ekklesia* (the Church) exists as the continuation, expansion and renewal of Israel from the old covenant to the new. This plan had formerly been a mystery, but God revealed it to him, and he presents it openly in this letter.

---

[150] The NIV puts Israel in Eph. 3:6, although it is not in the Greek. However, it arises out of the context of the passage and the meaning of co-heirs etc.

Chapter 10

Israel in Hebrews

There would appear to be some uncertainty over the authorship of the letter to the Hebrews, and it is generally considered today that it was not the apostle Paul, although for a good deal of Church history the letter was attributed to him.[151] Eusebius suggested that the letter was written by Paul in Hebrew and translated into Greek by either Luke or Clement, which would perhaps explain some of the apparently non-Pauline phraseology. Eusebius favours Clement as the translator of Paul's letter.[152] There is no mention in the letter itself of the author's name, but it would seem that it was someone at least close to Paul because the theology contained in the letter covers many of the same themes as Paul's teaching. Furthermore, it does tell us that it was written from Italy, and it expresses concern for Timothy, Paul's beloved co-worker in the closing comments.[153] In other words, it has a typical Pauline ending if not a normal beginning. Perhaps the opening statement has been lost, or there are other reasons for its omission. In fact the theology of Hebrews may be seen in part as an extension of the doctrines presented in Galatians and Ephesians, particularly relating to the temple, to Abraham and Isaac, and also in terms of the place of the Jews within the new covenant.

The new teaching is also expounded with Pauline boldness as the writer implores Jewish converts not to turn back to their old practices in Judaism. Who would dare to write such a letter to the Hebrew people, knowing that riots might ensue? Paul had such experiences simply from his very presence in the temple area, but he pressed home the message nonetheless. The content of Hebrews then

---

[151] See for instance, Davies, J.H. *A Letter To Hebrews, The Cambridge Bible Commentary*, London: Cambridge University Press, (1967), pp.9-11. It is likely that it was written before AD 70 because it makes no mention of the destruction of the Temple - see Davies, pp. 8-9

[152] Eusebius of Caesarea, 'Ecclesiastical History' Book III, Chapter XXXVIII, translated by Cruse, C.F. *The Ecclesiastical History of Eusebius Pamphilus*, 1850, reprinted Grand Rapids:Baker Book House, (1995), p. 124.

[153] Paul Finch, *Beyond Acts: New Perspectives in New Testament History*, Florida:Sunrise Publications, (2003) pp. 172-176 believes that Hebrews 6:1-3 contains a similar order to the teaching in Paul's other Epistles with Repentance, Faith, Baptisms, Laying on of Hands to receive the Holy Spirit, Resurrection of the Dead, Eternal Judgment, Perfection.

contains a message that is very close to Paul's teaching, a message that Paul said was given to him by revelation from God. If it wasn't Paul it was someone very close to him, although I tend to believe it was Paul.[154]

In a number of places in the letter the writer calls readers to persevere and not turn back to the old ways in Judaism that had now been fulfilled by Christ's work on the cross. Although the letter was written to the Hebrews of the first century Church, particularly in Jerusalem prior to its destruction, the subject matter is still relevant to us today. The central theme of the letter is the person of Jesus Christ; who he is, and what he has done in fulfilment of Old Testament writings and prophecies, especially as the practices of the new Church relate to the fulfilment of temple worship and practice.

At the start of the letter Christ is presented as the co-worker with the Father in the act of creation, and therefore he is higher than the angels as the Son of God, and the exact representation of the Father, sustaining all things by his powerful word (Heb. 1:1-14). Next we see Christ as the son of man, but noting also that everything is subject to him. In this position, as both God and man, Christ made the perfect sacrifice for sin for all time, with the purpose of bringing many men and women to the same glory that Christ possesses. As the argument of Hebrews develops it becomes clear that the glorification of the new

---

[154] Another possible candidate for authorship of Hebrews who has been mentioned in historical texts is Barnabas. Tertullian, writing in *De Pudicitia* around AD 220, mentioned an Epistle to the Hebrews written by Barnabas, although this may be a reference to another second century letter. Barnabas would certainly fit the bill; he was from the Levitical line and was a close companion of Paul as both shared in ministry, even travelling together for a while; that is until the dispute over Mark's departure caused a temporary parting of the ways. Mark was a nephew of Barnabas, but later Paul is reconciled to Mark, and asks for him to come to him in prison, commenting on his usefulness to him (2 Tim. 4:11). This position in the early Church, and lineage with the Levitical priestly line, would have given Barnabas sufficient weight amongst his hearers, especially those Jewish converts from the priesthood. He would therefore have been a suitable candidate for writing such a letter, as the purpose was to encourage Jewish believers to remain with the Christian faith and not revert back to their former legalistic practices of worship in times of trouble. Apollos is another possible candidate, and the one generally accepted today, but Luther was the one who first proposed him and Clement and Origen do not mention Apollos. See Davies, *Hebrews*, pp.9-11. The question of authorship though remains controversial and I believe that Paul may indeed have written it in the way Eusebius asserts, although I will refer to the author as the writer of Hebrews in this chapter section.

temple, that is the Church, is of central importance. In order to bring glory to the new temple it was necessary for Christ to become fully human so that he could set people free from sin's bondage. In doing this Christ was acting as the perfect high priest, enabling redemption for all.

In the next chapter Jesus is presented as being greater than Moses, and a high priest appointed over the house of God; that is the Church (Heb. 3:6). The converted Jews were further exhorted not to harden their hearts and turn back to the old ways as they had now heard the message of the gospel. In this exhortation they were urged not to be like the Israelites who had heard God in the desert and then wanted to go back to Egypt, thus failing to enter into God's rest (Heb. 3:7-11; Ps. 95:7-11). And this I think is a very important point in relation to this discussion; that God's rest for Jews is now found in Christ, not in the possession of land. The letter urges its hearers to continue in Christ and in this way they will find their true rest. But to hanker after the old ways of Judaism, with its desire for possession of the city and land, is akin to going back to Egypt. The author compares the Old Testament rest in respect to the possession of the land with the new covenant rest in Jesus. Of course today many Jews still seek a physical return to the land, but what is needed instead for true rest is faith in the Messiah.

Later in Hebrews (13:11-14) the Jewish believers are told not to hold on to the old city of Jerusalem because it is not an enduring city. Instead they should go outside the camp to the Messiah and look for the city that is above and cannot be shaken. The Jewish hearers are told that Christ suffered sacrificially outside the city, and so they should also be willing to suffer Christ's disgrace outside the camp with him. The message for the Hebrews then is to go forward into Jesus leaving the old city of Jerusalem and temple behind for good. In doing this they will not go back to Egypt. This is a pertinent message for Christian Zionists.

Jesus is further presented in Hebrews as the great high priest, not of the order of Aaron, but of the order of Melchizedek. God made an oath by his own name to Abraham, promising to bless him and give him many descendants. While the Law was given through Moses, the one acting as mediator, the oath that God gave to Abraham was by his own name and therefore greater. Under this blessing Abraham gave a tenth of the plunder to Melchizedek the kingly priest, thus showing that Melchizedek was a greater priest than Levi because Levi was a descendent of Abraham (Heb. 7:6-9).[155] The Levites had collected tithes

---

[155] O Palmer Robertson, *The Israel of God*, Phillipsberg, P&R Publishers, (2000) pp. 62-63 notes that some see Melchizedek as the pre-incarnate Christ. However, Robertson considers this unlikely, and points out that some rabbinical sources instead believed that Melchizedek was the biblical Shem

from the children of Abraham, but Melchizedek was presented with a tithe from Abraham showing him to be greater than the Levitical priesthood. Melchizedek was appointed as a priest by God, and therefore as one who did not have to trace his human ancestry in order to justify his position. The other mention of Melchizedek is in Psalm 110:1-4, and this is interpreted by the writer of Hebrews as applying to the Messiah who is seen as a majestic sceptre and a 'priest for ever.'

Psalm 110:1-4 is also the passage that Jesus points to concerning himself in Matthew 22:44 in discussion with the Pharisees. Psalm 110:1-4 reads as follows

> The Lord says to my Lord: Sit at my right hand until I make your enemies a footstool for your feet.'
>
> The Lord will extend your mighty sceptre from Zion; you will rule in the midst of your enemies.
>
> Your troops will be willing on your day of battle. Arrayed in holy majesty, from the womb of the dawn you will receive the dew of your youth.
>
> The Lord has sworn and will not change his mind: You are a priest for ever, in the order of Melchizedek.

Melchizedek is presented as a king meaning 'king of righteousness' and he exercised his rule over Jerusalem the city of peace. Because of the play on words on the name Melchizedek he may be considered as a king of righteousness and of peace, and the writer of Hebrews would most likely have expected the Hebrew readers to understand this.[156] Jesus is also seen as the sceptre ruling from the New Jerusalem in the vision of John in the book of Revelation (Rev. 21:1-5). But the writer to Hebrews considers Jesus to be a perpetual king and priest in a different and greater capacity to that of the Levitical priesthood, and one ruling from Zion, which is the New Jerusalem.

Whereas the sacrifices made by the Levites were always incomplete the new covenant of Christ was perfect. The former

---

(also in the Book of Jasher). This view was supported by Jerome and Luther, but rejected by Calvin. Calvin observed that Melchizedek had no stated ancestry in Scripture (Heb. 7:1-3) whereas Shem clearly did. However, the context is really that of not having gained the priestly line through ancestry as the Levitical priests had done. Jesus, who is called a priest of the order of Melchizedek, has known human ancestry on his mother's side. So Shem could feasibly have been Melchizedek even if his human ancestry is known.

[156] See Davies, *Hebrews*, pp. 65-67, i.e. *melek* = king; *sedeq* = righteousness; *shalom* = peace.

covenant given to Moses has therefore been 'set aside' (Heb. 7:18). The true tabernacle then is not a building, or a tent, made by human hands, but is now one made by God (Heb. 8:2), and thus Jesus' ministry is far superior to that of Moses.

The writer to the Hebrews also appeals to the writing of Jeremiah to make the point that God has promised a new covenant to the people of Israel (Heb. 8:8-12; Jer. 31:31-34).

> "The time is coming," declares the LORD, "when I will make a new covenant with the house of Israel and with the house of Judah.
>
> It will not be like the covenant I made with their forefathers when I took them by the hand to lead them out of Egypt, because they broke my covenant, though I was a husband to them," declares the LORD.
>
> "This is the covenant I will make with the house of Israel after that time," declares the LORD. "I will put my law in their minds and write it on their hearts. I will be their God, and they will be my people.
>
> No longer will a man teach his neighbour, or a man his brother, saying, 'Know the LORD,' because they will all know me, from the least of them to the greatest," declares the LORD. "For I will forgive their wickedness and will remember their sins no more."

Because the sacrifice of Jesus is so much better than the requirements of the Mosaic Law, then the new covenant that Jesus established has made the old Mosaic one 'obsolete' (Heb. 8:13). The tabernacle, that is Jesus, is without blemish, and he took his own blood in and made the perfect sacrifice (Heb. 9:11-12), thus providing the cover of righteousness forever for those who are being made holy. The new covenantal promise has thus made Christians heirs of an eternal inheritance (Heb. 9:15), and the Law of Moses was merely a shadow of the greater things that were to come (Heb. 10:1).

Importantly, the letter to the Hebrews comments that Jesus provided everything for the establishment of the new covenant, and all of this was according to the promise freely given to Abraham. Jesus provided the perfect sacrifice with his own blood and has become the great high priest ministering in the heavenly tabernacle, which is also his own body, the Church.

In Hebrews we are told that God's plan was much more than merely bringing a single nation into a particular land. It was always about extending divine blessing to all nations on earth; this under a heavenly kingdom according to God's promise through Abraham's seed. Many of the patriarchs received promises that they did not see fulfilled in their own time. They believed them by faith, but their hope was for a heavenly kingdom being 'aliens and strangers' (Gk: *ethnoi kai parepidemos)*; that is, living as aliens away from one's own people while residing on the earth (Heb. 11:13). Abraham went to the land of promise in faithful obedience to God, but lived in a tent like a stranger in a foreign land, as did Isaac and Jacob (Heb. 11:8-10). Abraham 'was looking forward to the city with foundations, whose architect and builder is God' (Heb. 11:10) and to a 'better country – a heavenly one' (Heb. 11:16). We may see then that the promise to Israel is that Jews, Israelites and Gentiles in Christ have come 'to Mount Zion, to the heavenly Jerusalem, the city of the living God' (Heb. 12:22) and that this city cannot be shaken as an earthly city can (Heb. 12:27-28).

I believe that this letter is particularly pertinent to those Christians and Jews who are now placing their hope and faith in the re-establishment of a worldly State of Israel. Their hope is for earthly blessings and an earthly city of Jerusalem with the re-instatement of temple worship. However, we are told in Hebrews that this earthly city is not enduring, and is ruled over by men and women who are in opposition to the message of Christ. It cannot provide the true rest that God planned in Jesus, and Christians are called to live apart from that old city, the capital of Israel. Those of faith should instead follow the example of the patriarch Abraham and place their trust in the Messiah, thus looking forward to the complete fulfilment of his kingdom rule on earth from the heavenly Jerusalem.

The message of Hebrews is that Christ has done everything for salvation by providing the sacrifice, the priesthood, and the temple that is his own body. The true Church is also formed as the body of Christ. From this it may be seen then that the new Israel, or the New Jerusalem that is now identifiable as the Church, is being built up in unity in the body of Christ. The glory of God now resides in this tabernacle, which is the Church, and it is God's desire that his ancient people of Israel and Judah should be brought back into this spiritual fullness. But the desire of some Christian Zionists to rebuild an earthly temple in Jerusalem is in effect robbing Jews of their full promises in Christ. Instead the rule of Christ has already begun across the whole earth, although it will not be complete until he returns. God, through the biblical writers, promised a New Heaven and a New Earth ruled from the New Jerusalem under the authority of Christ.

Chapter 11

Israel in 1 Peter

It is noteworthy that Peter later wrote his first epistle to the Christians in Galatia, as well as in the area of Asia, Pontus, Cappadocia and Bithynia. These are places located in modern Turkey. I have already discussed the disagreement between Paul, Peter and the Jerusalem Church in Paul's letter to the Galatians. This related to the place of the Law amongst Gentile believers, and I believe that Peter and Paul had resolved their differences by the time he writes this epistle. In fact it was initially Peter who came to this same conclusion after the salvation of Cornelius and his family. So Peter and Paul were really in agreement, even if Peter was afraid to live it out because of intimidation from a Jerusalem faction. Therefore it would be wrong to try and find differences between Paul and Peter in these passages, as there is I think agreement here.

But we may note that Jews, Israelites and other converts were present in Jerusalem from these same areas on the day of Pentecost and heard Peter's preaching. And it is Messianic believers from these areas that he calls God's elect pilgrims (Gk; *eklektois parepidemois*) of the *diasporas* (1 Pet. 1:1). As noted, James (James 1:1) also writes to the 'twelve tribes in the dispersion' (Gk. *diaspora*). Now if we place ourselves in Peter's shoes in the first century, the Church to which he was writing was formed of Jews, dispersed Israelites, as well as Gentiles. And significantly Peter had the message of the prophets in mind, particularly Hosea (and this reflects Paul's use of Hosea in Romans). Peter writes that the prophets longed to see the salvation of Israel that would come through Jesus, and was now being fulfilled in his time through the Holy Spirit (1 Pet. 1:10-12).

Peter asserts in his letter that they are being built up into a 'spiritual house' and therefore form a 'holy priesthood' in order to offer spiritual sacrifices to God (1 Pet. 2:4-5). Jesus is the living stone that is set in Zion, and all of us are called to trust in him so that we might be built into God's house and not suffer shame before God. But to those who reject Jesus he has become a stumbling block (1 Pet. 2:6-8). He writes further that they are a 'chosen people [or race, Gk: *genos*], a royal priesthood, a holy nation [Gk: *ethnos*], a people [Gk: *laos*] belonging to God...' (1 Pet. 2:9). Echoing the same message of Hebrews, they are to be 'sojourners and aliens' (Gk; *paroikos kai parepidemous*) in the land in which they live; a people called out to dwell near to God, and away from their own natural people (1 Pet. 2:11). Peter in these verses is in fact referring to language from the Mosaic Law that is directed towards the people of Israel, but he applies it here to the Messianic community. God instructs Moses as follows

> 'Now if you obey me fully and keep my covenant, then out of all the nations you will be my treasured possession. Although the whole earth is mine, you will be for me a kingdom of priests and a holy nation. These words you are to speak to the Israelites.' [157]

In the next verse Peter (1 Pet. 2:10) alludes to a passage in Hosea where it was said that those who were not God's people, that is the exiled Israelites, would again be called the people of God (see Hos. 1:9-11). This passage was concerned with the eventual restoration and reunion of the house of Judah and the house of Israel. It is very likely that many of those addressed by Peter's letter were in fact Israelites of the Assyrian diaspora, and I think that Peter was fully aware of this. But equally those included in the Church in these areas of responsibility were from other nations, as well as the inclusion of Jewish converts.

It is noteworthy I think that Peter used language that clearly acknowledged and alludes to the identity of Israel and applies it to the Christian community in which Jews, Israelites and Gentiles are united together in the Messiah. In other words, Peter came to see that the Christian community represented the faithful part of Israel, but included all of these groups, as a people set apart to live near to God spiritually. This Israel exists as a body of believers that is extending across the whole earth, but was also still present in Jerusalem during Peter's time. However, Peter did not focus upon the possession of Jerusalem or the Holy Land as Christian Zionists desire, but called the believers to live close to God wherever they are placed, even away from their own people and land. Peter calls the Messianic community to live out their lives in faithful obedience to the established rulers as foreigners and exiles (1 Pet. 2:11). He does not seek to lead the Messianic community back to the Holy Land, but seeks to build a holy Israelite people dedicated to God in the land in which they dwell. This suggests that his vision was enlarged beyond the borders of Palestine. The new temple is being established as the Christian Church, the people of Israel living out their faith in the Messiah upon the whole earth.

---

[157] See for instance Deut. 7:6, 10:15, 28:9 and Exod. 19:5-6.

Chapter 12

Who Owns the land?

In this chapter I am going to consider the ethnic claims concerning the Jewish identity of those who reside today in the Holy Land, although I will restrict this discussion to the ethnicity of the Jewish population of the State of Israel, and to the historical Palestinian Christian community. This discussion leaves aside for now the question of who has legal rights to the land and the right to the birthright title of Israel.

As we have seen the descendents of Abraham were promised a specific piece of land by God; that is the land of Canaan, and the question of how this promise is to be interpreted within the New Covenant is the subject of this present chapter. This question is though made more difficult because seemingly Paul and the other apostles did not address it directly, although I think it is addressed nonetheless. This was most likely because both believers in the Messiah and those who rejected Christ were resident in the land in the time that much of the New Testament was written. However, there are some indirect references as I have shown in previous chapters and both Peter and Paul seem to place more emphasis upon the life of the Church in Jesus as opposed to regaining land. So, while a strong case is not presented it is possible to build an argument based upon an understanding that the promises of Abraham are fulfilled in Christ.

In this light I believe that ownership of the land is now in Christ, and indeed we can see from Scripture that the whole earth is the Lord's, and that must include the land of Canaan as well (Psalm 24:1). If we also look at this question from the context of the meta-narrative as discussed already we see that the whole of creation is for consummation in Christ. As Tom Wright has pointed out this Christian narrative should also be seen through the people of Israel who are now in Christ; Wright sees it as God's plan of redemption for the whole world that is through Israel. And echoing Hosea, Paul writes in Romans that the whole of creation is to be 'liberated from its bondage to decay and brought into the glorious freedom of the children of God' (Romans 8:21). From this Paul goes on to insist in chapters 9-11 that Jews and Gentiles together are God's people, but established upon an Israelite root. From this we can see that the Promised Land, as part of the earth, is for consummation in Christ through the children of God. The community of believers now include Gentiles and Jews brought together in Jesus.

Robertson and Holwerda have also addressed the question of land quite comprehensively.[158] For Robertson the redemptive work of Christ concerning the land means that it has been extended to encompass the whole earth. The promise of the land of Canaan was a mere shadow of the full light of Christ that was to come. Under the New Covenant we now have the fullness of what was only previously seen dimly. Holwerda believes also that the New Testament writers did not give up on land altogether in favour of spiritual promises, but that the land has been extended to cover the whole earth and that Paul's concern is for the new creation.[159] This is reflected in Romans 4:13 where Abraham's blessing is given for the world. All authority in heaven and earth has been given to Christ (Matt. 28:18) and the duty of believers is to bring all nations to obedience in him.

Holwerda points out though that the question of the ownership of the Holy Land is a very sensitive one for Jews and that they continue to remember the Promised Land in their prayers and rituals. Holwerda for instance quotes the common Passover saying 'next year in Jerusalem.' He refers to the views of Heschel who identified with the Jews believing that to give up on the land would be to reject their sacred promises revealed by God to Abraham. For Jews, Heschel believed that it would be a travesty of all they hold dear in terms of their beliefs and prayers to give up the hope of the land. Heschel points out that the land is not just a case of sentiment, but it is an imperative concern driven by the deepest of love.[160] So there is a very strong affinity for the land in Jewish thought. In Scripture we find that the promise of land was in fact an irrevocable promise to Abraham's offspring through Isaac and Jacob and one given directly by God (Gen. 26:3; 28:4; 28:13). This land was also said to flow with milk and honey (Exod. 3:17). However, while the land was give as a gift from God, residency in the land was conditional upon obedience to God through faith and was not a matter of human strength (Numb. 14:30). According to the Mosaic Law the holiness of the people was central to occupation (Lev. 18:28).

However, if it is argued that possession of the land of Israel is just a matter of birth then there are some further points to be considered. If ethnicity as a result of descent through Abraham, Isaac and Jacob counts as a right to settle in the land then I would argue that the Palestinians, especially the Palestinian Christian community also has a

---

[158] Robertson, *The Israel of God* pp. 3-32, and Holwerda *Jesus and Israel*, pp.85-112

[159] Holwerda, *Jesus and Israel*, pp. 101-112.

[160] Heschel A.J. *Israel: An Echo of Eternity* (New York: Farrar, Straus and Giroux, (1969), pp. 43f. See Holwerda, p. 86-111.

right as well as the Jews. This is because I believe that it can be shown that the ancient Christian community in the land too has ethnic Jewish roots.[161]

The Jewish Claim

The first question to consider is whether the population of the State of Israel today is really Jewish? At face value this may seem like a rather obvious question, but it is not quite as straightforward as many believe. Who are the people who make up the present day population of the State of Israel and identify themselves as Jews? Firstly, the Jewish nation in fact had forcibly assimilated the Edomites (descended from Esau, Jacob's brother) in 125 BC. The Edomites had a complex relationship with the Israelites, sometimes showing hostility, sometimes cooperation, but they always desired Jacob's blessing because they believed that Jacob had stolen it from their forefather Esau, and therefore they were willing to accept their forced conversion. Esau, as the first born son and heir of Isaac, had in fact sold his inheritance to his younger brother for the price of a bowl of lamb stew, and Jacob had obtained the blessing of his father by pretending to be his more hairy older brother. Esau pleaded with his father for some blessing, but all he received was that one-day he would cast off his younger brother's ascendancy and rule over him for a short time. Later the tribe of Edom came to rule Judea under the half Edomite King Herod the Great, and at last, at least in part, fulfilled the blessing Isaac had given to Esau for a short period of time (Gen. 27:40). The people of the land of Israel in the time of Christ were in part Edomite, as they are today, although equally they are in part Jewish.

There are a number of other important points relating to research on the people now residing in the State of Israel. A diverse ethnic grouping that appears to form the majority in Israel today are descended from the Caucasian Khazar people of central Asia, a people who converted to Judaism some time around the late eighth century or early ninth century AD. One Jewish historian, Arthur Koestler, has called these non-Semitic Jews, the Thirteenth Tribe.[162] The Khazar kingdom was positioned between the Christian centres of power in Europe and the growing power of Islam that was extending northwards.

---

[161] I am allowing here the idea that intermarriage with foreigners does not stop an ethnic claim to be of Jewish descent. But if we allow this clause we must apply it consistently to both Jews and Palestinians

[162] Koestler, A., *The Thirteenth Tribe*, Random House, 1976; See also; Brook, K.A. *The Jews of Khazaria*, Rowman & Littlefield Publ. 2006

Not wishing to join with either the Christians or the Muslims they sent for Pharisees and Rabbis to come to their land in order to teach them the ways of Talmudic Judaism.

Khazar descent is believed to be through Kozar a son of Togarmah, and as a nation they once formed part of the Gokturk Empire. For this reason some opponents of the State of Israel have suggested that the majority of the Israeli populace are in fact related in some way to Gog and Magog, which would put a different twist on the prophecy of Ezekiel (38-39). However, it is not possible to establish this claim authoritatively without further research and information, as there could be a number of possible candidates for Gog and Magog. This includes Turkish and Islamic forces that have invaded and ruled in Palestine in the period since the New Testament times, or perhaps it represents a Russian invasion from the north that is yet to come. God in fact slowly reveals the meaning of prophecy in the proper time, and the real identity of Gog and Magog will I believe also be revealed one day according to God's timeframe.

But what happened to the Khazar Jews? Although there is some disagreement, the general idea is that the Khazars spread to Poland when their empire collapsed and later became identified as Ashkenazi Jews. It is possible that there were already Jews living in Eastern Europe at this time and that these people later assimilated with the emigrating Khazar Jews through intermarriage. The fact that the Ashkenazi or Khazar Jews are partly Caucasian and not Semitic doesn't necessarily mean that the people of Israel today should not be identifiable as ethnically Jewish in part because of intermarriage. Such intermarriage with foreigners doesn't stop the community remaining a legitimate expression of Judah in an ethnic sense. The most ethnically distinct Semitic Jews today are Shepardi Jews who traditionally remained around the Mediterranean Sea coasts, but often found themselves expelled from their settled cities from time to time. Even in New Testament times Jews were living in many places around the Mediterranean Sea, and the apostles often preached to Jews first in order to establish a gathering in a particular place.

Although the Jews in exile retained their ethnic identity even through intermarriage, increasingly their beliefs moved away from a straightforward reading of the Torah in favour of the Talmud. The Talmud is a vast collection of writing that includes the *Mishnah*, which is a standardised form of the largely oral Pharisaic *Tradition of the Elders*. In the time of Jesus the Mishnah existed amongst the Pharisees and was passed down from father to son (Matt. 15: 2). Jesus in fact condemned this tradition because the Scribes and Pharisees were using it to nullify the Law of Moses for their own selfish ends. But not all

128

Jews accepted the Talmud with a number retaining their commitment to the Torah. A group called *True Torah Jews Against Zionism* for instance retains a commitment to the Torah and further argues that the State of Israel does not represent the true faith of Moses, or the real Jewish people. They are opposed to Zionism because they believe the modern State of Israel has not been sanctioned by God, or accompanied by repentance, but it is a human work. While the Torah Jews today hope for a full restoration of a Jewish state they believe repentance must come first according to the Mosaic Law (Deut. 4:29-31). It was incidentally the prophecy of Jeremiah that caused Daniel to repent on behalf of the Jewish people that then led God to heal and restore the Jews to the Promised Land at the end of their Babylonian exile (Jer. 29; Dan. 9). For this reason Torah Jews believe the State of Israel is illegitimate without repentance coming first.[163]

But the question remains regarding the Jewish identity of the modern day Israeli population. Ethnically, the resident people of Israel who claim to be Jews are at least in part Jewish under the traditional understanding. However, spiritually most are still living outside of God's promise to Abraham, a promise that can only be received through faith in the Messiah who was the true seed of Abraham. There are though some Jews in Israel who have found faith in Jesus as their Messiah, and they need the support and prayers of Christians as they seek to bring their kinsfolk back into fellowship with God's one olive root, that is only to be found in Jesus.

Jewish - Christian Presence in Palestine

The second question for consideration is the extent of the Jewish roots of the Christian Palestinian community. The Christian community residing in Palestine today covers various denominations and is known as Nasrani (from Nazareth) or Masihi (from Messiah) and they have always had great respect for the land, which they identify as the Holy Land. The earliest Jewish Christians were present in the land in

---

[163] Another point to consider is the origin of the six pointed Star of David, Shield of David or Magen David on the Israeli flag (and displayed prominently on the cover of Hagee's book *In Defense of Israel*). Although a beloved symbol of many Christian Zionists, it cannot easily be traced to Old Testament Judaism and it would seem that instead it was a Babylonian or Persian astrological symbol or amulet known as the 'King's Star' that became associated with Israel through occasional infiltration of pagan and Babylonian idolatry. Many Orthodox Torah Jews refuse to use it as a Jewish symbol believing it to be occult.

the first few centuries of the Christian era, later flourishing with the conversion of the Roman Empire to Christianity during and following the time of Constantine. Although many of these Christians were Jewish converts, a large number of Gentiles and undoubtedly some Israelites from the diaspora joined with them from various nations.

Eusebius in fact records much of the early history of the Jerusalem Church. He informs us that the early believers were commanded by the prophetic revelation of Jesus to flee the city as the trouble increased in Jerusalem, and that the whole Church crossed the Jordan and settled in a place called Pella for a period of time.[164] It was shortly after this that the Romans put to death hundreds of thousands of Jews, but the Jewish Christian community had escaped.

It is not clear to what extent this believing community returned to Jerusalem subsequently. F.F.Bruce for instance asserts that the believers retained only loose links with the city following its destruction although they retained their identity as the Jerusalem Church in Trans-Jordan.[165] Thus they maintaining their links with the land promised to Abraham. Some Christians however did return to Jerusalem after the troubles had settled down. Bruce also highlights the tension in Jerusalem prior to the events of AD 68-70 that existed between the Hellenistic Jewish Christian converts and the Hebrew Jews in the Church. This tension arose because of disagreements over the place of the Law in the life of the Gentile Church. James had though tried to hold both sides together as they tried to come to terms with the significance of the events that had occurred through the life and death of Christ. With the Greek faction in a minority and increasing numbers of Pharisees coming to Christ the legalists appeared to gain the upper hand prior to the exile and it was primarily this faction that fled to Trans-Jordan. The Greek speaking Jews would more likely have escaped westwards as the problems in Jerusalem intensified.

James the half-brother of Christ was the first bishop of Jerusalem, but he was thrown off the roof of the temple and stoned to death by the Jewish authorities shortly before the Roman invasion. The early Church then appointed Simeon the son of Cleopas to be the second bishop of Jerusalem, and he was the cousin of the Lord through the maternal side.[166] Eusebius writes that Simeon lived to the age of 120

---

[164] Eusebius, Book III Ch V

[165] Bruce, F.F. 'The Church of Jerusalem,' *Christian Brethren Research Fellowship Journal* 4, April 1964, pp. 5-14.

[166] Eusebius Book III Ch XI. He mentions that Hegesippus asserted that Joseph and Simeon were brothers, but John 19:25 records that it was the wives (both called Mary) who were sisters.

years and died a martyr's death during the reign of the emperor Trajan. During the time of Simeon there were several persecutions against the descendents of David, especially under Vespasian, Domitian and Trajan, and the followers of Christ were not exempt from suspicion. With Simeon killed, a Jew by the name of Justus was appointed as the third bishop of Jerusalem. Eusebius reports that Justus was one of a great number of circumcised Jews who were coming to faith in Christ at that time.[167] The first fifteen bishops were in fact Hebrews and Eusebius lists the following twelve as Zaccheus, Tobias, Benjamin, John, Matthew, Philip, Seneca, Justus, Levi, Ephres, Joseph and Judas, although collectively they seem to have covered only a short period of time.[168]

Due to continued revolt by the non-Christian Jews who had resettled in Jerusalem after AD 70, there was further violence against the Christens in the time of the emperor Hadrian. They were therefore expelled from Jerusalem in AD 135 and Jews were even denied the possibility of setting eyes on their much-loved city. This prohibition was maintained until at least the time of Constantine. Jerusalem's name was changed to *Aelia Capitolina* by Hadrian with many Gentiles settled in the place of the Jews who had been driven out. Subsequently the later bishops of Jerusalem were Gentiles with the first called Marcus.[169]

Bruce argued that the identity of the exiled Jewish Christian community in Trans-Jordan was gradually lost in subsequent centuries as they were under suspicion of heresy from the wider Christian Church; the Jews considered them to be apostates.[170] Although their Jewish identity may have become obscured I would argue that they must have retained some links with the Gentile believers in Jerusalem and believers in Galilee and elsewhere in the Holy Land.[171] So collectively they maintained a Christian witness in the land of Palestine through many centuries.

The Maronite Christians, centred now in Lebanon, trace their links back to the Church in Antioch. This city had a large Jewish presence in the first century and the founding Church had connections with Paul and Peter, but it is likely that the Antioch Church had a significant Gentile component. Following the fall of Jerusalem it gained greater importance in the life of the wider Church than the Jerusalem Church. They have though gained their name from the fourth century

---

[167] Eusebius, Book III Ch XXXV

[168] Eusebius, Book IV Ch V

[169] Eusebius Book IV Ch VI

[170] Bruce, *The Church of Jerusalem.*

[171] Bruce suggests that there were other Jewish Christians in Palestine, especially around Galilee, as a result of Christ's teaching.

Syrian monk St Maron, and formed a semi-independent Christian community speaking Aramaic. Later they accepted Roman Catholic authority, but maintained a degree of independence. In fact for a time following the Islamic conquest until the Crusades they were believed to have disappeared, but in fact they kept their Christian faith and identity in isolation.

From the fourth century to the Islamic influx and conquest in the seventh century Jerusalem was a prosperous centre of the wider Christian community in the land, although the Christian community did not seek to rebuild the temple as they were instead looking for the New Jerusalem. A Christian presence has remained in the wider land of Palestine through later centuries involving crusades and periods of Muslim rule, and during times of peace the community has flourished. Even by the time of the Ottoman Empire the numbers of Christians remained relatively high.

It is reported by Wagner that at the end of the nineteenth century under the Ottoman rule thirty percent of the inhabitants in Palestine were thought to be Christian. However, he observes that the number of Christians in the land has fallen dramatically in the past 100 years. By the time of the British Mandate rule in Palestine the number of Christians were of the order of 18 to 20 percent having fallen steadily from the Ottoman period, but remained fairly constant from 1922 to 1947.[172] Wagner reports that according to a British census the number of Palestinian Christians in Jerusalem in 1922 was around 51 percent of the population. Most were from the well-educated mercantile class. However, following the UN partition of 28th November 1947 between 725,000 and 775,000 Palestinians, including many Christians, were expelled. Wagner quotes the historian Sami Hadawi, who estimated that over 50 percent of Christians in West Jerusalem were expelled, which represented the largest reduction in Christian numbers in Palestinian history. More Jerusalem Christians were expelled than Muslims following the land grab of 1948-1949 with 37 percent of Jerusalem Christians becoming refugees. This disparity was because Christians were concentrated more in the western part of the city that was seized by Israel. Of the land seized by Israeli authorities some 34 percent had previously been owned by Palestinian Christian churches with no compensation given.[173] Between 1947 and 1950 both Christian and

---

[172] Wagner, D., "Palestinian Christians: An Historic Community at Risk?" *Information Brief,* No. 89, 12th March 2002; and Charles M. Sennot (2007) *The Body and the Blood: The Middle East's Vanishing Christians and the Possibility for Peace.* Public Affairs, 22
[173] Wagner, *Palestinian Christians,*

Who Owns the Land?

Muslim Palestinians were expelled throughout the Israeli controlled areas. According to the Israel State's own statistics there were only 35,000 Christians remaining in the Jewish controlled area in 1950, representing some 3 percent of the total population. Seemingly, hundreds of thousands of Christians had been forced out. By 1995 the number of Christians in the State of Israel had increased to 160,000 people, but little change in percentage terms.[174]

Sociologist Bernard Sabella of Bethlehem University reported that in the Palestinian controlled areas of the West Bank, East Jerusalem and Gaza the number of Christians had declined from 18 percent in 1947, to 13 percent in 1966, and a massive fall to only 2.1 percent by 1993, and 1.6 percent by 2002. This fall is attributed to the Israeli military occupation by Wagner, and a lack of security and economic stability in Palestinian areas caused by Muslim terrorism, which has led to continuous emigration of the Christian people out of the land.[175]

So I would argue that there has been a continual presence of Christians in the Holy Land from the time of Christ, and that in part this community in Palestine has Jewish roots. If we consider that the promise of land to Abraham in Genesis 17 is binding because it is wholly dependent upon God's Word, then I believe that it has been fulfilled through the last 2,000 years in the Christian Church. However, we should not forget also that Christ is the seed of Abraham and so when we ask who owns the land the answer is God because the whole earth is the Lord's. The calling of Jesus is to make disciples of all nations, including the government of the State of Israel and Palestine. In other words, I believe it is clear that some sections of the Church are wrong to teach that the State of Israel can be in covenant relationship with God when the state ignores the teachings of Christ.

---

[174] Population by Religion and Population Group, Israeli Central Bureau of Statistics, 2004 [http://www1.cbs.gov.il/shnaton56/st02_01.pdf] Accessed Sept. 2008

[175] Wagner, *Palestinian Christians*.

Understanding Israel

Chapter 13

What Promises Remain for Jews?

While I believe that a straightforward reading of many of the Old Testament prophecies relating to Israel are being fulfilled in the Christian Church (that is, I believe, spiritually, legally and ethnically a union of Judah and Israel together with Gentile believers) Jesus said that the fig tree, representing unrepentant Judah, would again appear bearing green leaves, but not fruit. This is, I believe, what we see today in the State of Israel, a state identifiable as ethnically Jewish in part, but in many ways secular and rejecting the teachings of Christ and nullifying the writing of Moses. Instead there is a continued interest in the Talmudic interpretation of the Mosaic Law that developed out of the Tradition of the Elders. The State of Israel shows outward glory, but does not see the necessity for bringing forth the fruit of the Spirit that Jesus desired and required.

But that is clearly not the end of the matter. Paul wrote in the letter to the Romans that in the end all Israel will be saved because of the promise of God to Abraham. This is to happen once the full measure of the Gentiles has been brought into the Kingdom of God. Paul further exclaims; '...how much greater riches will their fullness bring!' and comments that if 'they do not persist in unbelief, they will be grafted in again' (Rom. 11: 23). According to Paul 'Israel has experienced a hardening in part until the full number of the Gentiles has come in. And so all Israel will be saved...'(Rom. 11: 25-26). Paul also noted that '...they are loved on account of the Patriarchs... (Rom. 11:28)' and, '...they too...may now receive mercy as a result of God's mercy...' (Rom. 11: 31).

In the present time it is to be hoped that this promise is not far off from being fulfilled. Christians should support the work of evangelism to the Jews taking place in Israel under very difficult circumstances and urge the Jewish authorities to remove legal restrictions. Such laws are preventing Jews from receiving the promise of God given through their forefather Abraham, and fulfilled through Christ. Some Christian Zionists are also hindering Jewish people from receiving the full promises of God by suggesting that they can still approach God through the Mosaic legal sacrifices, and urging Christians not to witness to, or evangelise Jews in Israel, or elsewhere. However, the perfect, loving sacrifice that Jesus made upon the cross is for all Jews and Gentiles, given according to God's own promise. With similar sentiments, the North American grouping of the Lausanne Consultation on Jewish Evangelism recently issued a statement on the importance of evangelism to Jews following its 26th annual meeting (2-4 March 2009) in Pheonix, Arizona. The statement rejects dual covenant theology and reasserts that the gospel is for Jews, both in the land of Israel and elsewhere, even as a priority, commenting further that to deny the gospel to Jews is not a loving response and is detrimental to their best interests.

Abraham received a seven-fold blessing that is for all Israel and this covenant is greater than the Law of Moses, both to Jews and Gentiles, according to their faith. Genesis (Gen. 12: 1-3) records this blessing, but notes that the blessing is not just for Abraham and his direct descendents, but that all people on earth will be blessed through him. The fruit that God requires is that the blessing is shared and passed on.

> 'I will make you into a great nation, and I will bless you.
> I will make your name great, and you will be a blessing.
> I will bless those who bless you, and whoever curses you I will curse;
> and all peoples on earth will be blessed through you.' (Gen 12: 2-3)

Paul, in the letters to the Romans, Galatians and Ephesians, notes that this blessing has passed to the Gentiles through Christ, but that in the end all Israel will partake in the blessing because of what Christ has done, and because of God's own promise. In the end the once rejected remnant of Jewish people will receive grace to believe in Christ. There is only one rootstock as a channel of grace and God's desire is to bring Jews and Gentiles together in that united olive tree, which is today the Christian-Messianic community of believers.

One fear though today that many are concerned about is that Israel is in danger from its Islamic neighbours. Neither does modern Israel appear to rely on the grace of God for its defence, but believes that its own power and strength can save it from harm with help from a powerful and wealthy America. Israel is multiplying its armaments in contradiction of God's command to trust him, also forgetting that Jacob was given his new name of Israel because of the necessity for reliance upon God for blessing and protection, unlike the younger Jacob who tried to fix his own blessing. It would though be a great tragedy if the State of Israel suffered major loss before the Jews in Palestine receive their promised blessing in Abraham through Christ. There is great danger for the people in the State of Israel today who live outside of Christ.

There are many people from around the world who have hoped and prayed for the conversion of Jews in Israel, but that has not happened yet to any great extent, even after sixty years of nationhood, and there is much resistance to evangelism in both Israeli society and in legislation. God, in his mercy, has so far protected Israel from serious harm, but that mercy is so that the Jews in Israel might turn to him. The Israelis cannot resist God's grace forever through rebellion and reliance on their human strength without suffering the consequences, as their own biblical history attests to so clearly.

Tony Pearce, like Hagee, and many other supporters of the State of Israel, applies the blessing of Abraham to the modern State of Israel, and develops the theology of the pre-tribulation rapture in his book The Omega Files,[176] but unlike some of the more extreme Christian Zionist teachers, he recognises the problem of unbelief in Israel today. For Pearce, Israel will sign a false peace treaty with the antichrist in order to escape destruction at the hands of the global enemy. However, they will be betrayed and suffer major loss. According to Pearce, it will be out of that suffering that the Jews of the world will finally accept Jesus as the Messiah. This, according to Pearce, will then herald in the final part of the second coming of Christ.[177]

While I do not necessarily agree with this scenario, it is of interest in order to highlight the fact that many Christian Zionists do not think through the eschatological consequences of what is being taught, but simply have placed their hope and trust in the visible State of Israel as evidence of God's activity in the world, instead of placing their hope and trust in the presently invisible Messiah. It is almost as if Israel, as a visible state, has replaced the Messiah in the minds of many Christians. There is danger in this I believe, not least because Christians run the risk of being deceived by false teaching. Christianity in the West is already under attack from many sides; the new atheists are writing and selling books by the million, and the faith of other Christians has grown faint with a deistic spirit having replaced the dynamic faith of the first century Christians. As a result of the activity of militant atheism that is undermining people's faith, new age or neo-pagan groups seem to be attracting many supporters with their post-modern beliefs and ideas, and

---

[176] Pearce, *The Omega Files*. New Wine Press
[177] Pearce, *The Omega Files,*, p. 79.

the concept of truth itself is being lost.[178] Christians are also being wearied by economic crises and war in the Middle East where the supporters of political Zionism are fighting the forces of militant Islam. There has been recent war in Iraq, and continuing conflict in Afghanistan, and talk in the press at this time concerning America and the West engaging in war with Iran to prevent that Islamic state obtaining nuclear warheads. Pakistan is also unstable with its dangerous nuclear weapons at risk of falling into the hands of the Taliban. A war with Iran would be for the stated purpose of protecting Israel from a possible future nuclear strike, but there are great risks in such an endeavour apart from the serious ethical problems.

As well as the obvious concern about this scenario, a second concern then is that if Islamic forces were to succeed in destroying the State of Israel then it could prove a fatal blow to the faith of many Christians, this because those Christians have placed such high hopes and faith in Israel believing the nation is fulfilling a divine plan, and not really understanding the complete theology of Christian Zionism and what it entails.

Islam too is greatly feared in the western world, although I think such fears are over exaggerated. The strength of the Church has always been in humble service, love and forgiveness, while building goodwill for Christ amongst the people of the world. Islam instead lacks the ability to generate sufficient goodwill and unity needed for world domination. For these reasons, I do not believe that Islam can ever spread across the world by force of arms because it does not create that goodwill, but only a grudging and hateful compliance to brutal dictatorial rulers. By seeking to conquer by force, the Islamic people lose their God given humanity not recognising that truth cannot be imposed by force of arms. The truth of God can only be received by revelation from God. But equally the western world and Israel cannot defeat Islam by force, but only by showing the love of Christ to Muslims while engaging in respectful dialogue, thus preaching by deeds not only by words. This was the mistake of the Crusades; Christians only empowered Islam by seeking to impose their Christian will on them by force and the western nations are making the same mistake today (although in reality the West is so secular these days that it would be more accurate to say that it is secularism that is seeking to impose its will on Islam by force at the present time).

---

[178] The meaning of 'truth' in atheism is merely illusionary, because atheism ultimately destroys the notion of meaning and logic. The atheists have no consistently logical and objective way of establishing their claims.

Promises for Jews

Whatever happens to the State of Israel in the future, there will still be more Jews living outside of Palestine and the gospel will continue to go out to them until Christ returns, and right up to the end they will continue to be offered grace to believe in Christ. The land of Palestine was always too small to contain the full promise given to Abraham, and God's purpose was to bless the whole world through his people by scattering them around the world and then bringing them to faith in Jesus Christ. The descendents of Abraham, especially through Joseph and Ephraim, were to become very numerous upon the earth. This is the promise of God to Israel today, but it is being fulfilled through Christ and the Church community. Jesus said to his disciples 'I tell you the truth, you will not finish going through the cities of Israel [preaching the gospel] before the Son of Man comes [returns]' (Matt. 10: 23). The promise to Jews today is the promise of restoration in Christ and the offer of being re-grafted back into their own natural olive tree; this by returning to Christ in obedience to God.

But how should we consider the status of the Jewish nation today before God? Has God abandoned the state completely and replaced it with the Church, or does God really have two groups of people on the earth under a dual covenant? If we consider the teachings of Hosea that were spoken against the Assyrian exiles, and apply them to the present day Jews, then it may be seen that the unrepentant nation is in effect being unfaithful towards God by rejecting Christ. And, just as God divorced the northern tribes of Israel for their pagan idolatry, God too has legally divorced the present day segment of Jews who rejected Christ (Hos. 2: 2-7 & Matt. 23). However, just as God sent the northern tribes of Israel away, he continued to remember and love them. In the same way, God also remembers and loves the present day Jews, just as Paul said in Romans, but the current status of unrepentant Judah is that of a divorced woman. Still loved on account of the Patriarchs, but presently legally separated. The only way for the Jewish people to be reunited with God's true community of believers is through acceptance of Christ's work upon the cross (Rom. 11: 31). In that way Jews may be remarried to God under the new covenant, there can be no way back to God through the old one.

As for seeking to understand God's plan for the present day State of Israel, I believe it is possible that God has brought Jewish people into the land so that he can pour out his Spirit upon the people living in the nation. And thus lead them to genuine spiritual revival, and also to a lasting and just peace settlement with the Palestinians, where Muslims also need to come to Christ. Without wishing to limit God's purposes in the world it should be acknowledged that it is possible that God desires that Jews live in the land under the new covenant. A

Christian vision for God's people in the Holy Land then should be one where Jews are to be re-grafted into their natural olive tree and thus become united with Palestinian Christians and other Gentile believers. The Christian-Messianic community in Palestine is, I believe, the true Israel in the land, not the secular, national and political State of Israel. I believe that support for this community should be the focus of Christian' support for Israel, and of those who feel called to love and work amongst Jews; that is a vision of peace, justice and reconciliation in Christ. It needs to be remembered that there is the great commission of Christ, that is to bring all nations under his governing authority, and that includes the nations and people of Israel and Palestine.

Chapter 14

Conclusions

This has only been a short study, but a number of points can be made. I do not believe that replacement theology as often characterised, or the theology of modern Christian Zionism, provide accurate theological frameworks regarding the place of Israel today; whether as a spiritual entity, or as a state in God's plan. However, there is in fact a wide spectrum of thought, and categorising individual opinion is problematic. However, from this study the following points can be identified and stated.

Point 1. What is often a hindrance to understanding the status of true Israel is an incomplete grasp of Old Testament history and the prophetic writings. As we have seen, the name *Israel* was originally given as a spiritual title upon Jacob when he came into submission to God. This was also Paul's understanding in the letter to the Romans wherein he affirmed that not all Israel is Israel, but only those called to a life of faithfulness to God. So, Israel is primarily a spiritual title conferred upon those in obedience to God's calling; today it is those who accept Jesus. While Abraham's blessing is known (and often misapplied), Joseph, Ephraim and Manasseh's possession of Israel's birthright is often missed, as is the northern exile of Israel in 721 BC by the Assyrians. This exile meant that the birthright was removed out of the land. The Israelites were then scattered across the earth as Jacob-Israel promised to Joseph's sons, especially Ephraim. God's plan, through Abraham and his descendents, was to bless the whole world. Biblical prophecy continued to speak about the northern tribes of Israel in exile, and the promise of their restoration (spiritual and otherwise) was even spoken of in the later period of the prophet Zechariah. Many supporters of Christian Zionism ignore the fate of the northern tribes of Israel, believing them to be replaced and rejected for good, and then misapply prophecies that relate to the scattered northern Israelites to the establishment of the modern State of Israel by the descendents of Judah. However, Judah did not possess the birthright, instead the Judaic tribe had the wonderful promise to bring forth the ruling Messiah.

Point 2. Furthermore, because supporters of Christian Zionism, such as Hagee, downplay the need for Jews to find the Messiah, which is perhaps an extreme form of Darby's dispensationalism, then it may be asked whether another gospel is being preached? Supporters of Christian Zionism need to be aware that this development is bound to invite another serious question; is the formation of the State of Israel really part of God's plan, or is it part of a deception that the apostles warned against that lead people away from the Messiah?

Point 3. I believe that a correct understanding of Scripture shows that the Christian Church is in a very real sense spiritual Israel because of the promises given to Abraham that are to be received by faith. Israel then continues as the Christian Church or Messianic community today. This does not replace Israel; instead it is an Israel where Jews, Israelites and Gentile believers dwell together, united in the one olive tree. As Paul noted, the true Israelites are those who have faith in Christ because of the promise given to Abraham, and Abraham was the man of faith whose trust in God was accredited to him as righteousness. So the Church is fulfilling and continuing the covenant of promise given, by God's own name, to Abraham, and under the promised Judaic-Davidic ruler, Jesus the Messiah. This covenant of promise cannot be replaced and is greater than the mediated covenant of Moses that has been rendered obsolete. What has been replaced then, by Christ's perfect sacrifice as the Lamb of God upon the cross, is the sacrificial requirement of the Mosaic Law whereby the blood of animals was necessary to take away the sins of the Jews and Israelites on an annual basis. Now Christians are to live by the spirit of the Law, which is love. That part of the Mosaic Law was only ever meant to be an interim measure to lead people to Christ when the time had come for Christ to be revealed. Christ came in fulfilment of the greater promise given to Abraham that has not been replaced, but continues in the Church through Christ and is received by faith. This global Church of Jesus is now spiritual Israel and the kingdom of heaven upon the earth where the new Israel is being built up together as God's perfect tabernacle in Christ's own body.

Point 4. The Christian Church is also ethnically related to both Judah and Israel; it is in part a Messianic community of ethnic Jews. The first Christians were Jews, and many of the early converts were also from the exiled northern tribes of Israel who were dispersed among the nations, and Jesus sent his disciples to them and to scattered Jews during his ministry, and for the first few years after his ascension. It was only after Peter's vision to take the gospel to the household of the Gentile Cornelius, (where God says he has made the repentant Gentiles 'clean') and Paul's calling to preach to the Gentiles, that the Church's ministry was extended to Gentiles. This may be seen as a fulfilment of Old Testament prophecies relating to the reunification of Israel and Judah, (and there are a number of them that form a consistent pattern as has been shown from Jeremiah, Isaiah, Hosea, Zechariah and Ezekiel etc), together with an ingathering of many Gentiles into the initially Jewish

Conclusions

Church. Later this Israel, that is the Christian Church, resettled Palestine and established communities in the land as a literal fulfilment of prophecy, but the real kingdom of God that Jesus spoke of in his parables was a spiritual kingdom that would grow and extend across the earth, as for instance a mustard tree grows across the whole garden, but also where the wheat and the weeds would grow up together (Matt. 13). In other words, although Jews and Israelites joined the Church at its instigation, they were resettled into God's kingdom as spiritual Israel; a body of believers that was growing across the world and extending to Gentiles, and not just resettled as a small ethnic group into a single nation in a small piece of land in the Middle East.

Point 5. The Christian Church, as spiritual Israel, did resettle Palestine following the overthrow of the Jewish nation by the Romans in AD 68-70 in a literal fulfilment of prophecy. The true Israel, as well as spreading across the world, today maintains continuity in the Holy Land from the first century. It also follows from this that the present day Palestinian Christian community continues this lineage and needs the support of other Christians. Encouragingly, some Messianic Jewish believers have been grafted back into their natural olive root also, and they too need the love and support of Gentile Christian believers.

Point 6. The Christian Church is also legally Israel in terms of the covenant of Abraham because Jesus, through the apostles he sent out, shepherded the flock of the house of Israel. In doing this he reunited the Israelite northern tribes that included Ephraim and Joseph (who were scattered, but possessed the birthright), with the remnant of Judah (who brought forth the Messianic Sceptre), together with the in-grafted Gentiles. In other words, the legal birthright that Jacob-Israel possessed from Isaac and Abraham, and passed on to Joseph and Ephraim, is now in the Christian Church because Jesus brought the remnant of Joseph and Ephraim under his governing authority according to scriptural prophecy. The first disciples also formed a properly established Jewish community with 120 men according to custom. I want to emphasise though that while these legal and ethnic arguments are important, the spiritual aspect is of greater importance. When we come to the present day status of the State of Israel and the Church there are a number of further points that need to be considered.

Point 7. God clearly has allowed a Jewish State of Israel to arise and exist within the last one hundred years, although the reasons for this are not entirely clear. While this state legally exists in human terms, and seems to have been given an opportunity to fulfil some form of divine purpose today because God has allowed it to exist, God's purposes are often difficult to understand until they are revealed in full. Today there is only a partial revelation regarding the identity of the

State of Israel. I believe that some of the teachings of Christian Zionism overlook the general thrust of God's purposes revealed through biblical prophecy and fulfilled in Christ and the Church. New Testament Pauline theology cannot be used to suggest that there will be a return to the old covenant system of worship, because Jesus has abolished that system for good by his perfect sacrifice.

According to the Gospels, Judaism cannot now bear the fruit that God requires without the Messiah, even though Jesus said that the fig tree of Israel would again appear sprouting more green leaves, but not fruit. According to the Mosaic Law the Jewish restoration to the land of Israel was to be accompanied first by repentance. Trying to establish the State of Israel apart from repentance and outside of Christ is in effect disobedience towards God. In other words, although God has permitted Israel to exist as a secular state for whatever reason, the state is not actually living in obedience to God's directive will and purpose. I do not believe that God will ultimately bless such a situation.

The idea that the State of Israel can exist as part of God's kingdom outside of the Christian Church goes against the clear teaching of Scripture, which teaches unity with one olive root on which all the branches of Israel and Judah must eventually be grafted. I do not believe that the State of Israel, as a nationalistic Zionist state, can fulfil a divine purpose today outside of Christ, and I question how Christians can rightly support nationalistic expansionism in the land against the Palestinians. However, this study has no interest in opposing the existence of the modern State of Israel as a political entity, I will leave that to God if there is any opposing to be done, but neither do I believe that Christians should support the State of Israel in that nationalistic sense. A Christian's first calling is to Christ and his spiritual kingdom, upholding it in love, justice and righteousness, and in this regard Christians and Messianic believers should provide a prophetic voice to the State of Israel, calling the state to obedience under the Messiah. It is important to love the unrepentant Jewish people as they, like all of us, are in need of salvation in Christ.

Point 8. The status of the two-third's part of the Jewish nation that rejected Christ, and therefore is not at present included in the Messiah, is akin to that of a legally divorced woman, as outlined by Hosea and Isaiah. They are therefore still loved by God on account of their forefathers, but not at present legally his people. God's desire is that Jews return to him and accept Jesus as their Messiah.

Point 9. There are many Palestinian Christians and Messianic Jews in Israel today seeking to witness to the Jews, and they need our support and prayers. Christians are called to love Jews, as Hagee rightly noted, but sadly some do not accept the Messianic witness to Jews.

Conclusions

However, some biblical prophecies (Rom. 9-11, and Zech. 12: 10) point to the conversion of Jews in the last days and this should be a matter of encouragement and prayer. Jesus also asserted (Matt. 10: 23) that the gospel message must continue to be preached to the Jews until he returns. This is because of God's promise to Abraham. Paul noted in Romans that the unrepentant Jews now are loved on account of the Patriarchs and will be offered grace to believe in the present time, and up until the end. Equally, the Palestinian Christians, need our love, support and prayers as they seek to live in difficult conditions. We cannot overlook their suffering either and as Christians we should seek to work for peace and justice in the land between both communities.

As noted, it is possible that God desires a Messianic community of ethnic Jewish believers in the land before Christ returns, but once again the Christian community should not be divided between Jews and Gentiles, between Jewish believers and Palestinian Christians. In fact those Israeli citizens who do accept Christ join with the true Israel of God in Palestine, and an expansionist and nationalistic State of Israel is wholly unnecessary for God's purposes to be completed.

I believe then that Jews need to accept Jesus as their Messiah in order to fulfil their purpose in God's plan; anything else would imply that God has two kingdoms under a dual covenant, but such theology divides Israel into earthly and spiritual entities, which is really a form of Gnosticism. But as Paul noted there is only one kingdom, one olive rootstock on to which both the Jews and Gentiles are to be grafted. It is also important to recognise that the Palestinian Christian community can be traced back to the earliest Christian believers, an ethic mix of Jews and Gentiles. This lineage I believe represents the true Israelite residence in the Holy Land in a literal sense. But it is also in a spiritual and legal sense as well as the ethnic one, as a continual resident people in the land according to God's promises, and also as part of the worldwide Christian community. Furthermore, it is legitimate to ask questions about the treatment of Palestinians, especially as it relates to the indigenous Christian community in Palestine.

It is being argued here then that the relationship between the Christian Church and historical Israel is one of unity and continuity where the Church is spiritually, ethnically and legally Israel, thus forming the faithful remnant of the true olive tree that is being built up together in Christ's body. God has indeed made a promise to Israel through Abraham that cannot be broken and is being fulfilled in the Christian/Messianic Church. The full promise to Israel though may be considered to be as part of the continual conversion of Jews to the Messiah, an ongoing process that is not yet complete. Christ's work on the cross was in fulfilment of the promise given to Abraham, but Paul notes that in the end all Israel will be saved, suggesting that the full measure of unrepentant Jews and Israelites will one day be united in accepting Christ, alongside the wider Christian community. This is, I believe, the remaining promise of God to all Israel, to Jews and Israelites inside and outside of the Middle East, and should be the focus of Christian love and concern for Jews.

A Vision for the State of Israel

Ideally, I would suggest that a Christian vision for governance of the Holy Land should be one that seeks to bring Israel, Gaza and the West Bank together, perhaps with a joint state with a confederate structure. We should seek greater unity between Jews and Palestinians, both communities united, working and living together in Christ. What is needed is spiritual expansion in Christ, not an expansion of the possession of land. Christians should further pray for the government in the State of Israel that it develops policies that are in line with Judeo-Christian truths and values. Such values follow the principles of the Law of Moses that have been interpreted by Jesus Christ in terms of love being the fulfilment of the Law. Christians should not oppose the right of the Israeli state to exist, such rights are given and taken away by God, and Christians are called to have a servant spirit, but with a prayerful, prophetic edge. In the same way, although the Old Testament prophets pronounced God's will to the Israelite rulers, they never opposed the nation in their own name. The same principle I believe applies to all states, whether secular western nations or predominantly Muslim nations as well. Those people and nations who oppose God's loving righteousness and justice will be brought to a place where they must account for their action and learn obedience through God's discipline.[179]

Whether the Jewish people inside the State of Israel take advantage of the opportunity to fulfil a divine purpose by receiving Jesus Christ as the Messiah and following his path of righteousness remains to be seen. Whatever happens to the State of Israel in the future, and there is concern over that question, there will remain an opportunity for Jews resident and living inside and outside of the State of Israel to receive their full promises, given to Judah and Israel, in Jesus Christ until He returns.

---

[179] There are Jews in Israel who too seek peace and justice for Palestinians. The Israeli Committee Against House Demolitions desires justice and a sustainable peace settlement for both sides; thus seeking 'security, dignity and freedom' as well as economic development, perhaps under a regional confederation of states [http://www.icahd.org/eng/about.asp?menu=2&submenu=1]

Appendices

Appendix 1. Jerusalem Declaration on Christian Zionism

Statement by the Patriarch and Local Heads of Churches In Jerusalem 22nd August 2006

> Blessed are the peacemakers for they shall be called the children of God. (Matt. 5: 9)

Christian Zionism is a modern theological and political movement that embraces the most extreme ideological positions of Zionism, thereby becoming detrimental to a just peace within Palestine and Israel. The Christian Zionist programme provides a worldview where the Gospel is identified with the ideology of empire, colonialism and militarism. In its extreme form, it places an emphasis on apocalyptic events leading to the end of history rather than living Christ's love and justice today.

We categorically reject Christian Zionist doctrines as false teaching that corrupts the biblical message of love, justice and reconciliation. We further reject the contemporary alliance of Christian Zionist leaders and organizations with elements in the governments of Israel and the United States that are presently imposing their unilateral pre-emptive borders and domination over Palestine. This inevitably leads to unending cycles of violence that undermine the security of all peoples of the Middle East and the rest of the world.

We reject the teachings of Christian Zionism that facilitate and support these policies as they advance racial exclusivity and perpetual war rather than the gospel of universal love, redemption and reconciliation taught by Jesus Christ. Rather than condemn the world to the doom of Armageddon we call upon everyone to liberate themselves from the ideologies of militarism and occupation. Instead, let them pursue the healing of the nations!

We call upon Christians in Churches on every continent to pray for the Palestinian and Israeli people, both of whom are suffering as victims of occupation and militarism. These discriminative actions are turning Palestine into impoverished ghettos surrounded by exclusive Israeli settlements. The establishment of the illegal settlements and the construction of the Separation Wall on confiscated Palestinian land undermines the viability of a Palestinian state as well as peace and security in the entire region.

We call upon all Churches that remain silent, to break their silence and speak for reconciliation with justice in the Holy Land.

Therefore, we commit ourselves to the following principles as an alternative way:

> **We** affirm that all people are created in the image of God. In turn they are called to honour the dignity of every human being and to respect their inalienable rights.
>
> **We** affirm that Israelis and Palestinians are capable of living together within peace, justice and security.
>
> **We** affirm that Palestinians are one people, both Muslim and Christian. We reject all attempts to subvert and fragment their unity.
>
> **We** call upon all people to reject the narrow world-view of Christian Zionism and other ideologies that privilege one people at the expense of others.
>
> **We** are committed to non-violent resistance as the most effective means to end the illegal occupation in order to attain a just and lasting peace.
>
> **With** urgency we warn that Christian Zionism and its alliances are justifying colonization, apartheid and empire building.

God demands that justice be done. No enduring peace, security or reconciliation is possible without the foundation of justice. The demands of justice will not disappear. The struggle for justice must be pursued diligently and persistently but non-violently.

> "What does the Lord require of you, to act justly, to love mercy, and to walk humbly with your God." (Mic. 6: 8)

This is where we take our stand. We stand for justice. We can do no other. Justice alone guarantees a peace that will lead to reconciliation with a life of security and prosperity for all the peoples of our Land. By standing on the side of justice, we open ourselves to the work of peace - and working for peace makes us children of God.

> "God was reconciling the world to himself in Christ, not counting men's sins against them. And he has committed to us the message of reconciliation." (2 Cor. 5: 19)

Authors: His Beattitude Patriarch Michel Sabbah - Latin Patriarchate, Jerusalem. Archbishop Swerios Malki Mourad, Syrian Orthodox Patriarchate, Jerusalem. Bishop Riah Abu El-Assal, Episcopal Church of Jerusalem and the Middle East. Bishop Munib Younan, Evangelical Lutheran Church in Jordan and the Holy Land.

Appendices

Appendix 2. Israel in the Prophets (table)

	1. Israel to be restored to the land under the Messiah	2. Israel and Judah to be reunited under the Messiah	3. The kingdom extending to the Gentile nations	4. The restoration of Israel under a new covenant
Amos	Amos 9: 11-12		Amos 9: 11-12	
Hosea	Hos. 3: 4-5	Hos. 1: 10-11	Hos 2: 21-23	Hos. 2: 14-20
Isaiah	Isa. 1: 12-16; 49: 5	Isa. 11: 10-12	Isa. 14: 1-2; 49: 6; 49:19-20; 56:3-8; 65:1-2	Isa. 49: 8
Micah	Mic. 2:12-13; 5:2-4		Mic. 5:4-5	
Jeremiah	Jer. 23: 5-6; 30: 8-10; 33: 17	Jer. 23:5-6; 30:1-4; 31:27; 31:31-34; 50:4-6		Jer. 31:31
Ezekiel	Ezek. 34: 11-24; 37:24-28	Ezek. 37: 15-23		Ezek. 34: 25-31 Ezek. 37: 24-28
Zechariah	Zech. 10: 1-5	Zech. 8: 13; 10: 6-12	Zech. 9: 11-14	Zech. 9: 11-13

This table is a summary of central themes relating to Israel in the Old Testament prophets as discussed throughout this book. What is shown consistently in the Old Testament prophets is that the promises of God included restoration of the northern tribes of Israel to God, together with reunification with Judah and union with the Gentiles. All of this was to take place under the new covenant that God was going to make with his people through the coming Messiah.

Although there was the promise to Israel that they would repossess the land, the land was considered too small to contain the large number of Israel's offspring. They had spread across the earth and multiplied, thus fulfilling the promises of God. These promises were to bless Abraham, Isaac, Jacob, Joseph and Ephraim with abundant fruit. Now through Christ, God has extended the borders of Israel to include all the earth, but within the new Jerusalem as the kingdom of God.

Appendices
Appendix 3. The Lost Tribes of Israel

It has been noted that there are similarities between some European names, and names relating to the tribes of Israel. Denmark, as a name, is suggested to be close to the tribe of Dan, Iberia, Ireland and Hibernia perhaps sound like 'Hebrew' and the Saxons and Scots could be identified as the Beth Sacae, or the house of Isaac, while others have claimed that the Celtic name Cymru (pronounced Cumri) relates to the house of the Israelite king Omri.[180] Further lines of evidence for this claim come from the discovery and translation of the Behistun Inscription, a multilingual inscription on Mount Behistun, which was written in antiquity before 400BC, and still exists along the ancient road from Babylon to Media. Henry Rawlinson translated the large text between 1835 and 1843, and it consists of the same statement in three languages, Old Persian, Babylonia and Elamite. The Old Persian and Elamite texts identify the Sacae, Saka or Scythian people with the Gimirri, or Cimmerian on the Babylonian part of the text. Furthermore, the Assyrians who conquered the northern tribes of Israel identified the people of Israel as the House of Khumri, named after Omri the notable King of Israel in the 8th century BC.[181] George Rawlinson commented that he thought he had;

> '...reasonable grounds for regarding the Gimirri, or Cimmerians, who first appeared on the confines of Assyria and Media in the seventh century B.C., and the Sacae of the Behistun Rock, nearly two centuries later, as identical with the Beth-Khumree of Samaria, or the Ten Tribes of the House of Israel.'[182]

However, while this may be of interest to some it really would require a thorough investigation of the evidence to establish authoritatively and is therefore beyond the scope of this present study. I also find these ideas too British or European centric, when in truth the exiled Israelites were scattered across the world, as far as India and

---

[180] These claims were made in the late 19th century by Sir John Rhys, *Early Celtic Britain*, pp. 142, 150 & 162-3

[181] For instance Capt. Raymond, E., *Missing Links Discovered in Assyrian Tablets* Artisan Pub, 1985

[182] Rawlinson, G., Taken from a note in his translation of *History of Herodotus*, Book VII, p. 378

China as well as Europe.[183] For these reason it is not the intention here to make such a link and thus I will leave aside the question of whether a link exists in reality. But, bearing in mind the fact that according to Scripture the Israelites were scattered across the earth, and Jesus' comments relating to the work of preaching to the scattered Israelites throughout the world (Matt. 10: 23), such a link would be entirely consistent with scriptural teaching (See also for instance the promise to Ephraim (Gen. 48: 15-16)).

So what happened to the lost tribes of Israel? A plain sense reading of Scripture suggests that many were subsumed into the emerging Christian Church, (a process that is not yet complete) and then gradually lost their separate Israelite identity. But it means that the Church is in part ethnically Israel (as well as having ethnic links with the first Jewish Christian believers). Some Christians may argue that this is quite a tenuous argument, but I would point them to study the words of the prophets in the context of the political and historical setting in which they wrote, as I have tried to do in this book. Furthermore, it also needs to be remembered that what is important to God is not ethnic identity, but spiritual identity in Christ, where the Church is being built up together as spiritual Zion with people from every ethnic group.

---

[183] In the 1920s Thomas Torrance for instance tried to identify the Chiang-Min people of West Szechuan Province in China as Israelite exiles.

Appendices

Appendix 4. Questionable Documents

There are a number of works that are worth mentioning that are of questionable origin and of a conspiratorial nature. The purpose of this is to shed some light on what are controversial documents, but for some appealing.

Protocols of the Elders of Zion

The first is the *Protocols of the Elders of Zion*. This work has long been considered a forgery, although sometimes those who object to their authenticity seem to protest a little too much. Whatever their origin, I doubt that they are truly of Jewish origin; perhaps instead they are the work of the Nazi fascist propaganda machine. There is no point in discussing the *Protocols* in further depth because they are of dubious origin and therefore a red herring and not central to the message of this book. Furthermore, discussing them tends to generate more heat than light.

Holocaust Denial

Another aspect for consideration is Holocaust denial that is increasingly common today. At times some have sought to downplay the Holocaust suggesting that six million Jews did not really die in the Second World War. In response, I would comment that there is no real reason to deny that millions of Jews suffered and died in the war, and there is no real reason to deny a figure of six million as a reasonable rounded estimate of numbers who died. Quite clearly many Jews have suffered greatly through history, and this needs to be acknowledged and remembered. Also, it needs to be recognised that undoubtedly millions of people died in the war from many other nations, as well as those who identified themselves as Jewish.

Third World War

The third point of interest is the letter from Albert Pike, a leading Freemason and Satanist, to the mafia boss Giuseppe Mazzini, dated to 15th August 1871. This letter allegedly involved a blueprint for three world wars.[184] The stated aim of the revealed plan was to bring

---

[184] Anyone wanting a reference can easily find the letter through an Internet search. But see for instance http://www.threeworldwars.com/albert-pike2.htm.

about the final destruction of Christianity and institute a religion of Lucifer in its place. However, the authenticity of the letter has not been established convincingly.

According to Carr the blueprint was worked out between 1859, and 1871. The letter was first mentioned by Cardinal Caro y Rodriguez of Santiago, Chile, in his book *The Mystery of Freemasonry Unveiled* in 1925. Rodriguez noted that the letter was in the possession of the British Museum. However, William Guy Carr, a former Intelligence Officer in the Royal Canadian Navy, obtained a statement from the British Museum asserting that they did not possess such a letter. Carr writes in a footnote to his 1959 book *Satan, Prince of this World*, that the keeper of manuscripts informed him that this letter is not catalogued in the British Museum Library, therefore its origin must be in doubt.[185] However, the Pike to Mazzini letter was first publicly discussed in 1925, after the first war, but before the second.

More recently Terry Melanson has done a good job in highlighting the problems with this thesis, suggesting the ideas are suspect because of the link to Cardinal Caro y Rodriguez.[186] However, Melanson's work is incomplete and the source of Carr's research has not yet been identified because Carr makes different claims than the threeworldwar website claims. So the mystery remains.

The letter comments that the purpose of the First World War was to overthrow the Russian Czars, and then build up atheistic communism in that land. Christianity would be weakened through the spread of communism. The Second World War was to be fought so as to strengthen political Zionism sufficiently to allow the formation of a sovereign state of Israel in Palestine. International Communism would be strengthened to balance the power of Christendom. It may be noted that the Second World War did indeed allow the creation of a Zionist State of Israel in 1948, partly because of a wave of sympathy for the Jewish people as a result of the Holocaust.

Communism was also strengthened when in 1945 the Potsdam Conference, held between Truman, Churchill and Stalin, handed over a large part of Eastern Europe to Russian control. According to the letter, these developments enabled plans for a third global war. Following the 9/11 events and the subsequent war on terror events could be seen to be moving towards greater conflict in the Middle East. The letter in reality highlights the threats and dangers faced by the people of Israel, and also

---

[185] See also; Carr, W.G., *Pawns in the Game* (CPA Book Publisher reprint (nd), (although Carr signs his introduction Oct. 13, 1958), p. XV

[186] See: http://www.conspiracyarchive.com/Articles/Pike-Mazzini_Three-World-Wars.htm

by Muslims and Christians, if the letter is an accurate reflection of what is happening today.

The letter states that the Third World War is to be fought by exploiting differences between political Zionism and the Islamic World, to the point where they 'mutually destroy each other.' The other nations would be forced to take sides and therefore lead to 'physical, moral, spiritual and economical exhaustion.' Christianity, with its increasingly weak deistic spirit, will be unable to withstand the new atheists and nihilists.

Today, the State of Israel is at times waging war against its Islamic neighbours, who are slowly gaining in organisation and strength, and now increasingly threaten the existence of Israel as a state. With so many Arab and Palestinian Muslims hardened by war, there seems little for them to lose, and they are increasingly turning to desperate measures. In response the State of Israel seems to be fighting back with greater force.

While the letter is of questionable original, there are people, ironically even some Christian supporters of Israel, who seem to be interested in driving events in a similar direction towards war. Some Christian Zionists believe that the State of Israel has been established so that it will be eventually destroyed through another Holocaust. The Islamic world and its culture too is being destroyed and degraded by war and violence.

I believe that Christian supporters of Israel need to be aware and concerned that support for political Zionism with its expansionist vision against the Palestinians is in effect playing into the hands of those who seek to destroy the Jewish people, and Christianity. Whether the letter has a measure of authenticity and is attributable to the stated author, (which is in doubt) events seem to be playing out in that vague direction anyway. If that is a reasonable proposition, then it may be seen that the State of Israel is in great danger, as well as the Arab nations.

Also, the faith of many Christians who have placed a lot of trust in the State of Israel, believing it is fulfilling a divine purpose in this time, could be shaken. Can it possibly be that the emergence of an expansionist state in Israel is part of a deliberate plan of Satan to provoke war in the Middle East, and ultimately destroy the Jewish people and Christian faith? There is no definitive answer to this question at this time and the letter is of questionable origin, but it is something to be aware of. From this I would urge readers not to get too attached to particular eschatological schemes, especially those that involve a separate State of Israel, and a pre-tribulation rapture, because it may endanger their faith when the time of trial comes. The other message from this is that in light of such dangers there is surely a greater onus upon Christians to work for peace and justice between both the Jewish and Palestinian communities in the Middle East in order to bring about a lasting and sustainable peace settlement. Christians need to have a vision for the Holy Land that involves bringing the Jewish people and Palestinians together in the Messiah, and thus seek to avoid an apocalyptical catastrophe that is possibly being planned by some. Of course God is ultimately sovereign over the states of the world and events that unfold, but Christians have a clear mandate in terms of going throughout the earth and making disciples of all nations seeking to bring all into God's kingdom.

Selected Bibliography

Brockway, A et al (1988) *The Theology of the Churches and the Jewish People,* Geneva: WCC Publ.

Bruce, F.F (1964) 'The Church of Jerusalem,' *Christian Brethren Research Fellowship Journal* 4, April, pp. 5-14.

Calvin, J. (1961) *The Epistle of Paul the Apostle to the Romans,* Edinburgh: St. Andrew's Press

Carroll, J., (2001) *Constantine's Sword: The Church and the Jews,* Boston: Houghton Mifflin

Carter, J, (2006) *Palestine: Peace not Apartheid,* New York, Simon and Schuster

Cohen, J. (1991) (ed.), *Essential Papers on Judaism and Christianity in Conflict: From Late Antiquity to the Reformation,* New York: New York University Press

Davies, J.H. (1967) *A Letter To Hebrews: Cambridge Bible Commentary,* London: Cambridge University Press

Eusebius of Caesarea, (translated by Cruse, C.F. (1850)), The Ecclesiastical History of Eusebius Pamphilus - Bishop of Caesarea, In Palestine, reprinted (1995) as *Eusebius' Ecclesiastical History,* Grand Rapids: Baker Book House

Finch, P. (2003), *Beyond Acts: New Perspectives in New Testament History,* Florida: Sunrise Publications

Hagee, J., (2008) *In Defense of Israel,* Grand Rapids: Zondervan

Heshcel A.J. (1969) *Israel: An Echo of Eternity,* New York: Farrar, Straus and Giroux

Holwerda, D.E (1995) *Jesus and Israel: One Covenant or Two?* Grand Rapids: Wm B Eerdsman Publ. Co.

Hood, J.Y. B., (1995) *Aquinas and the Jews,* Philadelphia: University of Pennsylvania Press

Jacobs, J, (1925) 'Tribes, Lost Ten,' in Singer, I., and Adler, C (ed.) *Jewish Encyclopaedia,* Vol.12, New York: Funk and Wagnalls

Jones, S.E., (2002), *The Struggle for the Birthright,* God's Kingdom Ministries, USA

Josephus, (1987) *Antiquities of the Jews, The Works of Josephus*, (Trans.) Whiston, Hendrickson Publishers

Kraus, Hans-Joachim, (1989) 'Israel in the Theology of Calvin - Towards a New Approach to the Old Testament and Judaism', *Christian Jewish Relations*, Vol. 22, No. 3 & 4

Lindsey, H. (1974) *The Late Great Planet Earth*, Grand Rapids: Zondervan

Motyer, S. *Israel in the Plan of God*, Leicester: IVP 1989

Novak, D., (2004) 'The Covenant in Rabbinic Thought,' in Korn, E.B. (ed.), *Two Faiths, One Covenant?: Jewish and Christian Identity in the Presence of the Other*, Rowman & Littlefield

Pawson, D. (2008). *Defending Christian Zionism*, Bradford on Avon: Terra Nova Publ.

Pawson, D, (2009) *Israel in the New Testament*, Bradford on Avon: Terra Nova Publ

Pearce, T., (2002) *The Omega Files*, New Wine Press

Prasch, J (2009) 'Apostolic Jewish-Christian Hermeneutics and Supercessionism', in Smith, C (ed.) *The Jews, Modern Israel and the New Supercessionism*, Lampeter: King's Divinity Press, pp. 47-62

Robertson, O.P., (2000) *The Israel of God*, P & R Publ.

Rowdon, H. (1967) *The Origins of the Brethren*, Pickering and Inglis

Sennot, C.M. (2007) 'The Body and the Blood: The Middle East's Vanishing Christians and the Possibility for Peace', *Public Affairs*, 22

Sizer, S., (2004) *Christian Zionism: Road map to Armageddon?* Nottingham: IVP

Sizer, S., (2007) *Zion's Christian Soldiers? The Bible Israel and the Church*, Nottingham: IVP

Smith, C (2009) (ed.) *The Jews, Modern Israel and the New Supercessionism*, Lampeter: King's Divinity Press

Soulen, R.K., (1996).*The God of Israel and Christian Theology*, Minneapolis: Fortress Press

Steer, R. (1997) George Muller, Christian Focus Publications

Stott, J. (2007) 'The Place of Israel', in, Sizer, S. *Zion's Christian Soldiers? The Bible, Israel and the Church*, Nottingham: IVP

Bibliography

Torrance, D.W., & Taylor, G., (2007) Israel God's Servant, London: Paternoster Press

Wagner, D., (2002) "Palestinian Christians: An Historic Community at Risk?" *Information Brief*, No. 89, 12th March

Walker, A, (1985) *Restoring the Kingdom*, London: Hodder and Stoughton

Wiener, P.F. (1985), *Martin Luther: Hitler's Spiritual Ancestor*, Gustav Broukal Press. Originally written during World War II as a Win the Peace Pamphlet, No 3, Hutchinson and Co., London.

Wilkinson, P.R. (2007) *For Zion's Sake, Christian Zionism and the Role of John Nelson Darby,* London: Paternoster

Wolvoord J.F. and Wolvoord J.E. (1974) *Armageddon: Oil and the Middle East Crisis,* Grand Rapids: Zondervan Press

Wright, N.T. (1999) *The Way of the Lord: Christian Pilgrimage in the Holy Land and Beyond.* 1999, London: SPCK; Grand Rapids: Eerdmans

Wright, N.T. (2009) *Justification: God's plan and Paul's Vision*, London: SPCK

Scriptural References and Index

Scripture References

Scripture

1 Chron. 5: 1-2 – Israel's birthright passes to Joseph 69
1 John 2: 22-23 – Warning against those who deny Christ 52
1 Pet. 1:1 123
1 Pet. 1:10-12 123
1 Pet. 2:10 124
1 Pet. 2:11 124
1 Pet. 2:4-5 123
1 Pet. 2:6-8 123
1 Pet. 2:9 123
1 Peter 1: 1-2 – Peter writes to Israelite Diaspora in Turkey 90
2 Cor. 5: 19 – God is reconciled to the world through Christ 47, 148
2 John 1: 7 – Warning against those who deny Christ 52
2 Kings 17: 6 – Israelites exiled to Assyria and Media 72, 89, 90
2 Tim. 4: 11 118
Acts 1: 6-8 90
Acts 10: 2 13
Acts 15: 16-17 – Gentiles convert to Christ as David's tent is rebuilt 72,
   91
Acts 2: 14 90
Acts 2: 14-39 – Peter addresses the crowd on the day of Pentecost 90
Acts 2: 22 91
Acts 2: 36 – All the 'house of Israel' should know that Jesus is the
   Christ 91
Acts 2: 38-39 91
Acts 2: 5 89
Acts 2: 5-12 88
Acts 2: 9-10 – Parthians and Medes (See 2 Kings 17: 6) 89
Acts 9: 15 91
Amos 9: 11-12- David's fallen tent rebuilt along with the Gentiles -
   quoted by James in Acts 15: 16-17 .... 72, 91, 149
Amos 9: 13-15 – Israelite exiles return, together with Gentiles, when
   David's tent is rebuilt – fulfilled in Christ 72, 91
Amos 9: 8-9 - Israel rebuilt after being shaken 72
Col. 2: 11-23 115
Dan. 2: 31-35 – God's rock will break idolatrous worldly kingdoms .. 85

Dan. 9...129

Deut. 27: 26 – The Law brings a curse - See Gal. 3: 10...................113

Deut. 4: 29-31...129

Eph. 1:10 – All things brought together under Christ......................115

Eph. 1:20-23 – Christ head of the Church....................................115

Eph. 2:11-13 – Gentiles brought near to Christ.............................115

Eph. 2:14-16 – God is making one 'new man' between Jews and
Gentiles..116

Eph. 2:19-22 – The Church is Christ's body, the holy temple, being built
in unity...116

Eph. 2:4-6 – Jews and Gentiles reconciled in Christ......................115

Eph. 3:1-6 – Gentiles heirs together with Israel.............................116

Ezek. 1: 4-6 – Ezekiel bears the sins of Judah 40 days.....................82

Ezek. 34: 11-12 – God searches for Israel's lost sheep (See Matt. 10).82

Ezek. 34: 1-12..88, 94

Ezek. 34: 1-31 – Assyrian exiles considered a flock of neglected sheep
....82

Ezek. 34: 13-16 – Lost sheep brought back to the land......................82

Ezek. 34: 1-6 – Israel, God's flock, is scattered across the earth without
a shepherd..82

Ezek. 34: 17-24 – Israel ruled over by the shepherd 'David'..............82

Ezek. 34: 25-31 – God makes a covenant of peace with Israel....82, 149

Ezek. 36: 23-24 – Israel to be brought back....................................82

Ezek. 36: 25-26 – Israel given new heart and spirit..........................82

Ezek. 36: 27 – God's Spirit placed in Israel bringing obedience.........82

Ezek. 37: 11-14 – Dry bones of Israel come back to life....................83

Ezek. 37: 15-17 – Judah and Israel to be reunited............................83

Ezek. 37: 15-28 – Israel and Judah reunited....................................83

Ezek. 37: 18-23 – Judah and Israel reunited....................................83

Ezek. 37: 24-28 – Judah and Israel reunited under the Messiah -........83

Ezek. 39: 23-29...83

Ezek. 4: 1-5 – Ezekiel bears the sins of Israel 390 days....................82

Ezek. 43: 7 – The new temple...83

Ezek. 47 – River running out of the new Temple..............................83

Gal 4: 21-31 – The old covenant has been replaced by a new one.......53

Gal. 1: 11-12..112

Gal. 1: 7..112

Gal. 1:7...112

Gal. 2:1-10...112

Scriptural References and Index

Gal. 2:11-13 112

Gal. 2:9 – Paul submits his message to Jerusalem leadership 112

Gal. 3: 10 – The Law brings a curse 113

Gal. 3: 13 – Christ has redeemed Christians from the curse of the Law
.... 113

Gal. 3: 14 – Abraham's blessing comes upon the Gentiles 49

Gal. 3: 16 – Jesus the seed of Abraham 113

Gal. 3: 17-18 – Abraham's covenant given to Jews and Gentiles 114

Gal. 3: 17-20 114

Gal. 3: 19 – Jesus ends the curse of the Law 113

Gal. 3: 21-24 114

Gal. 3: 26-29 114

Gal. 3: 6 – Abraham the father of faith 112

Gal. 3: 8 – All nations blessed through Abraham 112

Gal. 3: 9, 14 – Abraham's blessing comes upon the Gentile believers
.... 112

Gal. 4: 21-26 – Sarah represents the new heavenly Jerusalem that is free,
Hagar the old Jerusalem that is in slavery 114

Gal. 4: 28-31 114

Gal. 6: 16 115

Gen 12: 2-3 – The seven fold blessing given to Abraham 49, 136

Gen 17:15-22 66

Gen. 15:5 113

Gen. 17:3-8 113

Gen. 27: 40 – Esau's blessing 127

Gen. 32:22-32 – Jacob is named Israel 103

Gen. 49: 10 68

Gen. 49: 22-26 – Joseph's birthright and blessing 68

Gen. 49: 8-12 – Jacob's blessing upon Judah was that the ruler would
come through his line 52

Gen.15:19 65

Gen.17:5-8 65

Gen.41: 42,52 – Joseph names Ephraim 68

Gen.48:15-16 – Ephraim's blessing 68

Heb. 1:1-14 – Christ upholds all things by his word 118

Heb. 11:10 – God is the architect of the heavenly temple 122

Heb. 11:13 – Patriarchs waited for the promise of Christ 122

Heb. 11:16 – Looking for a heavenly country 122

Heb. 11:8-10 122

Heb. 12:22 – Zion is now the heavenly Jerusalem 122
Heb. 12:27-28 122
Heb. 3:6 – The Church is the new temple 119
Heb. 3:7-11 – Jews urged not to turn back to old ways 119
Heb. 7:18 – Mosaic covenant set aside 121
Heb. 7:6-9 119
Heb. 8: 8-12 80
Heb. 8:13 – The Mosiac covenant is now obsolete 121
Heb. 8:2 – The new tabernacle is not made by human hands 121
Heb. 9:11-12 – Jesus made a perfect sacrifice with his own blood 121
Heb. 9:15 – Christians have an eternal inheritance 121
Hos. 1: 10 ....73, 149
Hos. 1: 10-11 – Reunion promised between Judah and Israel, but they
    would be as numerous as the sand 73
Hos. 1: 11 83
Hos. 1: 2-3 – Hosea marries the adulterous Gomer – symbolic of
    rebellious Israel 73
Hos. 1: 4-9 – Scattered Israelites to become very numerous 73
Hos. 1:9-11 124
Hos. 2: 14-17 – God promises to remarry Israel in righteousness 74
Hos. 2: 14-20 – Israel remarried under a new covenant 74, 149
Hos. 2: 21-23 – Restoration of Israel 74
Hos. 2: 23 73
Hos. 2: 2-7 – Israel divorced and sent away 73, 139
Hos. 3: 4-5 – Israel reunited with Judah under 'David' 74
Isa. 10: 20-25 – Only a remnant of Israel will be saved 104
Isa. 11: 10-12 – Root of Jesse - a banner for the nations & Israelite
    exiles brought back from Assyria 75
Isa. 11: 1-2 75
Isa. 11: 12-16 – Northern exiles return from Assyria under the Messiah
    ....75, 104
Isa. 14: 1-2 – Israel is promised resettlement in the land with the
    Gentiles 75, 149
Isa. 14: 3-16 75
Isa. 27: 6-9 – repentant Israel fills the world with righteousness
    (fruitfulness) 76
Isa. 29: 10 104
Isa. 35: 1-10 – Zion as spiritual Israel 42
Isa. 49: 1 76

Scriptural References and Index

Isa. 49: 11 – God will make pathways for the Israelites 76
Isa. 49: 1-2.. 76
Isa. 49: 12 – Israelites return from north and west, and Aswan 77
Isa. 49: 13.. 77
Isa. 49: 14-18 77
Isa. 49: 19-20 – The land is too small to contain God's people 77
Isa. 49: 22-23 – Gentiles will help bring Israel back 77
Isa. 49: 24-25 77
Isa. 49: 3.. 76
Isa. 49: 5 – Israel to be re-gathered under the Messiah..................... 76
Isa. 49: 6 – The Messiah is also a light to Gentiles 76
Isa. 49: 7 – Kings will see the Messiah 76
Isa. 49: 8-10 – The exiles to return.. 76
Isa. 54: 5-10 – A young wife (Israel) brought back with compassion.. 74
Isa. 56: 3, 6 – Foreigners gathered with Israel – not excluded........... 77
Isa. 56: 8 – others gathered alongside Israel 77
Isa. 56: 9-12 – God saddened by unfaithful shepherds 77
Isa. 62: 1-2 – Zion will be given a new name 78, 94
Isa. 62: 3-11 – God promises to remarry Israel –a banner to the nations
    78
Isa. 65: 1-2 – The obstinate people of God to rejected 78
Isa. 7: 14 – Jesus called Immanuel 93
Isa. 9: 3, 7 – Messiah to sit on David's throne, with an enlarged nation
    of Israel 75
Isa. 9: 7 – The Messiah will sit on David's throne........................... 52
James 1: 1 – James writes to the 'twelve tribes' of Israel 91, 123
Jer. 23: 5-6...52, 81, 149
Jer. 23: 5-6 – Israel and Judah restored under 'David' 79
Jer. 23: 7-8 – Israelites gathered out of the north (Assyrian exiles)..... 80
Jer. 24: 1-10 – Two baskets of figs; one good, one rotten................. 96
Jer. 29 129
Jer. 30: 1-4:- Judah and Israel to be restored.................................. 80
Jer. 30: 17-19 – Jacob's tent restored.. 80
Jer. 30: 8-10 – Judah and Israel will serve the Messiah 80
Jer. 30-33 80
Jer. 31: 12.. 80
Jer. 31: 1-6 – northern exiles of Israel loved by God and restored 80
Jer. 31: 18-21 – Ephraim repents and is restored to the land 80
Jer. 31: 27 – Israel and Judah restored together............................... 80

Jer. 31: 31-34 – New covenant with Israel and Judah - quoted in Heb. 8: 8-12 80
Jer. 31: 35-37 – Israel will never cease to be a nation before God 81
Jer. 31: 8 – Northern exiles of Israel brought out of the north 80
Jer. 31: 9-10 – Ephraim 'my first born son' restored to God who will be a shepherd to them 80
Jer. 32: 37-41 – An everlasting covenant given to Israel 81
Jer. 33: 15-16 81
Jer. 33: 15-18 52
Jer. 33: 17 81
Jer. 50: 4-6 – Judah and Israel reunited under the Messiah with a new covenant 83, 88, 94
Jer. 7: 11 – Alluded to in Matt. 21: 18-22 96
John 15:5 14
John 18: 36 51
John 8: 42-47 – Pharisees accused of being children of the devil 97
Lev. 19: 19, 23 95
Luke 1: 33 – Jesus to rule on David's throne over the house of Jacob (Israel) 93
Luke 1: 54-55 52
Luke 1: 67-72, 76 – John the Baptist prepares the way 93
Luke 1: 67-79 52
Luke 2: 25-32 – Jesus a light to Gentiles, a consolation to Israel 94
Luke 2: 27-32 53
Luke 2: 34-35 – Some will rise and some fall because of Christ 94
Mark 11: 12-21 95
Mark 13: 28 99
Matt. 1: 21 – Jesus will save his people from their sins 93
Matt. 1: 23 93
Matt. 10: 23 – Christians will continue to go to Israelite cities until he returns 88, 139, 145
Matt. 10: 6 – Disciples sent to the lost sheep of the house of Israel – (See Ezek. 34: 1-12) 88, 94
Matt. 11: 1 88
Matt. 12: 38-41 – Gentiles stand in judgement over unrepentant Pharisees 52
Matt. 12: 39-40 51
Matt. 13: 10-15 – Callous hearts would not understand Jesus' parables 95
Matt. 13: 10-17 35

Scriptural References and Index

Matt. 13: 24-30 – Kingdom parables 94
Matt. 13: 31-33 – The kingdom of God like a mustard seed that spreads
beyond its boundaries.. 95
Matt. 15: 2 – Tradition of the Elders 128
Matt. 15: 24 88
Matt. 16: 6... 97
Matt. 2: 6 – Born in Bethlehem to be a shepherd to his people........... 93
Matt. 21: 12-14.. 95
Matt. 21: 1-6 – Jesus enters Jerusalem on a colt (See Zech. 9: 9) 95
Matt. 21: 18-22 – Jesus curses the fruitless fig tree – representative of
Scribes and Pharisees 95
Matt. 21: 33-42 – Pharisees knew who he was, but planned to kill Jesus
.... 96
Matt. 21: 9 – Messianic statement – 'Blessed is he who comes in the
name of the Lord' 95
Matt. 23: 1-38 – Jewish authorities rejected – house left desolate....... 97
Matt. 23: 32 98
Matt. 23: 39 97
Matt. 23: 39 – Messianic blessing concerning Christ 52
Matt. 23: 8 98
Matt. 24: 15-22.. 99
Matt. 24: 2 – The temple to be destroyed 98
Matt. 24: 32-33 – Fig tree only produces green leaves, not fruit – sign of
second coming 99
Matt. 5: 9... 147
Matt. 8:11.. 27
Mic. 2: 12-13 – God's flock of Israel to be restored 79
Mic. 3: 10 – People condemned for building Zion with bloodshed 78
Mic. 4: 1-2 – The Law will go out to the nations............................. 79
Mic. 4: 3 – Promise of peace for the nations.................................. 79
Mic. 4: 6-7.. 79
Mic. 5: 2 – The King comes from Bethlehem 79, 93
Mic. 5: 3-4 – Israel restored and shepherded again......................... 79
Mic. 5: 4-5 – The greatness of the Shepherd will reach the ends of the
earth.. 79
Mic. 6: 8 – God requires justice and mercy be given to non Jews living
in the land.. 12
Mic. 7: 1-7 – God desires fruit 'early figs' 96
Ps. 95:7-11 - Israelites urged not to turn back to old ways.............. 119

Rev. 17: 5, 18 – Mystery Babylon 98
Rev. 18 98
Rev. 2: 9 97
Rev. 21-22 83
Rev. 7: 1-8 – 144,000 people from the twelve tribes of Israel............91
Rom. 10: 11-13 105
Rom. 11: 11 – Paul hopes that Jews will be envious of Christian's faith
   104
Rom. 11: 15 .... 11, 110
Rom. 11: 23 .... 107, 135
Rom. 11: 25-26 – All Israel will be saved in the end 135
Rom. 11: 28 .... 103, 107
Rom. 11: 31 – Jews loved on account of the Patriarchs – may now
    receive mercy 135, 139
Rom. 11: 4 – A remnant of Israel to be saved 104
Rom. 11: 5 104
Rom. 11: 7 .... 103, 104
Rom. 11:11-24 – Gentiles grafted into the Jewish vine......................23
Rom. 11:25-26 – All Israel will be saved in the end.........................27
Rom. 3: 21-31 – A righteousness from God by faith, and apart from
    Law 105
Rom. 4: 1-25 – Abraham to be the father to the whole world 110
Rom. 9: 11 – An elect of Jews receive grace 103
Rom. 9: 25-27 .... 73, 104
Rom. 9: 6 – Not all descendants of Israel are Israel........................103
Rom. 9: 6-9 – Not all descendants of Israel are Israel........................71
Rom. 9: 7-9 – Only those born of God's promise are Israel 103
Rom. 9-11 78
Zech. 10: 1-5 .... 84, 149
Zech. 10: 6 – God promises to restore the house of Joseph 84
Zech. 10: 6-12 – Joseph (Ephraim) and Judah restored from Egypt and
    Assyria 84
Zech. 11: 4-17 – God revokes his old coventant - 84
Zech. 12: 10 145
Zech. 12: 10-14 – mourning for the one they pierced with cleansing
    from sin 85
Zech. 12: 2-3 – Jerusalem (new Jerusalem) to become an unmovable
    rock 85
Zech. 12: 6-8 – God will save Judah 85

Scriptural References and Index

Zech. 13: 1-2 – Mourning for the one pierced, and then cleansing from sin.. 85

Zech. 13: 7 – two thirds will fall into further judgment and scattering 85, 105

Zech. 13: 8-9 – One third refined as silver and gold 85

Zech. 13: 9 – A remnant of Israel-Judah saved 105

Zech. 2: 11 – Many nations to join with reunited Judah-Israel 84

Zech. 2: 6 – Both Judah and Israel to be restored 84

Zech. 2: 8 – Zion is the apple of God's eye 84

Zech. 8: 12-14 – Judah and Israel to bear fruit in righteousness 85

Zech. 8: 1-3 85

Zech. 8: 13 – Judah and Israel to be restored 84

Zech. 8: 20-23 – Gentiles will look to Jews for knowledge about God 85

Zech. 8: 7-8 85

Zech. 9: 10... 84

Zech. 9: 10-14 – God will rule over the whole earth........................ 84

Zech. 9: 11-13 – Judah is a bow, Ephraim God's arrows, as God extends his peace across the earth 84, 149

Zech. 9: 9 .... 84, 95

Understanding Israel

Index

Aaron, 119

Abel, 97

Abraham, 12, 27, 39, 48, 65, 93, 107, 109, 114, 121, 117–24, 128, 135, 136

blessing of Abraham, 42, 49, 75, 92, 96, 136, 137

blessing to all nations, 73

children of Abraham, 57, 71, 92, 112

covenant of Abraham, 28, 57

man of faith, 142

promise to Abraham, 52, 77, 78, 95, 100, 112, 129, 135, 139, 142, 145

seed of Abraham, 73, 113, 122

adversus Judaeus, (against the Jews, 26

Albury conference, 35, 38

Alcazar, 33

Alexander the Great, 82

America, 17, 49, 136, 138

Amos, 71, 75

Anabaptists, 16, 25

anti Zionists

also. see replacement theology

fulfilment theology, 19

liberal theology, 19

liberation theology, 19

antichrist, 34, 41, 52, 137

deceivers, 52

anti-Semitic, 10, 50

apartheid, 10

Arab, 155

Arab Christians, 13

Arabia, 114

Armageddon, 14, 46, 147

Armenia, 90

Asenath (Joseph's wife), 68

Asherite poles, 76

Asia Minor, 90

Assyria, 72, 75, 82, 84, 90, 151

atheism, 50, 137, 138

Augustine of Hippo, 22, 26, 47

Baal, 12, 74, 104

Babylon, 13, 39, 75, 79, 81, 84, 97, 151

Babylonians, 82

Balfour Declaration, 45

Barmen Declaration, 7, 16

Barnabas, 91, 112, 118

Barth, Karl, 16

Behistun Inscription, 151

Ben Ezra. See Lacunza, Manuel de

Benjamin, 53, 71

Bethesda, (Brethren assembly), 43

Black Sea, 88

Bonhoeffer, Dietrich, 16

Brethren, 42, 43

Exclusive Brethren, 42, 44

Open Brethren, 42, 43, 44

Plymouth Brethren, 31, 36

British Mandate, 12, 132

cabalism, 35

Calvin, 26

Calvin, John, 26, 27, 28, 39, 42

Calvin's covenant theology, 26, 39, 41
Cappadocia, 89, 90
Carter, Jimmy, 10
Caspian Sea, 88
Catholic Apostolic Church, 31, 38
Catholic, Roman, 24, 25, 36, 112, 132
Clement (first century), 117
Confessing Church, 7, 16
Constantine, Roman Emperor, 23, 24, 130
Cornelius, 13, 142
Council of Nicea, 24
covenant
    dual covenant, 107, 145
    dualistic theology (See also dualism), 107
covenant theology. See Calvin's covenant theology
Craik, Henry, 43
Crusades, 138
Cuninghame, 33
Cyprian of Carthage, 22
Daniel, 85, 129
Darby, J.N., 10, 31, 33, 36, 37, 38, 39, 40, 41, 42, 43, 159
David, 35, 52, 57, 72, 75, 85, 91, 93, 94, 96, 100
    David's covenant, 28
    house of David, 85, 93
    Messianic reference, 74, 79, 80, 81, 82, 83, 88, 92, 95
Dead Sea, 83
Diaspora, 90, 130
    Gk. diaspora, 91, 123

Gk. diasporas, 90
dispensationalism, 10, 31, 35, 37, 38, 39, 43
    Church of Scotland, 31
    preparatory dispensation, 21
donkey, 97
    foal, 84
Drummond, Henry, 31, 34, 35, 38, 39
dualism, 40, 41, 69
Edom. See Esau
Ekklesia, (referring to the people of God in the Old and New Testament),, 28
election, 107
Elijah, 104
Ephraim, 67, 68, 75, 80, 83, 84
Esau, 66, 103, 127
eschatology, 9, 32, 33, 39, 43, 45, 46, 137
Esdras. See Ezra
Euphrates, 89
Eusebius, 53, 99, 117, 157
Ezekiel, 45, 46, 81, 82, 83, 142, 149
Ezra, 89
fascism, 51, 153
fig tree, 95, 99, 135, 144
    green leaves, 99
Frey, Joseph, 32
Galatians, 45, 111, 112, 117, 136
Gamaliel, 97
Gaza, 12, 133
Gentiles, 33, 39, 42, 43, 45, 46, 49, 51, 53, 71, 72, 76, 77, 78, 88, 91, 94, 96, 101, 104, 105, 107, 110, 112,

114, 116, 122, 130, 135, 136, 142, 149
Gnosticism, 23, 47
　Gnostic teachings, 41
　quasi-gnostic, 23
Gog and Magog, 46, 83, 128
Gomer, (Hosea's wife), 73
grace, 26, 28, 39, 41, 44, 84, 85, 103, 104, 107, 110, 112, 114, 115, 136, 137, 139, 145
Graves, Richard, 36
Groves, Anthony Norris, 36
Hagar, 53, 114
　slavery, 53
Hagee, John, 7, 13, 52, 48–54, 129, 141, 144
Hebrew, (language), 52
Hebrews, 45, 80, 83, 117, 118, 119, 121, 122
Herod the Great, 93, 127
Herzl, Theodor, 45
Hitler, Adolph, 16, 50
holocaust, 41, 42, 46, 153, 155
Holy Land, 54, 77, 129, 147, 148
Holy Spirit, 12, 34, 38, 47, 85, 91
Hosea, 72, 73, 75, 78, 106, 142, 149
Ibn Ezra, 27
Iran, 138
Irenaeus of Lyon, 21
Irving, Edward, 32, 33, 34, 35, 38, 39
Isaac, 27, 39, 48, 114, 117, 122, 127, 151

Isaiah, 33, 45, 46, 74, 75, 76, 78, 92, 142, 149
Ishtar, 12
Islam, 12, 46, 127, 138, 155
　Allah, 12
　Islamic, 46, 136
　Islamic conquests, 13
Israel
　Eretz Israel, 48
　house of Israel, 82, 88, 91
　kingdom of God, 94, 135
　kingdom of heaven, 94
　national calling, 40
　northern tribes of Israel, 78, 87
　spiritual Israel, 9, 20, 22, 57, 142, 143
　State of Israel, 9, 11, 12, 13, 15, 16, 31, 33, 37, 45, 46, 48, 49, 51, 54, 68, 99, 122, 125, 127, 128, 129, 133, 135, 136, 137, 139, 141, 143, 144, 146, 154, 155
Jacob, 27, 48, 52, 75, 76, 77, 78, 80, 83, 93, 103, 122, 127
James, brother of the Lord, 24, 53, 91, 123
Jeremiah, 19, 79, 80, 81, 121, 129, 142, 149
Jerusalem, 33, 35, 39, 47, 48, 51, 53, 78, 83, 84, 85, 89, 90, 91, 95, 97, 98, 112, 114, 122, 132, 133, 147, 148
　Christian Patriarchs and leaders of, 47
　Council of Jerusalem, 91

New Jerusalem, 53, 85, 114, 122, 132
Jesus Christ, 12, 13, 27, 47, 88, 112, 113, 116, 118, 139, 146, 147
Jews, 10, 12, 13, 14, 18, 21, 22, 23, 24, 25, 28, 31, 37, 40, 43, 45, 46, 67, 88, 89, 97, 99, 103, 104, 105, 107, 110, 112, 114, 115, 117, 118, 119, 122, 125–34, 135, 136, 137, 139, 142, 157, 158
  Jesus' disciples, 70
  Messianic Jews, 144
  remnant of Jews, 73
Jezreel (God scatters (sows) the Israelites), 73
Joel, 90
John the Apostle, 51, 83, 97, 98
John the Baptist, 93
John, Apostle, 52
Jonah, 51
Joseph, 67, 68, 83, 84, 93, 94
  birthright of Joseph, 57, 141, 143
Josephus, 89, 158
Judah, 52, 53, 57, 69, 70, 71, 73, 75, 76, 78, 79, 80, 81, 82, 83, 84, 85, 87, 88, 89, 90, 93, 95, 96, 99, 100, 121, 128, 135, 142, 146, 149
Judaism, 9, 10, 17, 23, 24, 35, 47, 53, 117, 118, 127, 129, 144, 157
Judeo-Christian, 57
Justin Martyr, 20

Kant, Immanuel, 25
Kerala, southern India, 90
Khazaria
  Ashkenazi Jews, 128
  Khazar Jews, 128
  Koestler, Arthur, 127
  Thirteenth Tribe, 127
Lacunza, Manuel de, 32, 33, 35
Lausanne Consultation on Jewish Evangelism, 14, 136
Law of Moses, 9, 24, 112, 113, 114, 121, 128, 136
  Levitical Law, 13
  Mosaic Law, 12, 18, 95, 105, 114, 121, 129, 135, 142, 144
Lebanon, 82, 131
Levantines, 13
Levi, 53, 119, 120
Lindsey, Hal, 99, 158
Lo-Ammi, (Israelites to greatly increase), 73
Lo-Ruhamah, (Israel rejected for a time), 73
LSPCJ, London Society for Promoting Christianity Among the Jews, 32, 35, 36, 37, 43, 44
Luke, 52, 88, 93, 117
Luther, Martin, 16, 25, 27
MacDonald, Margaret, 34
Magi, 93
Magnificat, 52
Manasseh, 68
Mark, 118
Maronites, 13, 131
Mary, the mother of Jesus, 93

Scriptural References and Index

Matthew, 27, 88, 93, 94, 95, 96, 98, 100
Media, 89, 151
  Medes, 73, 89, 90
Melchizedek, 119
Messiah. See Christ
Micah, 12, 75, 78, 96, 149
Middle East, 46, 78, 132, 138, 143, 146, 147, 148, 154, 158, 159
Mishnah. See Talmud
Molech, 12
Mount Sinai, 39, 114
Muller, George, 44
Muslims, 12, 128, 132, 138, 155
mustard tree, 95
nationalism, 11, 16
Nazareth, 48, 129
Newton, Benjamin Wills, 37, 43, 44
Nineveh, 51, 52
olive tree, 23, 104, 107, 110, 140
Omri, King of Israel, 151
Origen, 21, 26
Ottoman Empire, 132
Palestine, 10, 13, 31, 32, 45, 68, 69, 77, 87, 88, 91, 97, 110, 128, 129, 132, 136, 139, 143, 145, 147, 154, 157
  Palestinian, 12, 16, 132, 133, 145, 147, 155, 159
  Palestinians, 10, 11, 12, 13, 16, 54, 132, 145, 148
pantheism, 50
Parthians, 89

Paul, 27, 49, 53, 71, 73, 78, 91, 101, 104, 105, 107, 109, 111, 112, 113, 114, 115, 116, 117, 118, 135, 136, 142, 145
Pawson, David, 11, 42, 49, 52, 68
Pearce, Tony, 137
Pentecost, 85, 89, 90
Persians, 82, 90
Peter, 89, 90, 91, 112, 142
Pharisees, 52, 54, 91, 94, 95, 96, 97, 98, 100, 128
Positive Christianity, 16, 50
Potsdam Conference, 154
Powerscourt conferences, 37
Powerscourt, Lady, 37
racism, 11
rapture, 32, 34, 37, 40, 41, 42, 43, 137
  abomination that causes desolation, 99
  pre-tribulation, 34, 39
  secret rapture, 34, 35, 39, 43
Rashi, 27
Rawlinson, George, 89, 151
Rawlinson, Henry, 151
Reformation, 16, 23, 112, 157
replacement theology, 9, 23, 25, 50, 141
  economic supersessionism, 18
  punitive supersessionism, 18
  strucural supersessionism, 18
  substitution theology, 17

supersessionism, 17

Revelation, 33, 41, 91, 97
  harlet riding the beast, 98
  Mystery Babylon, 98

Riberia, 33

Roman Empire, 24, 33, 54, 130

Romans, 27, 45, 78, 89, 101, 107, 109, 135, 136, 143, 145

Russian pogroms, 32

Samaria, 73, 80, 90, 151

Sanhedrin, 97

Sarah (Abraham's wife), 114

Schleiermacher, Friedrich, 25

Scofield, Cyrus, 44
  Scofield Reference Bible, 44

Scythians, 90

Septuagint, 28

silver
  thirty pieces of silver, 84

Sizer, Stephen, 10, 27, 158

Soulen, R.K, 18

Soulen, R.K., 17

Star of David, 14
  Shield of David, 129

Stephen, martyr, 24

super-apostles, 111

Syria, 82

tabernacle, 39, 121, 122

Talmud, 14, 24, 128

temple, 24, 39, 93, 96, 132
  third temple, 41

Tertullian, 22, 118

The Morning Watch, 34, 35, 38

Third International Christian Zionist Congress, 47

Thomas, Apostle, 90

Timothy, 117

Torah, 14, 98, 129

Tradition of the Elders, 14, 128, 135

Tregelles, Samuel, 43

Way, Lewis, 32

West Bank, 133

Westminster Confession, 26, 28

Wilkinson, Paul, 26

Wolff, Joseph, 35

Zealots, 111

Zechariah, 52, 84, 85, 91, 93, 95, 97, 105, 142, 149

Zionism
  Christian Zionism, 9, 10, 16, 20, 25, 27, 45, 46, 47, 48, 69, 138, 141, 144, 147, 148, 158
  Christian Zionists, 11, 13, 15, 26, 41, 45, 70, 76, 85, 87, 99, 101, 107, 122, 129, 135, 137, 144, 155
  Christians United For Israel (CUFI), 48
  classic Zionism, 42
  First Zionist Congress (1897), 45
  political Zionism, 10, 37, 45, 138, 154
  Protocols of the Elders of Zion, 153
  Zion, 77, 78, 79, 80, 85, 94, 95, 122
  Zion's new name, 77

Other books by Andrew Sibley

Restoring the Ethics of Creation

Published 2006 by Anno Mundi Books, P.O. Box 752, Camberley, England, GU17 OXJ. Paperback, 5.5 x 8.5", 316 pp. ISBN 13: 978-0-9543922-2-2 / ISBN 10: 0-9543922-2-1

This book argues that as a result of the rise of the Darwinian faith system and belief in the certainty of technological progress and unrestrained capitalism, we have lost a proper respect for nature and humanity. Ethical standards are now based on subjective criteria where each person is able to decide his or her own conduct, often living for self in a grand struggle for survival. No more is seen the providential God who offers blessing and grace to mankind, nor the divine Sovereign who requires people to live in partnership with his will and purpose.

However, the Christian tradition known as Natural Theology has seen in nature the appearance of design, but more than that, it has pointed to the power, wisdom and goodness of the Designer and goes on to inform our conduct as Paul noted in Romans 1:20. When properly formulated, this twin book approach enriches our lives, with the book of Scripture in the one hand, and the book of nature in the other, giving mankind rights, duties and a purpose in caring for one another and for creation.

If as Christians we are really concerned with ethical standards, then we need to restore and develop a proper understanding of the Natural Theology tradition, both in terms of the appearance of design seen in nature, and also in terms of our response to the Creator. This book also addresses the problem of suffering and brokenness in nature and considers the question of the place of miracles in creation

Other books by Andrew Sibley

Cracking the Darwin Code

Published 2013 by Fastnet Publications (13 Jun 2013)
ISBN-10: 0956214614 / ISBN-13: 978-0956214614

This book examines the foundations of evolution and deep-time from non-Christian cultures in the Ancient Middle East and Indian Sub-Continent. It then examines how such pagan-religious beliefs were brought into the emerging scientific arena by Enlightenment philosophers who had an interest in Greek paganism and Hinduism - men such as Erasmus Darwin, David Hume and Benoit de Maillet. It then looks in detail at developments in the 19th century with references for instance to the writings of Charles Darwin, Charles Lyell and Thomas Huxley.

www.ingramcontent.com/pod-product-compliance
Lightning Source LLC
LaVergne TN
LVHW051408080426
835508LV00022B/2993